INVESTING
and the
IRRATIONAL
MIND

INVESTING

and the

IRRATIONAL

MIND

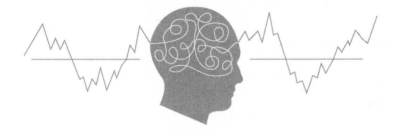

*Rethink Risk, Outwit Optimism,
and Seize Opportunities Others Miss*

ROBERT KOPPEL

NEW YORK   CHICAGO   SAN FRANCISCO
LISBON   LONDON   MADRID   MEXICO CITY   MILAN
NEW DELHI   SAN JUAN   SEOUL   SINGAPORE
SYDNEY   TORONTO

The *McGraw·Hill* Companies

1 2 3 4 5 6 7 8 9 10   DOC/DOC   1 6 5 4 3 2 1

ISBN: 978-0-07-175337-1 (print book)
MHID: 0-07-175337-0

ISBN: 978-0-07-175343-2 (e-book)
MHID: 0-07-175343-5

Design by Mauna Eichner and Lee Fukui

This publication is designed to provide accurate and authoritative information in regard to the subject matter covered. It is sold with the understanding that neither the author nor the publisher is engaged in rendering legal, accounting, securities trading, or other professional services. If legal advice or other expert assistance is required, the services of a competent professional person should be sought.

> —*From a Declaration of Principles Jointly Adopted by a Committee of the American Bar Association and a Committee of Publishers and Associations*

Library of Congress Cataloging-in-Publication Data
Koppel, Robert.
   Investing and the irrational mind: rethink risk, outwit optimism, and seize opportunities others miss / Robert Koppel.
      p. cm.
   ISBN 978-0-07-175337-1 (hardback)
   1. Investing—Psychological aspects. 2. Investing—Decision making. I. Title.
   HG4515.15.K67 2011
   332.601'9—dc22   2010047185

McGraw-Hill books are available at special quantity discounts to use as premiums and sales promotions or for use in corporate training programs. To contact a representative, please e-mail us at bulksales@mcgraw-hill.com.

This book is printed on acid-free paper.

Contents

Foreword

WILLIAM J. BRODSKY
Chairman and CEO, Chicago Board Options Exchange

Over the years of helping to guide the development of several U.S. exchanges—currently as chairman and CEO of the Chicago Board Options Exchange, and before that at the Chicago Mercantile Exchange and the American Stock Exchange—I've had the pleasure of getting to know a long list of professional traders and investors. In addition, I am an avid personal investor.

Many of the professionals I know—several of whom are profiled in this book—have become legends for their trading prowess. Their successes, however, rather than being a series of endless profitable trades, were peppered along the way with some failures, followed by a good dose of learning and personal introspection. Others—some professional traders and many more who are part-time investors—have not been as successful; they have had to learn the hard way that without "emotional intelligence," even the best-thought-out strategy can unravel during times of market upheaval. John Maynard Keynes admonished that the markets have the ability to stay irrational longer than investors can stay solvent, and for those who are unable to digest that warning, the journey toward becoming a successful investor or trader may be short-lived.

This book also suggests that neither formal education nor raw IQ appears to be the biggest factor in achieving market success. In his inimitable down-to-earth style, Warren Buffett may have said it best: "Investing is not a game where the guy with the 160 IQ beats the guy with a 130 IQ. . . . What's needed is a sound intellectual framework for making decisions and the ability to keep emotions from corroding that framework."

And that, in its broadest sense, is what Bob Koppel's book explores. Contained in its 250 fast-reading pages are fascinating examples and insights into how the brain works, drawn from studies of some of the best scientific minds in behavioral economics and psychology.

This book differentiates itself from others that concentrate on either nuts-and-bolts analytical and strategic skills (the stuff of the left brain) or simple formulas for market mastery. Taking an entirely different path, our author and the experts he cites suggest that investors' emotions cannot and should not be ignored, with all market decisions being left to automated trading systems. Instead, the underlying theme is that the best investors are able to recognize their emotions and use them to their advantage without allowing those emotions to overpower them.

In his introduction, Koppel states that he has "come to believe that the market is truly a Rorschach test"—a way to see himself clearly in the mirror, with all of his personal beliefs, emotions, and inconsistencies in how he deals with the markets laid out before him. He is able to expertly express why these human factors may be inextricably linked to a better chance of success in the markets.

The good news, as Bob points out, is that even "old dogs" can learn new tricks about investing. We can master new skills, alter old ones, overcome crippling emotions, and, through experimentation, teach ourselves psychological responses and styles that can become automatic. And we can do this because, as the latest findings on the "plasticity" of the brain prove, we continue to change.

Readers of this book will find within these pages new truths—in the form of a sort of investor's "field manual"—that will help transform their thinking on an important subject. I believe that this is as relevant as, or more so than, today's latest investment strategies, trading systems, or technical chart formations. It is yet another successful endeavor for Bob, whose books offer lessons that could be extremely invaluable throughout one's investing life.

Preface

MING HSU

Director, Neuroeconomics Laboratory,
Haas School of Business,
University of California, Berkeley

For many people around the world, the 2008 financial crisis produced much personal misfortune and hand-wring-
ing. For many economists, however, there was a sense of
existential crisis that shook a belief system that had been carefully
cultivated over years, if not decades. This belief system is based,
more or less, on the following: economic models are flawed, as all
models are flawed, but, like good models, they retain the correct
stylized facts about the real world. Among this set of models, few
are so influential, both within the professional world and with the
broader public, as the efficient market hypothesis. Understanding the marketplace in real life, however, means understanding
the interaction of a multitude of distinct groups of players. These
individuals vary in their risk attitudes, market experience, and
financial sophistication. They may exhibit cognitive biases and
fallacies that can be far removed from the rational investor that
standard economic and financial theories assume.

In the past, it has been convenient to sweep these differences under the rug with the useful fiction of "efficient markets." As we are increasingly learning, however, and as has been dramatically illustrated by events over the past two years, many of these biases, rather than being a series of random mistakes by novice and unseasoned investors, are deeply ingrained in human psychology and biology. In some cases, people (including economic theorists!) persist in such behavior even when they are confronted with persuasive logical arguments to the contrary, and indeed cannot offer a clear rationale for their behavior.[1] In the delightful words of Daniel Ellsberg, which would appear very much out of place in today's academic journals, the theorists, "having looked into their hearts, found conflicts with the axioms and decided . . . to satisfy their preferences and let the axioms satisfy themselves."

In the past two decades, researchers have started to put back the psychological foibles of decision makers. This injection of psychology into economics, popularly known as "behavioral economics," has become influential enough that Cass Sunstein, coauthor of the book *Nudge* with behavioral economics pioneer Richard Thaler, is now "regulatory czar" under President Obama.[2] One has even heard the proclamation that "we're all behavioralists now." More recently, the introduction of brain research has given rise to yet another field, "neuroeconomics." Indeed, at this point there is a veritable flood of tools from the biological sciences, from genomics to pharmacology, waiting to enter the fertile grounds of neuroeconomics. Perhaps surprisingly, it has been the economists who are most active in resisting these new entries. Unlike the natural sciences, where the growth of interdisciplinary fields such as biophysics and physical chemistry is rarely greeted with tomes discussing the philosophical underpinnings, behavioral economics and neuroeconomics are criticized for not being sufficiently like the good old-fashioned economic theories that rest on the assumptions of the rational man and infinite cognitive capacity. Old habits apparently do die hard.

Still, no matter how persuasive and formidable the intellectual edifice may be, this new science of decision making will be judged based on both the accuracy of its predictions and the practical applications that it engenders. It is therefore gratifying to see an experienced author and market veteran like Bob Koppel bridging the gap and translating what has been almost exclusively academic research to a practical level that will appeal to investors, novice and experienced alike. In his latest book, *Investing and the Irrational Mind*, Koppel marshals an impressive array of evidence from the latest research in behavioral economics and neuroeconomics. This is research, particularly in neuroeconomics, that few investors have heard of, much less know how to use to their advantage.

This is not to say that behavioral economics and neuroeconomics provide facile answers or magical formulas for success. Indeed, such wishful, fallacious thinking is amply documented in this book and is partly to blame for our current economic malaise. And in any case, we are still in the early days of behavioral economics and neuroeconomics. As I see it, the success of intellectual ideas is not altogether different from the diffusion of new products in the marketplace, and it goes through several distinct stages. First, the intellectual edifices are built, but they are known by only a small group of academics or leading industry users. Next, they become the domain of early adopters, in this case perhaps some vanguard group of investors. Finally, and only for the most successful ideas, their use becomes so widespread that entire institutions are built around these ideas. Quantitative finance provides a perfect illustration of this process. Beginning with luminaries such as Harry Markowitz and Fischer Black, we have now reached a point where it is difficult to imagine life without the institutions that have been built upon financial models of risk and valuation. Behavioral economics, I think, has now reached the second stage, while neuroeconomics is still in the first stage with glimpses of moving to the second.

It is difficult, however, to see behavioral economics and behavioral finance moving squarely into the third stage. Behavioral economics has remained a collection of findings and treatments, albeit powerful ones, that do not lend themselves to the type of systematic day-to-day operations that distinguishes institutions. The great promise of neuroeconomics is that it will one day provide a rich array of quantitative information that can be integrated into the day-to-day operations of a trading floor. That is, one day we may be able to build institutions that take into account the individual or collective genetic, physiological, and brain responses of the individuals that make up the institution, in the same way that financial instruments litter the current investment landscape.

That day remains a twinkle in the eyes of a small group of academics and forward thinkers like Bob Koppel. In the meantime, Bob has given us a work that presents a plethora of new ideas and data in an enjoyable and accessible manner. Simply put, to succeed in today's market, an investor needs to not only digest the relevant information from the market, but also take into account the imperfect machinery that is his own brain. This book provides a guide to doing that.

Acknowledgments

I want to thank the individuals who, despite demanding schedules, agreed to be interviewed for *Investing and the Irrational Mind*. I deeply appreciate their expertise, candor, and insight into the role of psychology in financial decisions. I wish also to acknowledge all those who graciously offered comments on how to improve the original manuscript. In particular, thanks go out to Bill Brodsky, Ming Hsu, Tom Grossman, Robin Mesch, Howard and Alex Abell, Tom Shanks, Yra Harris, Judd Hirschberg, Mox Tan, Jennifer Lerner, Scott Gordon, Denise Shull, Antoine Bruguier and Rick Kilcollin. Thanks also to **Kate Darcy**, John Conolly and Robert Guardi of the CME Group for their early support and the production of the *Investing and the Irrational Mind* video for the Exchange website.

I would like to thank Mara Koppel for once again demonstrating her fine editorial skills. Thanks also to my family, Lily and Niko Koppel and Tom Folsom, all professional writers, for their comments and technical assistance. My agent and former editor Cindy Zigmund deserves high praise for wise counsel and encouragement.

Finally, I would like to thank my editor at McGraw-Hill Mary Glenn and her staff, Daina Penikas, Joseph Berkowitz, Ann Pryor and Sara Hendricksen, for their uncompromising belief in this book. Their enthusiasm throughout is warmly noted.

INVESTING
and the
IRRATIONAL
MIND

Introduction

Shortly after the events of September 11, I left New York and returned to Chicago. I thought that I was done writing about the psychology of money forever. As the author of more than half a dozen critically acclaimed books on investing and money issues, what more did I have to say? Yet, with the global financial meltdown brought on by a new breed of traders fueled by greed, testosterone, and genius-level IQs, I once more felt the urge to enter the fray. A few years ago, who could have imagined the near demise of the financial world at the hands of traders trained as mathematicians and theoretical physicists?

It is only a recent phenomenon that the threat of "black swans" disguised as mortgage-backed securities or "quants gone wild," discussed in the news, could have been considered anything but a remote possibility. The problem was neither the disastrous effects of quantum physics and differential calculus, nor a global think tank run amok by a handful of whiz kids from Harvard, MIT, and Princeton.

What is to blame for the recent economic upheaval is our basic understanding of finance and market psychology, and those mysterious and unconscious forces—human emotions, social norms, and delusional expectations—that guide our investment decisions. In retrospect, we should have heeded Warren Buffett's warning to "beware of geeks bearing formulas" and taken into account the systematic and predictable irrationality of our brains when confronted with financial decision making.

FUNDAMÉNTALLY IRRATIONAL

Born out of the desire of economists going back to the eighteenth century to have their field regarded as a natural science, explanations of financial activity have traditionally been understood as fundamentally rational. In finance, people widely subscribed to the "efficient market hypothesis," first expressed by French mathematician Louis Bachelier, which holds that markets are "informationally efficient," with the prices of invested assets reflecting all publicly available information. Yet this rational model is coming increasingly under fire as eye-opening revelations provoke a deeper examination of us as market participants. The real question is whether we act in our own portfolio's best interests.

Benefiting from the latest insights in the fields of behavioral finance and neuroeconomics, today's market psychology has come a long way since the days of hard-and-fast investment axioms and reliance on pop psychology hawked by trading gurus and coaches. Today, it seems that almost anyone who has a large grant and Ivy League cred is demonstrating just how fundamentally irrational we really are—in love, in our business relationships, but especially when it comes to our pocketbooks, as this book will investigate. Studies released regularly from institutions such as Harvard, Caltech, Duke, and Berkeley note our ever-inventive expressions of herd behavior when it comes to spending our hard-earned cash and making financial decisions. For any doubters, everything from brain imagery to "theory of mind"—both of which we will discuss later—proves the point. A recent study from the University of Illinois has even shown that our brains know the market not as an orderly algebra class, but as the wild jungle.

In *Predictably Irrational: The Hidden Forces That Shape Our Decisions*, MIT professor Dan Ariely explored how our choices in everything from occupational preferences to sex partners are derived from deep-seated emotions, misunderstood beliefs, and cultural norms that, as his title suggests, are not senseless or random, but are to be expected: inevitable and irrational. His work builds on the insights of behavioral economists and psychologists, among them several Nobel laureates: Daniel Kahneman and Amos Tversky, Herbert Simon, Richard Thaler, Robert Shiller, and Andrew Lo.

In this book, which focuses on how to overcome our irrationality when managing our trading and our investment portfolios, I will explore at length this group's contributions to the field of behavioral finance and what we can learn from them, and ourselves, to become better investors.

MY EXPERIENCE

The German philosopher Arthur Schopenhauer, his hair in two white tufts on either side of his elastic mind, once wrote, "Every truth passes through three stages before it is recognized. In the first it is ridiculed, in the second it is opposed, in the third it is regarded self-evident." When it comes to behavioral finance, after a long period of buffoonish laughter and academic criticism, we have now arrived at Stage 3. In truth, understanding the financial arena in psychological terms has been how I have always viewed markets from my earliest days trading foreign currency, interest rate, and equity futures on the floor of the Chicago Mercantile Exchange.

Since my start in the trading pits, there always seemed to be something undeniably irrational about the markets, my fellow traders, and myself. Although I came to the exchange with little practical financial training, beyond degrees in economics, philosophy, and group behavior from Columbia University, my greatest asset was a burning need to discover what made this place thrive. What unseen forces controlled whether or not we survived in the financial jungle? My quest for competitive intelligence was often not shared by my rivals. I was more anxious to learn than they were to teach.

Today, I have the perspective of being a market veteran who has spent more than 30 years trading equities and futures, long and short term, utilizing technical and fundamental analysis, and a range of financial instruments. I have been an exchange member trading my own account, as well as a principal in a CME Group clearing firm, where I hired and managed a team of proprietary traders who were market makers in every pit of the Chicago Mercantile Exchange and the Chicago Board of Trade, which today make up the CME Group, the world's largest futures exchange. I have also run, along with my business partner, Rand Financial Services' Innergame Division, which is recognized as one of the premier firms in the industry, executing trades and clearing for institutional clients with $50 million to several billion dollars under management. In New York, I was a principal in a $300 million hedge fund, where I supervised and created risk parameters for our team of proprietary traders. In addition, I have enjoyed friendships and conversations and conducted hundreds of in-depth interviews with top traders, hedge fund managers, and financial experts that were developed into my books, including *The Inner Game of Trading*, *The Intuitive Trader*, and *Money Talks*. I continue to work with traders to develop models and trading programs, and I advise others on trading strategy and risk management. In addition to all this, I've had my own ups and downs in the market.

Over time, I have learned that the stock market is a Rorschach test. The more I look, the more I see myself. The market is a mirror of complexity, inconsistency, irony, and paradox. Now, as validated by behavioral economics and neuroscience, investing is recognized as having less to do with the science of computation and more to do with the art of managing one's outlook, emotions, and consciousness. It involves invention, imagination, and know-how, and the courage to exploit the hard edge of a price chart—the action on the right-hand side that reveals the stock market's next unexpected move.

MAKE PROFITS, REDUCE LOSSES, AND GROW CAPITAL

Investing is a microcosm of life. Within it, we experience joy, uncertainty, frustration, and struggle. It requires courage, optimism, humility, and the desire to succeed. It would also be wise to refer to our army field manual on jungle survival, as at times there are predators as fierce as biting ants, spiders, and snakes.

Our challenge is made all the more difficult because our decisions are under assault from our brains. As economist Richard Thaler, best known as a theorist in behavioral finance, has pointed out, we are bounded by rationality, willpower, and self-interest. We fluctuate irrationally between an aversion to losing and our own delusional optimism.

In this context, irrationality means poor decisions, systematic errors, market inefficiencies, herd behavior, and the hasty, often detrimental collective decisions of "groupthink," a mode of thinking in which the members of a group strive for unanimity by overriding their motivation to appraise alternative courses of action realistically, with the resulting loss of individual creativity, uniqueness, and independent thinking. This leads us, like lemmings, to inevitable bubbles and crashes. Our brain's hardwiring predisposes us to misconceptions of reasoning, aggravated by emotional triggers and deviations in judgment: biases, fallacies, illusions, and paradoxes. Why? Because we ache for certainty, control, and the validation that we are right.

Our minds are messy, confusing, and ambiguous, mirroring the market, which is messy, confusing, and ambiguous. Behind this paradox is our deep-seated fear of losing. Losing draws down our account and, worse, provokes thoughts of insolvency and failure. Within our repertoire of responses are denial, inaction, confusion, and anger. Loss burns into our psyches. We feel its effects in tightened muscles, sweaty palms, and shallow breaths. It makes us anxious and on edge. We can see, hear, and even taste past mistakes and visions of doom. It makes us think less of ourselves, leading us to confuse our investment decisions with our self-worth. Obviously, this is not the desired end result of investing.

Beginning with a subjective, concise history of investor psychology, I will draw on behavioral finance to explore, and then demonstrate how to apply, state-of-the-art concepts. By the end of this book, you will know how to overcome debilitating emotions, irrational biases, and investment fallacies and arrive at an understanding of overall market risk through an approach that identifies, assesses, and controls losses. It is only through the development and implementation of focused, disciplined, patient, and confident market behavior—important internal skills that have been recognized as essential for nearly as long as there have been markets—that investors from small-share traders to billion-dollar hedge fund managers can make profits, reduce losses, and preserve and grow capital.

Insights from top traders, behavioral economists, risk managers, and neuroscientists further serve to illustrate the latest thinking, such as the work of Joseph Stiglitz, winner of the Nobel Prize in economics, whom the *New York Times*'s Paul Krugman calls "an insanely great economist, in ways you can't really appreciate unless you're deep into the field." Building on such brilliant analysis, I will ask some of the basic and provocative questions needed to arrive at an understanding of the source of market failure, relating it to the individual investor and emphasizing the persistent need for scrutiny, regulation, and oversight of our own decisions. Financial meltdown and flawed response is not a phenomenon that occurs only on the macro level.

Just as life doesn't come with instructions that, once followed, will enable you to sink baskets like Kobe Bryant or sing like Bono, in my experience knowing and working with many of the world's top traders and investors, I have come to realize there is no winning algorithm, no blueprint to explain peak performance. Unfortunately, knowing all the rules or mastering an objective system is about as far removed from the experience of optimum investing as painting by numbers is from producing a Picasso.

While it would be grievously incorrect to deny or underestimate the importance of reason or logic, as we will see, successful investing involves far more than specific analytical and strategic skills. It requires the development, cultivation, and conditioning of habits, thought patterns, and creative attitudes that influence the way we think and act in the market.

It is my goal in *Investing and the Irrational Mind* to answer the most fundamental question about financial decision making: how does the investor overcome habit-driven behaviors and ordinary reasoning, and move forward to achieve the psychological freedom to invest? In other words, I will reveal how we can master our irrational minds to gain the skills necessary to control our financial decisions.

Perceiving a situation seems, at first glimpse, like a remarkably simple operation. You just look and see what's around. But the operation that seems most simple is actually the most complex, it's just that most of the action takes place below the level of awareness. Looking at and perceiving the world is an active process of meaning-making that shapes and biases the rest of the decision making chain.

—DAVID BROOKS, "THE BEHAVIORAL REVOLUTION"

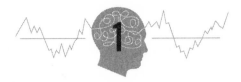

A Concise History of Investor Psychology

I n May 2008, in an interview with the *New York Times*, Kenneth C. Griffin, president and CEO of the $20 billion Citadel Investment Group, a leading global financial institution, offered some pretty harsh words about Wall Street. His gripe was with the Street's prevailing psychology of reckless and excessive risk taking. He called for an immediate overhaul of its mindset. No stranger to placing big bets, Griffin knew what he was talking about. While an undergraduate at Harvard, he had started two hedge funds from his dorm room, installing a satellite dish to channel real-time market data so that he could trade between classes. Founded in November 1990 with a little over $4 million, Citadel is now the world's eleventh largest hedge fund, earning Griffin a reported $900 million in 2009, after a double-digit drawdown in 2008.

Upset by the failure of Bear Stearns and the mistakes of big-name money managers and CEOs who assumed catastrophic risks that led to the evaporation of billions from their balance sheets and whose actions eventually led to the disappearance of Lehman Brothers and the near collapse of the financial system, he made an assessment that was blunt and to the point. "We, as an industry, dropped the ball," he said. "We have a responsibility to manage risk in a way that is prudent."

Was Wall Street once again guilty of hubris? According to Griffin, the problem was a market psychology that allowed for too much risk compounded by weak government oversight. "When you read that UBS did not even view parts of its mortgage portfolio as having risk," he said, "it becomes very obvious that a number of firms were not dotting the i's and crossing the t's when it comes to risk management."

He also cited the additional problem of youth and inexperience. "Walk across any of the trading floors—they are full of twenty-nine-year-old kids," he explained. "The capital markets of America are controlled by a bunch of right-out-of-business school young guys who haven't really seen that much. You have a real lack of wisdom."

THE QUANTS

Wall Street Journal reporter Scott Patterson's electrifying portrait, *The Quants*, describes how a group of brilliant, gutsy traders, composed of math geniuses and physicists, first earned their chops through gambling, then moved to take on Wall Street. Accentuating the quirky intrigue of this group, Patterson details the personalities and temperaments of its characters. Its principal figures included Citadel's Ken Griffin; chess master Boaz

Weinstein of Deutsche Bank; Peter Muller, manager of Morgan Stanley's secretive hedge fund Process Driven Trading (PDT); Cliff Asness, the founder of the nearly $40 billion fund AQR Capital Management; and Ed Thorp, an MIT-trained mathematician and card shark, hedge fund manager, and author of *Beat the Dealer*, the first book to statistically prove that the house advantage in blackjack can be overcome by card counting.

This story opens not long ago in the Versailles Room, which is as posh as its name suggests, in Fifth Avenue's storied St. Regis Hotel. Beneath a gilded ceiling, antique floor-to-ceiling mirrors revealed the players, the quants, competing at Wall Street Poker Night. These yearly red-carpet events and tournaments, benefiting Math for America, brought together quants and professional poker players, surrounded by beautiful women, to play high-stakes, blue-chip poker. "The small group of wealthy and brilliant individuals . . . had, through sheer brainpower and a healthy dose of daring, become the new tycoons of Wall Street," reports Patterson. "Few people outside the room had ever heard their names. And yet, behind the scenes, their decisions controlled the ebb and flow of billions of dollars coursing through the global financial system every day." This was not Gordon Gekko's 1980s game of liar's poker.

More than anything else in the world, the quants were searching for their truth. For the quants, it was revealed in the obscure patterns of the market, which could be discovered only through mathematics. These young masters of the universe devised an appropriate name for it: alpha. Alpha, Patterson explains, is defined as a "code word for an elusive skill certain individuals are endowed with that gives them the ability to consistently beat the market."

MARKET PSYCHOLOGY
IN A NUTSHELL

The desire to beat the market is not a new idea, nor has it been limited to quants or to capital markets. When it comes to speculation, we are looking at a dramatic history of booms and busts. Our minds are irrationally fueled by the prospects of quick enrichment through such things as tulips in Holland, gold in Louisiana, real estate in Florida, art, Internet stocks, and mortgage-backed securities. We are driven by greed. We are panicked by fear.

Combining psychology, economics, and neuroscience, the recent field of neuroeconomics studies how people react in these emotionally exuberant situations. Looking at the role of the brain, researchers examine how we evaluate investments, categorize risks and rewards, and interact with one another in our economic transactions. However, the story of our attempt to comprehend the relationship between investing and the irrational mind begins much earlier.

Since the inception of modern markets, investors have sought to understand the factors that assured profit and prevented individuals from getting caught up in a psychological ricochet between euphoria and depression. One of the first attempts was made by Dickson G. Watts, president of the New York Cotton Exchange from 1878 to 1880, a great arena of economic activity in America. In *Speculation as a Fine Art and Thoughts on Life*, in his list of essential qualities of the speculator, Watts wrote, "Those who make for themselves an infallible plan delude themselves and others."

Watts identified five qualities that he believed were key for success: self-reliance, judgment, courage, prudence, and pliability.

Summing up, he wrote, "The qualifications named are necessary to the makeup of a speculator, but they must be in well-balanced combination. A deficiency or an overplus of one quality will destroy the effectiveness of all. The possession of such faculties, in a proper adjustment is, of course, uncommon. In speculation, as in life, few succeed, many fail."

It was a good early attempt to understand a near chaotic speculative environment, one that relied heavily on nineteenth-century moralistic teachings and everyday common sense.

THE BOY PLUNGER

These observations won Watts the attention of young Jesse Livermore, who learned a lot about markets and himself from the slim volume, as revealed in Livermore's classic 1923 work on the art of speculation. *Reminiscences of a Stock Operator*, the fictionalized biography of the Boy Plunger, as he was known, charts the first-person experiences of Lawrence Livingston, a thinly disguised Livermore, through his progress in mastering Watts and the world of stock speculation to become one of Wall Street's most successful traders.

First appearing as a series of 12 articles in the *Saturday Evening Post*, *Reminiscences of a Stock Operator* was published under the name of its editor, journalist Edwin Lefèvre, a friendly newspaperman whom Livermore used as a source of information and as a plant to disseminate favorable news items. The book chronicles a trajectory of speculation that begins in the New England "bucket shops," brokerage firms, now illegal, that took the opposite side of customers' orders without having the orders actually executed on an exchange. The term itself derives from the fact that customers' orders went "in the bucket," having never been executed by the pseudo brokerages.

Starting off as a quotation boy, Livermore developed a "feel" for the market and began to trade for himself. After considerable trial and error, he arrived at crucial insights about the market that allowed him to build a million-dollar fortune while he was still in his twenties. Unfortunately, he lost that fortune and several more. But with each mistake, he extracted a lesson that he shared with his readers, often explaining that his lack of adherence to his own rules was the source of his most devastating losses.

"It never was my thinking that made the big money for me. It always was my sitting. Got that? My sitting tight! It is no trick at all to be right on the market," Livermore says. "You always find lots of early bulls in bull markets and early bears in bear markets. I've known many men who were right at exactly the right time, and began buying or selling stocks when prices were at the very level which should show the greatest profit. And their experience invariably matched mine—that is, they made no real money out of it. Men who can both be right and sit tight are uncommon."

It is the very psychological nature of Livermore's insights combined with great storytelling that make his ideas so compelling, as in this other example: "There is profit in studying the human factors—the ease with which human beings believe what it pleases them to believe; and how they allow themselves—indeed urge themselves—to be influenced by their cupidity or by the dollar-cost of the average man's carelessness. Fear and hope remain the same; therefore the study of the psychology of speculators is as valuable as it ever was."

This advice is as useful today as it was when it was written nearly 90 years ago, perhaps even more so in the wake of the meltdown of Bear Stearns and Lehman Brothers and a global economy that is still struggling to apprehend irrationality's meaning. Livermore was particularly wary of tips and their ruinous effects, another unfortunate lesson that many are now learning at the cost of their jobs and their homes. "Tips! How people want tips! They crave not only to get them but to give them. There is greed involved, and vanity."

Livermore made $3 million after the panic of 1907 and $100 million in the 1929 stock market crash, an astonishing sum for the time, and subsequently lost both fortunes. His greatest legacy appears to be the dissemination of a practical investment philosophy and a cautionary tale that a life in the market is not all beer and skittles. His battle-tempered perceptions about maximizing profits and reducing losses provide evergreen market advice. In the best-selling classic *Market Wizards: Interviews with Top Traders*, which delves into the minds of some of the world's most successful traders, *Reminiscences of a Stock Operator* was cited as the major investment primer for the traders that author Jack Schwager interviewed.

In March 1940, Livermore published, under his own name, *How to Trade in Stocks*, an attempt to codify all that he had learned in his long life of speculation. He wrote, "All through time, people have basically acted and reacted the same way in the market as a result of: greed, fear, ignorance, and hope. That is why the numerical formations and patterns recur on a constant basis." The book did not sell well; the prospects of war were high, and interest in the stock market was low.

Largely dismissed by the market gurus of the era, Livermore's effort to systematize his methods was viewed as being outside of

Wall Street's orthodoxy. It is ironic that as late as 2009, when two MIT neuroeconomists, Andrew W. Lo and Jasmina Hasanhodzic, published their book on Wall Street's leading technical analysts, including John Murphy, Stan Weinstein, Bob Farrell, Paul Desmond, and Ralph Alcampora, their title was *The Heretics of Finance*, indicating the level of esteem still accorded to these market professionals.

On November 28, 1940, Jesse Livermore fatally shot himself in the cloakroom of the Sherry-Netherland Hotel in New York. In a leather-bound notebook found in his pocket was a letter addressed to his fourth wife. It read, "My dear Nina: Can't help it. Things have been bad with me. I am tired of fighting. Can't carry on any longer. This is the only way out. I am unworthy of your love. I am a failure. I am truly sorry, but this is the only way out for me."

Seven years earlier, Livermore had married 38-year-old Harriet Metz Noble in Geneva, Illinois. It was his third marriage and her fifth. Despite Livermore's battle-tested risk acumen, he hadn't hesitated in his choice of Harriet, whose previous four husbands had committed suicide. Trusts and cash assets at Livermore's death totaled more than $5 million.

Although Livermore ultimately did not follow his own advice, and often acted erratically, his psychological insights have provided fertile ground for generations of investors.

THE LONE WOLF OF WALL STREET

A friend and colleague of Livermore's, who had also earned a fortune by short selling in the 1929 market crash, was stock trader

Bernard Baruch, later a financier and statesman who advised presidents Woodrow Wilson and Franklin D. Roosevelt on economic matters. Baruch's keen observations demonstrate the volatile nature of the market and the mindset required to master it. Today his name decorates a branch of the City University of New York. Like Livermore, he had read Scottish journalist Charles Mackay's 1841 book, *Extraordinary Popular Delusions and the Madness of Crowds*, which examined its subject in three parts: "National Delusions," "Peculiar Follies," and "Philosophical Delusions."

Among the financial manias that Mackay described were the South Sea Company bubble of 1711 to 1720, the Mississippi Company bubble of 1719 to 1720, and the Dutch tulip mania of the early seventeenth century. According to Mackay, during this bubble, speculators bought and sold tulip bulbs with abandon, even investing in futures contracts on them. Some varieties briefly became the most expensive luxuries in the world. Both Livermore and Baruch learned vital lessons from Mackay that they would bring with them to Wall Street.

Known as the Lone Wolf of Wall Street, Baruch earned a fortune before the age of 30. Famous for his razor-sharp observations, he is remembered today for pithy statements like his answer to the question of what was the key to his success in the market, "Selling too soon!" or "I'm not smart, but I like to observe. Millions saw the apple fall, but Newton was the one who asked why."

One of my favorites is Baruch's statement about self-reflection: "Only as you do know yourself can your brain serve you as a sharp and efficient tool. Know your own failings, passions, and prejudices so you can separate them from what you see." The full importance of this insight in light of recent developments in behavioral finance and neuroeconomics will soon become apparent.

Baruch provided his rules for successful investment:

▶ Don't speculate unless you do it full time.

▶ Resist so-called information or tips.

▶ Before purchasing a security, know everything you can about the company: its earnings and its capacity for growth.

▶ Never attempt to buy at a bottom or sell at a top of a market: this is a feat achieved only by liars.

▶ Take your losses swiftly and clearly. The first loss is your easiest loss.

▶ Don't buy too many securities. Focus on a few investments that can be monitored carefully.

▶ Periodically reappraise all your investments to make sure that they are appropriate for your particular strategy.

▶ Know when you can sell to your greatest advantage (of course, this also applies to buying).

▶ Never invest all your funds. Keep some liquid.

▶ Don't try to be a "jack of all investments." Stick to the field you know best.

A lifelong skeptic of both giving and taking advice, Baruch qualified his market rules with a caveat: "Being so skeptical about the usefulness of advice, I have been reluctant to lay down any rules or guidelines on how to invest or speculate wisely. Still, there are a number of things I have learned from my own experience that might be worth listening for those who are able to muster the necessary self-discipline."

MR. MARKET

The first serious attempt to distinguish between speculation and investment and to address the investor's natural inclination toward irrational investing was made by economist and professional investor Benjamin Graham, born Benjamin Grossbaum. "An investment operation is one which, upon thorough analysis, promises safety of principal and an adequate return," he wrote. "Operations not meeting these requirements are speculative."

Advocating what he called "value investing," Graham taught this approach at Columbia Business School and refined it over many editions of his famous book with David Dodd, *Security Analysis*, first published in 1934 and ever since considered to be a bible for serious investors. The idea behind value investing was to purchase stocks whose price was lower than their true value and then to hold them until the price returned to that value, earning a gain on the investment.

Graham's disciples make up a pantheon of professional investors, including Warren Buffett, Irving Kahn, William J. Ruane, and Walter Schloss. Buffett credited Graham with giving him the basis for his investment framework, describing him as the most influential person in his life after his own father. Irving Kahn and Buffett both named sons after him. Buffett describes

The Intelligent Investor, published in 1949, as "the best book about investing ever written." In it, Graham states that the investor should regard equity shares as offering part ownership of a business, making the stockholders focus on the long term, and cautioning against a short-term perspective that gets one bogged down in the erratic fluctuations of stock prices.

Graham's favorite allegory is that of Mr. Market, a fellow who turns up every day at the shareholder's door offering to buy or sell stocks at a different price. Often, the price quoted by Mr. Market seems plausible, but sometimes it is ridiculous, either way too low or way too high. The investor is free to trade at the quoted price or to ignore Mr. Market completely. But Mr. Market is agnostic, returning the following day to quote another price.

The point of this anecdote, then and now, is that the investor need not regard the arbitrariness of Mr. Market as the determining factor in the value of one's shares. The investor is advised to focus on the performance of his businesses and receiving dividends, rather than to concentrate on moody Mr. Market's fluctuations and irrational behavior.

THE WHIZZES

In 1988, futures trader Jack Schwager published *Market Wizards: Interviews with Top Traders*; this and subsequent editions focus on the trading philosophy, strategy, and psychology of a wide range of professional investors. Among those profiled were Michael Marcus, Bruce Kovner, Michael Steinhardt, Paul Tudor Jones, and computer trading pioneer and market guru Ed Seykota, famed for his statement, "Everybody gets what they want from

the market." The trading styles of a group of professional investors were also probed: commodities legend Richard Dennis; stock
selection expert William O'Neil; Chicago pit traders Tom Baldwin
and options market maker Tony Saliba; and James B. Rogers Jr.,
Quantum Fund cofounder with George Soros.

Schwager found that there was no single ingredient, algorithm, or market strategy that could sum up the amazing investment performance of this diverse group of professionals. They
employed a vast array of philosophies and methods, analyses and
time frames. "There is no holy grail in trading success," Schwager
concluded. "The methodologies employed by the market wizards cover the entire spectrum from purely technical to purely
fundamental and everything in between. The length of time they
typically hold a trade ranges from minutes to years. Although the
styles of the traders are very different, many common denomina-
tors were evident." What was shared, whether the approach was
based on macroeconomics or solely on price charts, hours long
or years in the making, was the psychology that allowed the investor to exploit opportunities, however he or she defined them.

Among the psychological qualities identified were desire,
confidence, perseverance, rigid risk control, patience, intellectual
independence, a love of investing, a strong loss threshold, and
discipline. Significantly, discipline was the most frequently mentioned attribute.

DISCIPLINE

Picking up on the psychological importance of discipline and the
difficulty of exercising it in the midst of financial decision mak-

ing, former stockbroker Mark Douglas wrote *The Disciplined Trader: Developing Winning Attitudes* in 1990, and followed it up in 2001 with *Trading in the Zone: Master the Market with Confidence, Discipline and a Winning Attitude.* Douglas proposed that the elements of character that produce success in most of life's endeavors are different from those that make for successful investment. The key was to maximize one's mindset. The essential work of the investor was to overcome psychological interference: internal conflicts, contradictions, and paradoxes.

When I interviewed Douglas in my office in Chicago's Art Deco Lyric Opera House, he told me that he believed there were certain characteristics of a mindset essential to creating success in the markets. For him, the key was consistency. He said to me, "There is an often-used saying on the floor of the exchanges that 'traders just rent their winnings.' As you know, there are many traders who have reached the stage of development where they can put together a substantial string of winning trades, days, weeks, or even months, only to lose all or almost all of their hard-won equity in a few trades and then start the process all over again."

One of the topics that we spoke about, which is currently an area of intense research in behavioral finance and neuroeconomics, is the relationship that the investor forms with the market. Douglas maintained that whereas most relationships imply two-sided or two-way interaction, this is not the case with the market. "Most traders have absolutely no control over the market's movement, and, by the same token, the market exercises no control over the trader," said Douglas. "From each individual's perspective, the market just generates information about itself and gives each trader the opportunity to make a successful trade on his own behalf." Douglas said that he taught investors that their results were a direct outcome of the number of distinctions that they made about the market's behavior, namely, "the quality of those distinctions, and how well they can act on them." He added that all these functions are internally oriented processes.

Douglas provided an interesting window into how investors could become disciplined traders, but he lacked the clarity to identify those internal elements convincingly or to provide a practical methodology. What was still needed was an approach that went beyond the mere description of the psychological problems associated with trading. Investors needed to know—through detailed exercises and illuminating examples—how to overcome debilitating behaviors in order to change their attitudes, sharpen their focus, and bolster their confidence.

In Chapter 2, we will consider the blueprint that offers solutions by modeling the beliefs, mental strategies, and internal dialogue of some of the world's best traders and investors. Enter the inner game.

The Inner Game

Z eroing in on the psychological elements of financial decision making that expose the investor to fear, greed, and a host of other irrational emotions, Howard Abell and I wrote *The Inner Game of Trading*. Writing primarily for fellow professional investors, we built on the concept introduced by Timothy Gallwey, once captain of the Harvard University tennis team, in *The Inner Game of Tennis*, published in the 1970s. Gallwey argued that games are composed of two parts, an outer game and an inner game. "The former is played against opponents, and is filled with lots of contradictory advice," he stated, "the latter is played not against, but within the mind of the player, and its principal obstacles are self-doubt and anxiety." As a critic later observed, it was sports psychology before the two words were codified into an accepted discipline.

Both my business partner and I had spent decades trading stocks as well as financial and equity futures on the floor of the Chicago Mercantile Exchange. I traded my own account, and Howard, who also managed a hedge fund, was the president of a large clearing firm, CSA Inc. Based on our observations of ourselves and of fellow traders, all of whom were professional investors, we recognized that there was a gap in the financial literature when it came to explaining the true nature of the market, its participants, and the idiosyncratic way in which trading decisions were made.

We plied our trade in a messy, sweaty, fiercely competitive world of organized confusion, where contradictory information and debilitating emotions were the rule. In *Bulls, Bears, and Millionaires*, I described my first impression of the floor as resembling the Great Barrier Reef, a "virtual kaleidoscopic swell of activity with traders, exchange employees and runners, color-coded in aggressive neon, scurrying about with all the single-mindedness of sperm cells; a teeming self-contained environment where only the most well-adapted life forms survive." To make it in this cutthroat environment was a constant psychological challenge.

Time and again I would hear from top traders who I interviewed, including George Segal, Jack Sandner, Toby Crabel, Tom Grossman, Patrick Arbor, Leo Melamed, and Jeffrey L. Silverman, that they knew or employed individuals who were as well or better versed than they were in the financial literature, some who could easily cite from memory insights from Watts, Livermore, Baruch, and George Soros's theory of reflexivity and its application to financial markets, but, interestingly, it was not this knowledge that made for a successful trader. So what does and what was their secret?

The answer was devilishly simple to articulate but painfully difficult to achieve. It was the ability to consistently make money based on an approach or system that they could execute with total confidence. They also remained upbeat after a series of losses, staying calm, focused, and analytical throughout the ups and downs of the market.

I often tell this story to new traders who ask what it takes to be a successful investor: John D. Rockefeller, the richest man in the world, was asked by a newspaperman in the 1920s what was the secret of his great fortune. The old man answered, "Three things. First, I always arrived at work early. Second, I was invariably the last to go home. Third, I struck oil!"

The point is that you have to work hard, but it doesn't hurt if you are also lucky.

One thing was clear to me: merely knowing what to do in the market wasn't enough. To be successful required a flexible, resourceful state of mind, allowing the investor to act effortlessly on his knowledge with intelligence and discipline, overcoming any irrational impulses that got in the way. I identified a set of psychological skills that could be learned and practiced, with specific suggestions for their application. These skills included compelling motivation, goal setting, confidence, anxiety control, focus, state management, self-talk, and mental conditioning. Through the prism of these skills, we get a glimpse into the internal terrain of consistent winners, how they overcome the psychological barriers and frustrations that hold most people back. What motivates them is not a love affair with risk taking. These are not the daredevils of the financial world. What they possess is the ability to overcome irrational biases and to keep moving forward—to learn from their mistakes, undeterred by setbacks.

High-performing investors are much like high-performing athletes. In fact, many top investors have had a history of sports success. In both pursuits, there is a definite psychological syntax that leads to a positive result. What we learn from them is that success provides its own arrangement of internal representations and concomitant proven market behaviors that are executed in a specific sequence of actions to achieve a profitable result. In contrast, the way most investors internalize market phenomena dictates an often indecisive, anxious, and confused response. The important point here is that we produce a predictable result—rational or irrational—that is true to our psychological syntax. In investing, the right mindset does not ensure a profitable outcome, but it does give the investor the ability to stay with the investment and realize its appreciation without getting bogged down in self-destructive feelings or thoughts.

The psychological syntax of a successful investor usually looks something like this: the investor identifies an opportunity, based on a tested methodology or approach; the execution is timely and decisive; the risk is well calculated, with a defined loss; and the investment is watched in a resourceful and patient state of mind. Irrational thoughts pop up, but they are regarded as being as random as a cell phone ringing in someone else's pocket. To quote Warren Buffett, "It's simple, but it's not easy."

The psychological syntax for successful investment applies as much to the short-term trader who is engaged in exploiting a sudden price anomaly in the market as it does to the long-term value trader. The key is to overcome predictably irrational behavior in the effort to achieve a rational financial goal.

Seth Klarman, founder and president of the Baupost Group, a Boston-based private investment partnership, wrote in the sixth edition of *Security Analysis* (2008), "The real secret to investing is that there is no secret to investing. Every important aspect of value investing has been made available to the public many times over, beginning in 1934 with the first edition of *Security Analysis*. That so many people fail to follow this timeless and almost foolproof approach enables those who adopt it to remain successful."

In stocks, as in sports, there is winning and there is losing. Success requires focused concentration that permits an unbiased perception of the market, fortified by a system of personal beliefs that allows the investor to simulate the feeling of being in control. All we can ever control is ourselves, but, as we shall see, that is more than enough.

THINKING AND REALITY

In 2009, the Soros Lectures at the Central European University were simultaneously broadcast to students at Fudan University, Shanghai; Hong Kong University; Columbia University; the London School of Economics; and MIT. George Soros stated his investment philosophy globally. It is one that has resonated with me, as it is consistent with my experience as a market participant because of its simplicity and fundamental truth. Soros spoke about how, over his life, he had developed a conceptual framework that helped him to make money as a hedge fund manager and to give money as a policy-oriented philanthropist. But he said that his conceptual framework itself is not about money. "It is about the relationship between thinking and reality," he said.

In crystalline form, this is the issue facing every investor, a subject that has been extensively studied by philosophers from early on. The relationship between thinking and reality reveals that we are fallible, caught in a labyrinth of uncertainty, where, true to Scottish philosopher and economist David Hume's observation, reason is the slave to passion. The structure of our brains leads us down a troubling path that is strewn with perceptual error and cognitive distortion. It makes us mistake-prone. Today, especially, investors are bombarded with sensory stimuli, often reaching the point of overload. Under the pressure of time, we order, condense, and oversimplify our experiences and the way we interpret data. It is no wonder that our intentions and actions don't always mesh.

ENTER THE BEHAVIORAL ECONOMISTS

Calling into question the traditional rational model of neoclassical economics, the field of behavioral economics has concentrated its research on the study of precisely these issues. Through surveys, experimental observations, and, recently, functional magnetic resonance imaging (fMRI), the field's objective is to better understand the economic decisions of consumers, borrowers, and investors and their effects on prices, investment returns, and the allocation of resources.

With the groundbreaking work of Nobel laureate Daniel Kahneman and Amos Tversky, cognitive models of decision making under conditions of risk and uncertainty present a challenge to accepted economic models of rational behavior. It is worth mentioning here that early economists, specifically Adam Smith and Jeremy Bentham, also wrote extensively on the influence of psychological factors, but as economics evolved into a discipline, this explanation lost out to ones that posited a rational *homo economicus*, or economic man. Richard Thaler, coauthor with Cass Sunstein of *Nudge: Improving Decisions about Health, Wealth and Happiness*, has quipped that, as the discipline of economics increasingly tied itself to the natural sciences, this rational agent more and more mirrored the economists who were inventing him, bearing little resemblance to real people.

Another notable exception was British economist John Maynard Keynes, whose ideas have profoundly affected modern macroeconomics, who referred to "animal spirits" to describe the quantifiable economic impact of our emotions on consumer confidence. Keynes held that, apart from the instability caused by speculation, there is the instability caused by the character of human nature, as a large proportion of our "positive activities depend on spontaneous optimism rather than mathematical expectations, whether moral or hedonistic or economic." He said that our decisions to do something positive can only be the result of these animal spirits, a "spontaneous urge to action rather than inaction, and not as the outcome of a weighted average of quantitative benefits multiplied by quantitative probabilities."

Appropriating Keynes's term, Nobel Prize–winning economist George A. Akerlof and Yale professor of economics Robert J. Shiller published a big-think book that became a favorite among members of the Obama administration. In *Animal Spirits: How Human Psychology Drives the Economy, and Why It Matters for Global Capitalism*, the authors focused on the role that emotions play in influencing economic behavior. They argue that, traditionally, economists have not placed enough emphasis on the importance of animal spirits, or the irrational emotional factors that drive our economic decisions. In this view, the government must act decisively to restore confidence, particularly at times like our recent financial crisis, thus capitalizing on the influence and effects of positive irrational impulses on the overall economy.

Seasoned investors who are in tune with their own animal spirits (the unforeseen but inevitable feelings and thoughts that motivate behavior) understand all too well the importance of the inner game and how irrational factors make or break a portfolio.

In Chapter 3, we will look to behavioral finance and neuro-economics for insights into our investment decisions based on the latest studies and findings about the structure of the mind, alerting us to the challenges of an irrational self.

Hardwired
and Irrational

I n an effort to better understand financial decision making in situations involving risk, Daniel Kahneman, Israeli psychologist, Nobel laureate behavioral economist, and professor emeritus at Princeton, and his longtime collaborator, the late Amos Tversky, developed prospect theory in 1979. In a departure from rationally oriented utility theory, which dates back to the late eighteenth and early nineteenth century, the researchers found that investors were more sensitive to a loss than they were to a gain of equal size. They also found that, while we are loss-averse, we are overconfident and risk-denying in our optimism. In a recent interview, Kahneman described his research colorfully: when it comes to investment decisions, he claimed, people hate losing more than they enjoy winning because "the emotional tail wags the rational dog."

Looking at and trying to make sense of the world is an active process that shapes and biases our decisions. As we will soon discover, true to *New York Times* columnist David Brooks's perception, "The operation that seems most simple is actually the most complex, it's just that most of the action takes place below the level of awareness."

Behavioral economists have shown that our financial decisions are often based not on detailed analysis, but rather on what are called heuristics, or rules of thumb. In addition, we are subject to a framing effect: the way an investment is presented determines its selection and outcome. We also experience a reflection effect whereby individuals make irrational choices to enter or exit an investment based on a subjective reference point determined by whether they have already experienced a gain or a loss. An example of this would be someone waiting for a "breakeven" price before exiting from an investment that is performing poorly rather than looking at the market objectively, without reference to the purchase price.

Richard Thaler is the director of the University of Chicago's Center for Decision Research. He humorously describes his studies of behavioral economics and the psychology of decision making on his Web site as "relaxing the standard economic assumption that everyone in the economy is rational and selfish, instead entertaining the possibility that some of the agents in the economy are sometimes human." Part of Thaler's research involves identifying market anomalies and cognitive biases that explain why our investment decisions are so often wrong.

When individual instances of economic behavior that violate traditional microeconomic theory are documented, the explanation for why they happen is often found in the following: (1) what sounds sensible may not be so, and (2) because of the way our brains are structured, we are subject to emotion and mistakes.

Speaking about the need for investors to overcome their natural tendencies to worry about small risks and not large ones, Thaler says that we are penny-wise and pound-foolish. To put it simply, our brains are hardwired for making irrational choices. Thaler identifies the most confident people as the ones who most often believe that they are *not* overconfident and are not wrong in their decision making. It is this very irony that may help shed light on the recent financial crisis. We experience reality not as it necessarily is, but as we expect it to be, with a clear preference for immediate gratification. This leads people to underindulge in activities that have immediate costs and delayed rewards, and to overindulge in activities that have immediate rewards and delayed costs. It also explains in part why investors tend to be risk-seeking when dealing with a perceived loss but risk-averse when dealing with a perceived gain. In the parlance of Wall Street, "You can't hold on to your losers and cut short your profits," and its corollary, "You can't eat like a bird and shit like an elephant."

THE FEAR SENSOR IN YOUR BRAIN

In a groundbreaking study, neuroscientists at the California Institute of Technology located our loss-aversion mechanism in a specific structure in the brain, the amygdala, two almond-shaped clusters of tissue located in the medial temporal lobes. Described in an article in one of the leading academic journals, the *Proceedings of the National Academy of Sciences*, the finding offers insight into economic behavior, and also into the role of the amygdala, which, according to the study, "registers rapid emotional reactions and is implicated in depression, anxiety, and autism." The study involved patients whose amygdala had been destroyed as a result of a rare genetic disease and individuals without amygdala damage, all of whom volunteered to participate in simple economic tasks.

The subjects were asked whether or not they would accept a variety of monetary gambles, each with a different possible gain or loss. For example, participants were asked whether they would take a gamble in which there was an equal probability that they would win $20 or lose $5 (a risk that most people will choose to accept), and whether they would take a 50/50 gamble to win $20 or lose $20 (a risk that most people will not choose to accept). They were also asked if they would take a 50/50 gamble on winning $20 or losing $15—a risk that most people will reject, even though the net expected outcome is positive.

The patients with amygdala damage took risky gambles more often than subjects of the same age and education who had no damage. The study concluded that the first group showed no aversion to monetary loss whatsoever, in sharp contrast to the control subjects. "We think this shows that the amygdala is critical for triggering a sense of caution toward making gambles in which you might lose," stated one of the researchers, professor of behavioral economics Colin Camerer. It may also be similar to the amygdala's role in fear and anxiety. He also added that while loss aversion has been observed in many economic studies, from monkeys trading tokens for food to people on high-stakes game shows, this was the "first clear evidence of a specific brain structure that is responsible for a fear of such losses."

THE RED WINE SNOBS
AND IRRATIONAL THINKING

Another study out of Caltech that was reported in *Psychology Today* in 2010 provides additional insight into how and why we invest and the irrational factors that guide our decisions. The experiment was conducted by a group of researchers under the leadership of Hilke Plassmann, whose research in consumer decision making and strategic marketing at the intersection of neuroscience, psychology, and economics has appeared in leading academic journals as well as being reported widely in the media. The purpose of this study was to examine the relationship between perception and taste. It poses the question, is taste more than just a matter of mere taste?

This study involved the Stanford wine-tasting group and several bottles of variously priced cabernet sauvignon. For the experiment, Plassmann and her colleagues told participants that they would be tasting five different wines in order to test the time it took individuals to detect different tastes for various flavors. In reality, the researchers were interested in something else. They wanted to analyze the connection between perceived flavor and the taster's knowledge of a wine's price.

To accomplish this, the researchers made sure that the participants were always aware of a wine's supposed value by presenting bottles that had retail prices of from $5 to $90 clearly marked. They also refilled the wine bottles in such a way that each participant would have to taste the same wine twice, once from a bottle that was marked as expensive, and once from a bottle that had a much lower price tag. Participants were led to believe that they were tasting five different wines, when in fact they were tasting only three different wines, two of them twice.

The first set of results was striking, but expected. The wine tasters remained oblivious to the researchers' manipulations and were not able to tell that they had tasted only three, instead of five, wines. Also, when tasting the same wine, the wine tasters invariably reported superior taste for the wine that came out of the $90 bottle than for the wine that came from the significantly cheaper bottle.

But there were additional data that made the experiment even more interesting. Since reported taste is a poor measure of true taste experience, researchers used functional magnetic resonance imaging (fMRI) scanning machines to image participants' brains as they tasted the wines, and what was revealed was fascinating. When a participant was tasting the wine out of the cheap bottle, the medial orbitofrontal cortex—an area of the brain that is strongly related to experiences of pleasure—showed little activity. But when the exact same wine was poured out of a $90 bottle, what do you think happened? The brain showed levels of activation that indicated that significantly more enjoyment was experienced from the exact same fermented grapes. The study made it clear that the price tag has a physiological effect on taste, and that expectations alone were sufficient to influence taste experience. The Stanford wine group expected the wine to taste better, and so it did.

What Sommeliers Have to Do with Market Wizards

As entertaining as this research is (you can try it the next time you have a dinner party), here is where the story gets even more interesting, with obvious implications for investors. Commenting on a brain imaging study with master sommeliers (think market wizards), titled "The Appreciation of Wine by Sommeliers: A Functional Magnetic Resonance Study of Sensory Integration," University of California professor of psychology Lawrence Rosenblum, referring to the Caltech wine-tasting experiment, offered an insightful observation that distinguishes the tasting experience of a master wine taster from that of an ordinary drinker. He shines a light on master sommelier Steven Poe.

Master sommeliers are considered the most knowledgeable wine experts. To give some perspective, Poe holds a title shared by fewer than 200 people in the entire world. His training involved years of education in taste, theory, and production, with a master examination involving a blind tasting at which the candidate must recognize the grape variety, region of origin, and vintage of six unlabeled glasses of wine. It is not unusual for candidates to take the test four or five times before they pass.

According to Rosenblum, Poe's knowledge is consistent with what is known about true wine expertise. Wine experts do not have more sensitive palates, per se. What makes Steven Poe an expert is how he brings his formal knowledge of wine production to what he tastes. For example, Poe is familiar with the flavor outcomes of *malolactic fermentation*, a process of secondary wine fermentation. In a blind tasting, he might notice one of the flavors associated with the process—a buttery texture, for example—and then attend to the other likely flavor results of the process, including hints of yogurt and sauerkraut. This could help Poe narrow down a wine's region and vintage.

And here is how all this relates to our investment decisions. There is a distinct cognitive and physiological difference in the way a master sommelier experiences the taste of wine. Rosenblum explains it as the "analytic, explicit knowledge component" of wine expertise, which is consistent with recent brain imaging research. This work shows that, relative to novices, when sommeliers sip, their brains show greater activity in regions associated with the higher cognitive functions (memory, language, and decision making). Increased activity in these regions probably reflects the expert's analytic tasting experience.

Rosenblum concludes, with obvious application to smarter financial decision making: "This is all good news for you. You may currently be tricked by a wine's label, price, and even color. But with some serious studying of wine production, along with practice in tasting, your brain can start lighting up like that of a master sommelier."

Seasoned investors experience their investments differently from the average investor, and one doesn't need to be aware of which area of the brain is being activated to appreciate and learn the difference. To quote Rosenblum, this is all good news. You may currently be being tricked by an investment's "label," its risks and rewards, and even the chances for its success, but with serious study of the market and the way that our minds work, your brain can start lighting up like that of an intelligent and accomplished investor.

THE EXCITEMENT FACTOR

When people become involved in markets, they are typically motivated to do so not only because markets are a source of potential riches, but because people find them exciting. It is easy to get caught up in the electricity and emotion of the stock market. Just think of Jim Cramer's *Mad Money* or CNBC's *Squawk Box*. The excitement factor can be motivating, but it can also be debilitating.

When I think about what first attracted me to trading when I set foot on the exchange floor more than 30 years ago, I realize that it was the feeling that each trade was like the deciding game of a seven-game World Series. I could practically feel the intensity pulsing through me on a molecular level. The same sentiment was expressed to me many times over by some of the country's top investors.

Toby Crabel, founder of Crabel Capital Management, a global investment firm with more than $1.6 billion under management, told me that his initial attraction to trading was the excitement that he experienced just setting foot on the trading floor. Before that, Toby had been a three-time All-American in tennis. Then he discovered commodity trading and found it electrifying. "I had this tremendous fascination with the trading floor. You would get this feeling that something big was happening here," he said. "Only later did I realize that aspect of trading is both positive and negative."

Tom Grossman, a former Goldman Sachs trader, now managing partner of Union Avenue Advisors' international equity fund, and a onetime business partner of mine, told me that his initial attraction to investing was what he referred to as "the hunt." He identified his early affinity for investing as a logical outgrowth of his participation in sports and an interest in gambling.

Like master sommeliers, seasoned investors like Crabel and Grossman rely more heavily on the cognitive, higher-functioning centers of their brains in order to attain their goals. When I asked Crabel, who has built a highly successful management company, if the market still held the same excitement for him, his answer was instructive. "The initial infatuation and excitement doesn't exist for me anymore," he said, admitting that it was an issue that he had had to deal with. "The course that I have taken is a much more methodical approach to the markets," he said. "The excitement comes from seeing my [capital] management business succeed."

Consistent with the idea of tamping down the emotional excitement of investing, Tom Grossman said that what has sustained his interest in the market is seeing what made money and what were the classical errors. "Just really thinking about the whole investment process and how many different and interesting ways there were to go about it," he said. "Learning what worked to make money consistently in the markets and what strategies and tactics meshed with my personality."

These responses express what Rosenblum referred to as "the analytic tasting experience." In a financial context, let's call this "the analytic investing experience" that allows for the empowering of our brains to master our financial decisions.

Socrates once famously said, "The unexamined life is not worth living," by which he meant that to enjoy a fulfilled life, we must question our thoughts and actions. With regard to money, we would all be wiser to say that the unexamined mind is not capable of successful investing. There is value in analyzing our motivation to invest, to inspect it critically, and to constantly ask ourselves the philosopher's simple question, why? Top investors spend their careers engaged in this practice, consciously and unconsciously, which, in my experience, accounts for their success. But unfortunately, even if you accomplish this, it is not enough.

BLACK SWANS

It is relevant here to bring up well-known scholar and trader Nassim Taleb's observation that, as investors, we overestimate the value of rational expectations and past data, and underestimate the importance of what he calls "black swans." These are crucial, high-impact, and "unknowable" events like the Kennedy assassination, Black Monday, 9/11, and the recent financial crisis; all of these are momentous, but in hindsight we convince ourselves that they are rational and explainable. Taleb identifies an issue of concern for investors that he has called the "ludic fallacy," the belief that the unstructured randomness found in life resembles the structured randomness found in games. This idea derives from the assumption that the unexpected may be predicted by extrapolating from variations in statistics based on past observations, especially when these statistics are presumed to represent samples from a bell-shaped curve. These concerns are particularly relevant in financial markets, where professional investors employ value-at-risk (VAR) models that imply normal bell-shaped curve distributions and underestimate the critical importance and impact of the outliers.

INTANGIBLE MOTIVES

We have seen how our brains often drive us in directions that are off our intended road map and how the map itself may be a poor representation of the territory. As behavioral economist Daniel Kahneman has observed, "Financial decision-making is not necessarily about money. It's also about intangible motives like avoiding regret or achieving pride." No wonder there is often a distance between our investment hopes and practices.

Almost all books on investing tell us to "buy low and sell high." Yet, most of us buy high and sell low. We also can't manage to set realistic and achievable goals and exercise that elusive, nearly mystical personality trait so often called upon by the likes of Warren Buffett and John Templeton: patience. Additionally, we are admonished not to listen to tips, like the one that your brother-in-law recently gave you, which was a guaranteed winner—before it went to zero. And to make things worse, the more we watch the news and keep up with how to invest, the more confusing the whole thing gets. Does any of this sound familiar?

What compounds the problem is the pop psychology finance literature that advises you to always keep an open and optimistic mind, which makes you feel like one of the characters nailed to a cross in the final scene of Monty Python's *Life of Brian*, asked to sing in the face of investor fear and frustration, "Always Look on the Bright Side of Life." Having an optimistic attitude may make you feel better, but it won't, by itself, turn you into a profitable investor.

The answer from neuroeconomics is that the best investment results come from understanding the irrational nature of our brains in order to strike the right balance between emotion and reason. This is easier said than done because the key to the dilemma goes beyond becoming a knowledgeable investor, which is a hard enough goal in itself. As they say on the trading floor, "The real frontier is between your ears." This phrase barely outlines the issues of human uncertainty, though, with all of its frailties.

Hawksbill Capital Management's CEO, Tom Shanks, brought the point into high relief in an interview when he described the process of introspection that he engages in after a period of market losses. "I think that anybody who goes through a drawdown questions whether what he's doing is correct and whether the systems are still viable, so there's a struggle with that," he said. "For me, experiencing a drawdown is a tremendous motivation to get back on track."

What Shanks made clear was that if you want to succeed at investing, the real challenge is to hold a mirror up to yourself and take a really hard look, stating, "You can't kid yourself in trading. You have to deal with who you really are, and take responsibility for all your shortcomings, which the market has a way of revealing rather starkly. You have to confront all your fears and tame them. You have to check your ego at the door."

In a follow-up interview in the summer of 2010, I wanted to know the toughest psychological issue that Shanks continued to struggle with—considering that his fund trades using a systematic program with a discretionary overlay. He said, "My biggest struggle is impulsivity. My instinct is to react to market action, and I've learned that it's much better to fight that impulse than to give in to it." He said that one thing that helps him keep it under control is being aware of the fact that the market usually behaves in a way that induces traders to do precisely the wrong thing. "I remind myself that the market action that gives rise to a strong impulse in me is having a similar effect on thousands of other market participants, and that's probably not a herd mentality I want to be a part of."

Referring to the fact that he was one of the highly selective group of traders, known as the Turtles, who were taught and capitalized by trading legends Richard Dennis and William Eckhardt in the 1980s, Shanks said, "I was always instructed to do the hard thing, which is an excellent maxim to follow, not just in trading, but in life." Shanks added that professional traders get paid for doing what others cannot do, for being psychologically tougher and more disciplined than the crowd. He then explained, "Most of the time that means forbearing to react to market action. If I feel I must trade, I believe it is always better to make the market 'prove' itself a little more by placing a stop—above the market if buying, below if selling—rather than a market order."

It is precisely because our brain is hardwired to respond in ways that it judges to be in our own best interest that it causes us to be impulsive, inconsistent, disorganized, and irrational in situations involving risk. That is also why, although you may be able to recite all the correct market axioms, it will always be difficult to put them into practice.

MARKET AXIOMS

Without blaming your brain too much, as you read through the following list of accepted market wisdom, ask yourself how many times you have violated these principles that are easier said than obeyed. Also, what were you thinking and why?

- ▶ Buy low, sell high.

- ▶ The trend is your friend.

- ▶ Avoid the crowd.

- ▶ Take small losses.

- Take big profits.

- Don't overtrade.

- Don't turn a profit into a loss.

- Don't be impulsive.

- Don't add to a losing position.

- Don't be stubborn.

- The market is always right.

- Trade liquid markets.

- Don't buy or sell on price alone.

- Preserve capital.

There are other profitable rules that are equally difficult to adhere to because of what we now know from neuroeconomics, namely, that when we invest, there are definite physiological reactions in our bodies and our brain that work against our conscious intentions.

When we are in a profitable position, our neural activity is indistinguishable from that of someone who is high on drugs. Brian Knutson, a professor at Stanford University and a pioneer in neuroeconomics, has imaged the brains of investors while they trade. "The more you think you can gain from the risk, the more you take the risk and the more activation in the circuitry," Knutson said. What he observed was that people who were trading actually got high, and irrational, on making money.

MONEY CAN BUY YOU LOVE

Another recent study that indicated that we are hardwired for irrational thought showed that our brains experience having money with the same feelings that we attribute to love. The research was conducted in China, where two groups of students were told that they would be participating in a test of finger dexterity. One group was given a pile of currency to count, and the other was given blank pieces of paper. Then they were asked to put their fingers in bowls of water heated to 122 degrees Fahrenheit and rate how uncomfortable it felt.

The subjects who had been counting money and then put their hands into the painfully hot water reported that the water didn't feel as hot to them as it did to people who had counted blank slips of paper. When imaged, their brains showed activity in the same areas that reflect "falling in love."

The experiment is described in a research paper titled "The Symbolic Power of Money," in the journal *Psychological Science*. Researcher Xinyue Zhou, of the department of psychology at Sun Yat-Sen University in China, described the findings: "We think money works as a substitute for another pain buffer—love."

In Chapter 4, we will discuss our brain and how to make the best use of it.

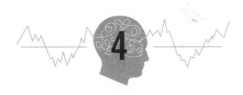

A User's Guide
to the Brain

As we saw in the Caltech amygdala study, we process risk in the same area of the brain that handles anxiety, depression, and threats of mortal danger. As a consequence, we are predisposed to seek instant gratification that we perceive to be pleasurable, and thus we are hardwired to misinterpret our investment expectations as what is really happening in the market. We also now know that anticipating profit and achieving it are experienced in vastly different ways in the brain.

Despite all these findings, market axioms still need to be obeyed to achieve a profitable outcome. Neuroeconomics has some encouraging ideas to offer on this point. It is possible to get off the treadmill of repeated investment error. The good news is that your brain is structured to help you accomplish this. According to Dr. John J. Ratey, clinical associate professor of psychiatry at Harvard Medical School, "The human brain's amazing plasticity enables it to continually rewire and learn—not just through academic study, but through experience, thought, action, and emotion." Neuroscience has clearly demonstrated that neural activity changes when we learn from our mistakes, as we saw with the brain activity of the master sommeliers. We possess the power to promote our brain's ability to regenerate through experience, thought, emotion, and action.

THE BRAIN IS NOT A COMPUTER

According to Dr. Ratey, "The brain is not a computer that simply executes genetically predetermined programs. Nor is it a passive grey cabbage, victim to the environmental influences that bear upon it. Genes and environment interact to continually change the brain from the time we are conceived until the moment we die. And we, the owners—to the extent that our genes allow it—can actively shape the way our brains develop throughout the course of our lives."

As your brain shifts the experience of investing from one of irrational pleasure to one of rational cognition, you are headed on a path to ensure a more profitable outcome. In order to accomplish this, you will need to learn how to do the following:

▶ Determine what kind of investor you are.

▶ Set realistic and achievable investment goals to earn higher returns.

▶ Learn how to be disciplined and patient.

▶ Manage risk effectively.

▶ Grow from your mistakes.

▶ Preserve your emotional and financial capital.

Neuroscience has now informed us that learning these skills provides us with the opportunity to better understand ourselves.

INVESTOR, KNOW THYSELF

In my association with top investors, the importance of self-knowledge and renewal has been a constantly stated objective. That is why I have found it so fascinating to excavate thoughts and emotions, and to explore how these individuals perceive their market experience as it relates to internal psychology and investing. The following is a list of words generated in my work with hundreds of major fund managers, as well as proprietary and independent traders. I asked them to write down the three words that best characterized "market wizards," and the words that appeared most often were *confident, disciplined, self-reliant, motivated, competent, self-aware, optimistic, intuitive, strategic, patient, hard-working, high-achieving, energetic, objective, proactive, organized, goal-oriented, self-contained, knowledgeable, open-minded, determined, enjoys investing, risk-managing, focused, independent, ambitious,* and *committed.*

The defining characteristic of the list is that the chosen terms are psychological in nature. Strategies and tactics are vitally important, but it is those qualities relating to moods, feelings, and attitudes to which these high performers attribute their success. A long-held belief among financial writers and many market participants is that in order to succeed in the market, it is essential to delete emotion from financial decision making. We now know, from neuroscience, that this idea is wrong.

The current research suggests that all we need to do to be successful investors is to keep the "good" emotions and get rid of the "bad" ones. And that's no joke. But for most of us, this is a nearly insurmountable proposition. The point is that our decisions are improved not by the elimination of all emotions, but by the harnessing of those emotions that are destructive and debilitating. A mere hunch can get you into trouble. A legitimate intuition may earn you a fortune.

This is a difficult point for many market participants to grasp. Dr. Ratey stated, "Contrary to the popular notion that decision-making requires a 'cool head,' it is feelings that point us in the right direction and help us make moral, personal, predictive and planning decisions." He described how feelings are produced when the brain senses the varying physiological states of the body.

Think about your recent purchase of a stock and the market's failure to gratify your expectation. Imagine for a moment that you are watching yourself clinically reacting to the loss. You may feel it in your stomach, in a shallow breath, or as tightness in the back of your neck. You have sweaty palms and a dry throat, and your mood is on edge.

Our body as represented in the brain is the basis for what we refer to as our "mind." Our physiology drives our mind, producing emotions that can make us do irrational things, but with an experienced awareness, we have the power to use our brains to overcome those anxieties that will lead us astray. When you look at yourself, watching your investment decline need not result in a loss or a mistaken action. Seasoned investors calculate losses *before* they happen. They are aware of the feelings and states of mind that a loss engenders. Yet, with strict risk management, they are able to override their natural inclination to flee from a psychologically and physiologically disturbing experience.

Many times a friend or colleague whom I have invited to the trading floor has remarked on the destructive level of stress that a professional must be feeling. That is because these observers "feel" themselves to be in an unfamiliar situation, where they are unaware of the hidden organization and structure. The trading floor appears to them to be an amphitheater of chaos and confusion. Without market knowledge or know-how, they perceive only threats lurking all around. Lacking a conceptual framework that would allow them to embrace risk, they don't sense opportunity. There is only danger. There are others who, unarmed with the background of how difficult a professional investor's work is, see only great rewards. Neither a mind filled with worry nor one fueled by wishful thinking is what good investing calls for.

Music and the Brain

An analogy that Dr. Ratey uses is to compare consciousness to a symphony orchestra. "At any moment the brain is receiving and generating all sorts of signals. Like musicians tuning up randomly on stage, the signals are constant but haphazard. However, when the conductor strikes the baton on the podium, the musicians suddenly all pay attention." By playing together, consciousness is created.

The psychologically aware investor learns to redirect those feelings and emotions that can be misguiding. In practice, this is an ideal that is never fully achieved. The challenge for the investor is to provide the internal opening downbeat so that what ensues will be in tune, played in harmony. A number of professionals whom I have interviewed in an effort to understand the workings of their minds have offered a similar analogy to music.

Leo Melamed, chairman emeritus of the Chicago Mercantile Exchange, described investing in our interview as being akin to music played on a rare violin. "A good trader is like a Stradivarius. You can play beautiful music on it, but, if it's out of tune, even a little bit out of tune, the music isn't very good." He added, "When you go through a difficult period, you get out of tune. Suddenly, something emotionally is wrong with your thinking and starts a process where your logic gets distorted."

Melamed went on to say that when logic gets distorted, an investor forgets his rules and violates investment principles that are known to be correct, resulting in a negative impact on the entire investment framework. "You're now doing things that you shouldn't be doing. If you think about it, you're reacting to emotions that you normally wouldn't react to. In other words, the Stradivarius is out of tune. That's the experience that every trader has encountered in one fashion or another."

Robin Mesch, president of an investment advisory firm working with proprietary traders worldwide, whom Bloomberg called one of the world's top minds in technical analysis, sounded a similar note in an interview. Trained as a musician, she stated that the pattern recognition skills that she used in her stock market price chart analysis were comparable to those employed in reading and interpreting musical scores. She told me, "Music creates a flow inside of you which creates the internal atmosphere for intuition," which Mesch cited as having a crucial role in her investing. She added, "You hear the music. There are certain qualities in musical phrases and tones; and connections inside the melodies."

This past summer, over dinner at Chicago's Le Colonial restaurant, I asked Mesch if she had any additional thoughts about the role of music in the way that she perceived markets. She said, "I've always thought of the markets as something you could hear, and what you are listening for is the sound of the order flow increasing or drying up. When the market is 'turning up or turning down the volume,' it creates a pattern or shape when organized on the computer screen. Music is really no more than organized sound, and like a composer, the role of the technician is to organize that sound of the order flow onto a screen so that the trader can read it clearly, engage with it, and bring her own meaning and understanding to the performance."

All of this awareness comes with a dividend. It places you on the road to making the right investment decisions without getting ambushed by an irrational mind. Emotional paleomammalian systems deep in our brains make us instinctively yearn for instant gratification, abandoning logic and reason to avoid whatever seems to be potentially risky. The relatively modern, analytical areas of our brain often provide weak resistance to the strong demands of an ancient mind. That's why knowing what to do in the market and knowing how to do it are so vastly different.

Patience and Diligence

In an interview with Tom Shanks of Hawksbill Capital Management, what came across to me from this thoughtful system trader was that he learned how to invest successfully by taking away lessons about the market and himself from each mistake that he made. He said, "Patience and diligence are rewarded.

Profits will eventually accrue if you do the right thing and stick with it. That's the most important thing."

The challenge is to marshal both our reflexive and our reflective brains to act in harmony in order to get in tune with the market. That is what the minds of the best investors know how to do. The research is clear on this point. Andrew Lo of MIT and Dmitry Repin of Boston University have studied traders to determine how stress and emotions affect investment returns. They monitored vital signs like heart rate, body temperature, and respiration as investors moved into and out of trades. Not surprisingly, they found that traders who get caught up in their emotions tend to fare poorly in the market, but traders who rely solely on logic do not fare well either. The most consistently profitable investors use their emotions to their benefit without letting their feelings overwhelm them.

"Professional athletes have the same reaction—they use emotion to psych themselves up, but they don't let those emotions take them over," Lo said. Of course, you don't need to be a neuroeconomist to arrive at this conclusion, as Warren Buffett has said, "Once you have ordinary intelligence, what you need is the temperament to control the urges that get other people into trouble in investing."

THEORY OF MIND

Neuroeconomics is also investigating whether the best investors, in addition to being aware of their own minds, are adept at reading the minds of others. *Theory of Mind* (ToM), also referred to as *mentalizing*, is the ability to attribute psychological states that we experience in the form of beliefs, desires, and pretense to the attitudes and motivations of others who have perceptions that are similar to or different from our own. Akin to empathy, theory of mind is concerned with experientially recognizing and understanding the states of mind and emotions of someone else, putting yourself in the shoes of another. It has been speculated that theory of mind exists on a continuum, which may explain why some investors are better at reading intentions and market behaviors than others.

NYU neuroeconomics professor Paul W. Glimcher suggests that we may be using two different strategies when we are inferring the mental states of others. In one strategy, we simulate the other person based on knowledge that we have about ourselves; with the other strategy, we assume, or infer, the mental states of the other person based on more abstract knowledge that we have about the world. He said that the second strategy "may also involve knowledge about stereotypes, and raises the interesting question as to whether judging another person's mental state may be biased in different ways depending on whether we perceive them as similar or dissimilar to ourselves."

The key point here is that success depends on a strong subjective awareness of yourself as well as an objective understanding of the market (which is made up of others), armed with strategy and risk control without fear or wishful thinking. In addition, when it comes to an understanding of the brain, it is useful to remember that our world has gone from flat to round. Current research has overturned the old neurological dogma that adult brains cannot regenerate. The brain's plasticity enables it to continually rewire and learn, which means that we can influence our brain's ability to overcome habit-driven behaviors and be renewed.

In Chapter 5, we will consider what the markets and our minds have in common with a tropical habitat. The purpose of the discussion is to improve financial decision making, because, if you haven't noticed, it is a jungle out there.

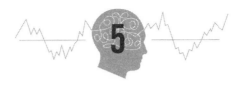

The Market:
It's a Jungle Out There

Studies from neuroeconomics offer counterintuitive ideas about the market and its participants that raise serious questions about the efficient market hypothesis (EMH). Stated simply, this hypothesis asserts that the market is "informationally efficient," and that investors cannot consistently achieve returns in excess of average market returns on a risk-adjusted basis. First suggested in 1900 by Louis Bachelier, a French mathematician, in his dissertation, "The Theory of Speculation," the idea was largely ignored until the 1930s. At the same time, research by economist and businessman Alfred Cowles, III maintained that professional investors were unable to outperform the stock market. Dedicated to raising economics to the level of a natural science, Cowles based his findings on his mathematical and statistical models. Added to this were independent studies that corroborated Bachelier's thesis and economic research that indicated that U.S. stock prices followed a random walk model.

EMH was developed by Eugene Fama at the University of Chicago's Booth School of Business as an academic course of study, was promulgated by Nobel Prize–winner Paul Samuelson and Stanford's Paul Cootner, and was widely accepted up until the 1990s. With the work of Daniel Kahneman, Amos Tversky, and others, behavioral economists uncovered serious flaws with the economic hypothesis predicated on the belief that prices on traded assets reflect all past publicly available information and that investors participate in markets with only rational expectations. Among the inefficiencies studied were those of price, such as the glaring divergence of stocks with low price/earnings and low price/cash-flow values, which outperformed other stocks, and those caused by cognitive biases, which demonstrated irrational decision making.

BIOLOGY AND THE MARKETS

MIT's Sloan School of Management professor Andrew Lo, a leading authority on hedge funds, specializes in quantitative global macro and global tactical asset allocation strategies. An expert on technical analysis, a market discipline that uses charts of past market prices and volumes to forecast future prices and market trends, Lo and his colleague Jasmina Hasanhodzic authored *The Heretics of Finance: Conversations with Leading Practitioners of Technical Analysis*.

Derived from hundreds of years of market observations and anecdotal information, the objective of technical analysis is to identify price patterns in financial markets in order to exploit these patterns to achieve a profitable return. Technical analysis had long been thought by academics as unworthy of serious consideration (in light of the principles of the efficient market hypothesis, which held that prices were random), and technicians were accorded the status of quacks. Lo and Hasanhodzic left no doubt about how, in their opinion, technical analysts have been traditionally regarded by mainstream economists. They pointed to the fact that technicians don't frequent the halls of academia, nor do they usually consort with finance professors or their students. In their view, "This separation is understandable given the disdain and disrespect most academics have for charting, which has been characterized by more than one academic with the following analogy: technical analysis is to financial analysis as astrology is to astronomy." The fact that some technicians have made use of astrological signs and rendered market predictions based on the alignment of price chart points with the phases of the moon has not furthered their cause in gaining greater acceptability.

Taking a heretical position, Lo has validated the practice of technical analysis by offering an alternative way to view the market. Drawing heavily on biology, he calls his theory the Adaptive Market Hypothesis. Applying the evolutionary principles of competition, adaptation, and survival of the fittest, Lo conceptualizes the market as a constantly changing living organism. Viewing the market in Darwinian terms is not exactly a new idea, but what gives Lo's theory added interest is its attempt to reconcile theories of market efficiency with the inefficiencies described in behavioral economics.

Lo's concept of the organic nature of our financial transactions bridges the divide between the neoclassical model and current behavioral models. He argues that much of what behavioral economics describes as irrational behavior can be reconciled with the efficient market hypothesis. According to Lo, the central idea of the efficient market hypothesis, that markets are informationally efficient and rational, withstands the challenge from behavioral economics, which argues that markets are driven by irrational forces. Lo said, "Recent research in the cognitive neurosciences suggests that these two perspectives are opposite sides of the same coin," and has proposed his framework to reconcile market efficiency with behavioral alternatives by applying the principles of evolution, competition, adaptation, and natural selection to our financial interactions.

Lo's point was that "prices reflect as much information as dictated by the combination of environmental conditions and the number and nature of 'species' in the economy." By "species," he means biological beings, of course (i.e., traders, investors, fund managers, and so on). In Lo's terms, efficiency is a dynamic and context-dependent concept that is heavily related to environmental factors affecting the market.

"Much of what behavioralists cite as counterexamples to economic rationality—loss aversion, overconfidence, overreaction, mental accounting, and other behavioral biases—are, in fact, consistent with an evolutionary model of individuals adapting to a changing environment via simple heuristics," said Lo.

THE ORGANIC RESHAPING
OF THE MARKET

The fundamental insight of the Adaptive Market Hypothesis is its emphasis on the constant organic reshaping of the market, where economic activity often does not exhibit equilibrium, or that point at which quantity demanded and quantity supplied are equal. In

Lo's theory, risk and reward are not necessarily stable over time, and arbitrage opportunities exist because prices are not random. It is in the market's reshaping that there is an underlying order to all financial activity and price action. Biological beings are rendering decisions that are influencing market outcomes. Behind every computer is a human being who is making a judgment.

In line with this perspective, there are, from time to time, inefficiencies that technical analysis and other qualitative and quantitative investment strategies can exploit. Since the market is in a constant state of flux, specific modes of analysis and execution will perform better or worse, depending on current conditions.

Underlying all of this is not the maximization of profit and utility, but rather the biological imperative of survival. Investors and markets are engaged in the naturally selective process of innovation, learning to adapt to a changing economic ecology. This idea echoes a comment made to me by market wizard Jeffrey L. Silverman, who coincidentally was educated at MIT. When I interviewed him in his Mercantile Exchange office, Silverman said, "Traders evolve and markets evolve. The role of the investor is just to evolve faster than everyone else." A longtime veteran of the financial markets, Silverman understood what he was talking about. Known for his keen eye and trading acumen, he had experienced the kill or be killed philosophy of markets on a daily basis over a long career.

SURVIVAL OF THE FITTEST

The notion that our brains relate to markets as if we were engaged in mortal combat rather than as a mathematical problem was the result of a research study led by Ming Hsu, head of the neuroeconomics laboratory at Berkeley's Haas School of Business. Professor Hsu's work focuses on decision making under uncertainty, moral decision making, and incorporating emotions and communication into strategic decision making. Although much is known about how individuals make decisions in situations of risk, less is known about the neural basis of decision making when risks are uncertain because of ambiguous or missing information. The results of Hsu's study suggested a general neural circuit that responds to degrees of uncertainty, contrary to traditional decision theory, which, in his words, "does not allow for degrees of uncertainty to influence decision-making."

A quick lesson about the brain highlights the findings. The prefrontal cortex is the anterior part of the frontal lobes and carries out the brain's executive function. It is here that complex logical reasoning, planning, and decision making occur. The central activity of this region is the orchestration of thoughts and actions in accordance with internal goals. According to clinical neuroscientist Daniel G. Amen, the medical director of the Amen Clinic for Behavioral Medicine in Fairfield, California, learning how to activate the prefrontal cortex in a positive way results in better internal supervision. Dr. Amen, an expert on the relationship between the brain and behavior and the author of several books about brain functioning, describes the various areas of the brain, stating, "Correcting abnormal brain functioning can change people's lives," and adding, "When your brain doesn't work right, neither can you."

Focusing on how to optimize brain function, he described the other areas of the brain. The parietal lobes integrate sensory information from the various senses. The temporal lobes, underneath the temples and behind the eyes, handle the senses of smell and sound, and are also responsible for processing complex stimuli, such as faces and scenes. When there are problems in this area, especially in the left temporal lobe, individuals are susceptible to rapid mood shifts and impairment of memory and learning. Both the parietal and the temporal lobes are also involved in decision making.

The basal ganglia are large structures deep within the brain that are responsible for the body's idling speed. When they are overactive, anxiety and feelings of panic result. When they are underactive, individuals wrestle with concentration and fine motor control.

At the center of the brain is the limbic system. Also known as the paleomammalian brain, it dates back to the earliest period of human evolution. When this part of the brain is out of kilter, the result is moodiness and negativity. The structures within this system include the hippocampus, the amygdala, the anterior thalamic nuclei, and the limbic cortex, which support a variety of functions, including emotion, behavior, and long-term memory. The striatum, a subcortical part of the forebrain, is a major input station for the basal ganglia. The striatum is activated by stimuli associated with reward by way of metabotropic dopamine receptors.

The cingulate run longitudinally through the center part of the frontal lobes. Dr. Amen refers to this area of the brain as the gear shifter, which allows for the transition of attention from thought to thought and between behaviors. "When this part of the brain is overactive, people have problems getting stuck in certain loops of thoughts or behaviors." It is responsible for rigidity and repetitive worries.

It is important to keep in mind that all these areas of the brain are interconnected, and none of them perform in a vacuum.

All systems are interrelated, so what affects one has implications for the others. There are also differences of opinion among neuroscientists about exactly how to separate the different systems.

With new findings appearing regularly, it is best to consider the perspective of neuroscientist Jonathan Cohen, who is the director of Princeton's Center for the Study of Brain, Mind, and Behavior, when considering brain function and its relationship to economic behavior. Cohen has collaborated with economists on several imaging studies. "The key idea in neuroeconomics is that there are multiple systems within the brain," Cohen said. "Most of the time, these systems cooperate in decision-making, but under some circumstances they compete with one another."

Bearing all this in mind, let's consider the results of Dr. Hsu's study. Using functional magnetic resonance imaging (fMRI) techniques, Hsu and his research team demonstrated that the level of ambiguity in choices correlated positively with activation in the amygdala and orbitofrontal cortex, and negatively with activity in the striatal system; and striatal activity correlated positively with expected reward. Also, neurological subjects with orbitofrontal lesions were insensitive to the level of ambiguity and risk in behavioral choices.

Hsu concluded, "Standard decision theory, however, precludes agents from acting differently in the face of risk and ambiguity. Our results show that this hypothesis is wrong on both the behavioral and neural level, and suggest a unified treatment of ambiguity and risk as limiting cases of a general system evaluating uncertainty."

This was a rather startling finding because the study suggested that investors' brains perceive the market more as a jungle than as an algebra class. In the language of neuro-economics, "Under uncertainty, the brain is alerted to the fact that information is missing, that choices based on the information available therefore carry more unknown and potentially dangerous consequences, and that cognitive and behavioral resources must be mobilized in order to seek out additional information from the environment." The important point here is that Hsu reached the conclusion that our brains view the market as an issue of life-or-death survival rather than one of arithmetic problem solving.

As a former floor trader, I can all the more appreciate the idea of our brain thinking of the market as a jungle. As someone once warned me early in my career, "The market's first rule is you eat only what you kill, and, if you act scared, stupid, or weak, you're someone else's dinner." In this sense, I believe that there is merit to Lo's notion of the market as an efficient and continually adaptive ecosystem in which Darwinian imperatives rule the day.

One of the particular advantages enjoyed by floor traders, which is borne out by a recent neuroeconomic study that focused on intuition and theory of mind, is that traders perform better when they have facial and additional physical cues at their disposal. These cues provide insight into other market participants' thoughts and intentions. The trading floor is rife with this type of material. In addition to monitoring order flow and the mood of the market, traders are always looking at other sources of human data in the form of who's buying and who's selling and which players are taking long or short positions. In the eyes of professionals, financial firms are often seen as falling into categories, such as dealers, brokers, investment banks, and hedge funds, and are ranked according to their past track records or their perceived record of recent success. It is all very subjective and irrational, and often highly useful.

Seasoned traders also intuitively examine one another on the trading floor, like scientists studying organic specimens. They tend to keep a mental list of perceptual data that range from a competitor's breathing to the way he holds himself to his manner of speech. We search for nuances and unconsciously ask ourselves questions: Is the breathing full or shallow? Is the body language confident or fearful? Is the manner of speech direct or anxiety-laden? Are the hand movements deliberate or fidgety? With each respiration or behavior, vital clues about strong resolve or self-doubt, concentration or inattentiveness, thoughtful decision or impulsiveness are offered to the market and can be acted on.

Personally, I would always look into the eyes of a trader who I thought may have been overcommitted to a particular position. I would study his stare or blinking for hints. I also looked for signs coming from the way someone shifted his weight, pulled too hard on an earlobe, or scratched at the corner of his mouth. A flushed face, as well as a visible pulse, could also be a reliable sign. In the jungle, all these subtle distinctions are made at the level of inference. Seeing and hearing trigger understandings for the floor trader that are not as readily available to market participants who are working in front of a screen.

Over time, off the floor, you also begin to learn how to read the tone and feel of a market. Does it look right? Is something not kosher? Seasoned traders routinely say that the market "stinks" or "smells fishy," and they are really sensing it—tasting victory, smelling blood. When this occurs, they are tapping into all five senses, not merely employing metaphor.

AN INVESTOR'S FIELD MANUAL

Since the market often looks and feels like a jungle, I thought it might assist us in our mission to learn how to become better investors to examine some tried-and-true strategies from the survival training source itself. The *U.S. Army Survival Manual* covers a broad range of proven survival techniques. It states that in order to make it in the wild, it is not enough to have the knowledge and skills needed to build shelters, get food, make fires, and travel without the aid of navigational devices. According to the field manual, a person's psychology is the defining indicator as to whether he will survive. It reads, "Some people with little or no survival training have managed to survive life-threatening circumstances. Some people with survival training have not used their skills and died. A key ingredient in any survival situation is the mental attitude of the individual involved. Having survival skills is important; having the will to survive is essential."

In a survival situation, soldiers face many stresses that ultimately affect their minds. The manual further states, "These stresses can produce thoughts and emotions that, if poorly understood, can transform a confident, well-trained soldier into an indecisive, ineffective individual with questionable ability to survive." To survive, a soldier needs to be aware of and able to recognize those stresses that are commonly associated with survival, as well as how to manage natural psychological reactions in order to stay alive.

Because of all the peril that abounds in the jungle, further reference to the field manual is useful. It states that, with practice, negotiating the thick undergrowth and dense foliage can be done efficiently; it also cautions soldiers to always wear long sleeves to avoid cuts and scratches. For the investor, I think the analogue is to have a trading plan and a system. To make it through the market's maze of ambiguous head fakes that inflict financial cuts and scratches, you need to know your financial goals, execute a thoughtful plan, and minimize the extent of bleeding through strict risk management.

The manual also states that to move easily, it is essential to develop what it calls *jungle eye*, which is the ability to look beyond what our innate perceptual bias has us focus on: the pattern of bushes and trees immediately in front of us. One needs to focus on the jungle further out and find natural breaks in the foliage. "Look *through* the jungle, not at it. Stop and stoop down occasionally to look along the jungle floor. This action may reveal game trails that you can follow."

The market also offers clues, both on and off the trading floor, everything from market fundamentals to technical information in the form of price levels and chart points, trend lines, continuation patterns, and areas of accumulation and distribution. There are also Elliott waves and fractals, Japanese candles and market profiles, esoteric forms of geometry, and algorithms that only someone with a genius-level IQ can fully appreciate. The key is, as in the jungle, that we move easily only when we begin to look beyond what our innate perceptual bias has us focus on. We must also keep in mind that sometimes the pattern we discover is not a true break in the foliage, nor an insight, but only a blind alley of our own making.

The most important thing, the field manual states, while monitoring psychological response to feeling at risk and emotional stress, is to be alert. Move with deliberation, stopping periodically to gauge your bearings. "Use a machete to cut through dense vegetation, but do not cut unnecessarily or you will quickly wear yourself out," advises the manual, adding, "Do not grasp at brush or vines when climbing slopes; they may have irritating spines or sharp thorns." It also warns, as in the market, that you should be on the lookout for biting ants, spiders, and poisonous snakes.

THE JUNGLE WITHIN THE JUNGLE

Our brain is anything but a neatly organized system. In fact, neuroscience has often compared it to a dense forest or "an overgrown jungle of 100 billion nerve cells, or neurons, which begin as round cell bodies that grow processes called axons and dendrites." Every cell has a single axon and as many as 100,000 dendrites. Neurons get their information from dendrites; it is the way that we learn, and axons are the way by which neurons pass on information to other neurons. "The neuron and its thousands of neighbors send out roots and branches—the axons and dendrites—in all directions, which intertwine to form an interconnected tangle with one hundred trillion constantly changing connections. There are more possible ways to connect the brain's neurons than there are atoms in the universe." These connections are responsible for our every thought, movement, and behavior.

As discussed earlier, until recently, it was thought that the brain was not engaged in an ongoing state of development—that, after childhood, the brain was hardwired as a result of assumed completed neural connections. According to the latest neuroscience research, we now know that our neural system is not fixed. It has the capability to reorganize and regenerate. "Thanks to sharp imaging technology and brilliant clinical research, we now have proof that development is a continuous, unending process." The important point here is that our brain's structure is not pre-determined. We can learn new skills and modify old ones, over-come debilitating emotions, and, through trial and error, teach ourselves psychological responses and styles that can become au-tomatic. We can do this because our brains are incredibly plastic throughout adulthood.

The difficulty for the investor is that, at moments of criti-cal decision making, the brain is often in competition with itself. Princeton professor Jonathan Cohen studied competing brain functions in a series of "ultimatum game" experiments. In these studies, a researcher offers a player a sum of money to divide in any way he chooses with a second player, who has the sole right to approve or disapprove the offer. If the second player approves the offer, the money is divided accordingly, but if the division is refused, neither player receives anything. It is called an ulti-matum game because, in effect, the first player gives the second player an ultimatum.

According to traditional game theory, any offer that provides profit should be accepted, as the alternative is that both players end up with nothing. When the game is played out, however, the results are strikingly different. Low offers, say of a dollar or less, are often rejected. Some players even reject higher sums. In an effort to understand what was happening, Cohen and several colleagues organized a series of ultimatum games in which half the players were placed in fMRI machines. At the beginning of a round, each player was shown a photograph of another player, who would make the first player an offer. The proposed division appeared on a screen inside the fMRI machine, and then Player 1 had 12 seconds in which to accept or reject the offer. Low offers were routinely vetoed, but what was most revealing were the brain scans of the respondents.

When a Player 1 received a stingy offer—one dollar for her, say, and nine dollars for the other player—she exhibited intense activity in the dorsolateral prefrontal cortex, an area associated with reasoning, and in the bilateral anterior insula, part of the limbic region that is active when people are angry or in distress. Researchers observed that the more intense the activity in the limbic area, the more likely the player was to reject the offer. Two regions of the brain were competing against each other to decide what to do: the prefrontal cortex wanted to accept the offer, and the insula wanted to reject it. "These findings suggest that when participants reject an unfair offer, it is not the result of a delibera- tive thought process," Cohen said. "Rather, it appears to be the product of a strong (seemingly negative) emotional response."

Taking ultimatum game research up a notch, Berkeley assis- tant professor Eduardo Andrade and MIT's Dan Ariely used the game-playing science experiment to show that not only are stingy offers refused when they are perceived to be unfair, but when emotional stimuli are present, players reject offers that would otherwise be accepted. They consistently found that emotion trumped self-interest. It is a painful lesson that many investors know too well: that anger is a powerful emotion that can cost you money.

To test how emotions influence the acceptance or rejection of an offer, Andrade and Ariely first made the subjects watch a "happy" video clip, a scene from the TV sitcom *Friends*, or an "angry" one, a confrontation from a movie in which an architect, after being fired, smashes a series of models. The outcomes were largely as one might expect. Given that individuals are willing to forgo self-interest when strong emotional stimuli are not present, it seems obvious that judgment is even more impaired when players are upset. Predictably, the players who saw the angry clip turned down offers that "happier" people accepted. Interestingly, when the experiment was repeated days or weeks later, without the reintroduction of the angry clip, the result was the same. The players who had been angry during the previous round rejected offers that were acceptable to similar, but less angry, people. The researchers surmised that playing the game revved up the same feelings of anger that players had experienced in the prior round. The implications for investing are pretty clear. In and out of the jungle, situations that set off feelings of anger and distress are breeding grounds for unprofitable decisions.

VARIATIONS ON A THEME

I was first introduced to the work of Dr. Jennifer Lerner through a *New York Times* article about why brooding shoppers tend to overpay. Lerner is a professor of public policy and management at the Harvard Kennedy School of Government, as well as director of its Laboratory for Decision Science, an interdisciplinary research center that she cofounded with two economists. Drawing on psychology, economics, and neuroscience, the Emotion and Decision Making Group's work centers on the study of human judgment and decision making.

Lerner's research explores the impact of specific emotions, such as fear, sadness, and anger, on our perception of risk and economic decisions. She has discovered that fear and anger have opposing effects on risk estimates: fear increases and anger decreases our perception of risk. The insights gained from this work have implications beyond how an individual's brain works. The data also provide knowledge that allows public officials to assess and communicate risk. According to Lerner, when we make decisions, our emotions act as a kind of weather system that overrides the accepted decision-relevant criteria.

To illustrate the impact of sadness and anger on financial decisions, Lerner conducted an experiment in which participants made simple economic decisions after viewing film clips that were designed to affect their mood, as in the Andrade and Ariely study. Subjects viewed a scene from either a tearjerker or a violent thriller before being asked to complete a simple task, unaware of the movie's influence on them.

The results for the effect of each emotion were both controversial and interesting. In the case of sadness, individuals became self-absorbed and liable to pay more for goods, in the unconscious belief that it would make them whole again. One reviewer quipped about the study's result with the tagline, "I have stuff, therefore I am." According to Lerner, "Another tempting belief is that one's mood (positive vs. negative), if it matters at all, would necessarily influence decisions in a mood-congruent way. So, many might suspect that being in a negative mood like sadness would trigger a negative outlook, encouraging devaluation. Here, again, the data contradict this belief. Sadness is a negative state but it does not trigger a negative outlook; instead it triggers increased valuation of commodities. People pay more to get things when they are sad."

When I spoke with Lerner, she suggested that the role of anger in decision making was more complex, as discussed in the findings in her paper "Portrait of the Angry Decision Maker: How

Appraisal Tendencies Shape Anger's Influence on Cognition." Lerner asserted, citing Aristotle, that angry decision makers have a difficult time being angry at the right time, for the right purpose, and in the right way, which hinders their ability to rationally enter a situation with objectivity. Instead, they make their decision with the tendency to feel confident, in control, and thinking the worst of others. These decisions often result in undesirable outcomes, such as aggression, unrealistic optimism, and overconfidence; however, in other situations, these decisions may result in desirable outcomes, inasmuch as anger can protect decision makers from indecision, risk aversion, and overanalysis. This too derives from the sense of certainty associated with anger, but may also be caused by a sense of optimism about the future.

Lerner said, "To be sure, the many judgment and decision outcomes associated with anger need to be documented and their normative status in diverse situations evaluated. It is now clear that one cannot reasonably cluster anger in with other negative emotions when making predictions. It is a unique and complex emotion." The upshot of the findings for both sadness and anger is, refrain from taking a big stab at the stock market if you are feeling depressed or in need of revenge.

THINKING LIKE A TRADER

When I spoke to Berkeley professor Ming Hsu, he suggested that I read a paper written by Peter Sokol-Hessner, entitled "Thinking like a Trader Reduces Individuals' Loss Aversion." Sokol-Hessner is completing a Ph.D. in psychology at NYU, where he is working on research that uses imaging technology to study the neural bases of financial decision making. He has conducted a series of studies in collaboration with Colin Camerer's lab at the California Institute of Technology, studying loss aversion using behavioral methods, physiological measurements, and imaging. He has also explored strategies in choice behavior, and has shown that people intentionally change how they make decisions in a very specific and reliable fashion, and that these changes result not only in changes in the decisions that they make, but also in their physiological reactions to profit and loss, and in their brain activity.

In his study, Sokol-Hessner asked participants more than 250 financial questions, posed as gambling choices, which were organized into two blocks. Individuals were instructed to answer the first set of questions as if each investment was the only one that they would make. In the second set of questions, participants were instructed to think of each bet not as an isolated gamble, but as part of a larger investment portfolio. The results demonstrated that people became less loss-averse when they believed that they were trading a portfolio of investments; shifting their mode of thinking, they believed that losses in one part of the portfolio would be mitigated by the profits in others. "Our research has shown that people can alter their own choice behavior in a systematic fashion," Sokol-Hessner said. "They can make themselves less loss-averse."

The results of the experiment suggested that individuals can respond to ambiguity and loss aversion with reasoning, potentially leading them to reject risky propositions; however, we need to be aware that the brain's first response to inconclusive data is usually one of fear. To illustrate this point, Caltech professor of behavioral economics Colin Camerer created a card game experiment.

Camerer was a child prodigy who, as an undergraduate, pursued quantitative studies at Johns Hopkins, followed by an MBA in finance and a Ph.D. in behavioral decision theory from the University of Chicago. Camerer and several colleagues performed brain scans on a group of volunteers while they placed bets on whether the next card drawn from a deck would come up red or black. In an initial set of trials, the players were told the number of red and black cards in the deck. This allowed them to calculate the probability of the next card's being a particular color. Then a second set of trials was held, in which participants were told only the aggregate number of cards in the deck.

The first scenario corresponded to the neoclassical economic model of rational investors facing a set of known risks. In the second set of trials, the players knew only something about what might happen, reflecting more of a real-world investment situation. As the researchers expected, the players' brains reacted to the two scenarios differently. With greater ambiguity, the players exhibited substantially more activity in the amygdala and in the orbitofrontal cortex. "The brain doesn't like ambiguous situations," observed Camerer. "When it can't figure out what is happening, the amygdala transmits fear to the orbitofrontal cortex."

THE EXHILARATION
OF THE SAFARI

As we are about to end our discussion about the market as a jungle, it will serve us well to remember how easily investors are seduced and injured by the call of the wild. Although investing can be very exciting, opportunities are best exploited without irrational exuberance. It is important to keep in the forefront of our minds that the market is driven by human emotion and that the ancient animal parts of our brains get as excited by money as by sex or drugs. In this regard, we are well advised to heed John Maynard Keynes's admonition that markets have the ability to stay irrational longer than we can stay solvent.

In Chapter 6, we will consider market psychology through the lens of behavioral economists Robert Shiller and Joseph Stiglitz and through a personal analysis, drawing on my experience of managing a team of proprietary traders and the essential psychological barriers that stand in the way of sound investing.

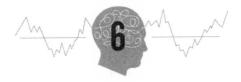

Things Fall Apart

The actions that led up to the subprime mortgage crisis of 2008 were based on the rational economic model that says that people make all the relevant financial calculations based on self-interest and logic. Accordingly, we were supposed to have made the perfect analysis of costs and benefits in our monetary decisions in order to optimize outcomes. But in the wake of this crisis and the financial meltdown that followed, we were brought to a deeper realization about human fallibility, risk taking, and a rational economic approach that fails to take our psychologically quirky behavior into consideration. According to Dan Ariely, "We were rudely awakened to the reality that psychology and irrational behavior play a much larger role in the economy's functioning than rational economists and the rest of us had been willing to admit."

In a congressional hearing on October 23, 2008, related to the financial crisis, former Fed chairman Alan Greenspan acknowledged that he was "partially" wrong in opposing regulation and that he was taken by surprise by what followed. He stated, "Those of us who have looked to the self-interest of lending institutions to protect shareholders' equity—myself especially—are in a state of shocked disbelief."

Greenspan was not alone in his opposition to regulation. In a 1999 government report that was a key factor in passing the Commodity Futures Modernization Act of 2000, allowing the rapid growth of over-the-counter derivatives, the ex-Fed chairman was joined by then Treasury Secretary Lawrence Summers, Securities and Exchange Commission chairman Arthur Levitt, and Commodity Futures Trading Commission chairman William Rainer.

In the same congressional hearing, Greenspan said of his belief in free markets: "I have found a flaw. I don't know how significant or permanent it is. But I have been very distressed by that fact."

Rep. Henry Waxman of California then pressed Greenspan to clarify. "In other words, you found that your view of the world, your ideology, was not right, it was not working," Waxman said.

"Absolutely, precisely," Greenspan replied, adding, "You know, that's precisely the reason I was shocked, because I have been going for 40 years or more with very considerable evidence that it was working exceptionally well." Greenspan admitted fault in opposing regulation and acknowledged that financial institutions hadn't protected shareholders and investments as well as he had expected.

IT CAN HAPPEN TO ANYONE

The first recorded speculative bubble is generally considered to have occurred when tulip mania erupted in the seventeenth century. At the height of the bubble in February 1637, some single tulip bulbs sold for more than ten times the annual income of a skilled craftsman. Underscoring the power of human emotions to drive markets, Yale economist Robert Shiller said: "People were buying tulips not because they liked tulips, but because the price was going up and they thought that they could sell them at a higher price." People tend to overreach because they fall prey to psychological biases that lead to groupthink and herd behavior.

We have seen throughout history that it is a lot easier to participate in an asset bubble than to avoid one. We also know that central bankers, regulators, and policy makers often set the stage for the exact economic conditions that they will later decry. So, how do you know when a bubble is forming? Perhaps, if we knew that, all of us could be spared a lot of financial misery.

During a panel discussion at the World Economic Forum in Davos, Switzerland, Shiller stated that economic bubbles could be diagnosed using the same methods employed by psychologists when diagnosing and treating mental illness. "After all, a bubble is a form of psychological malfunction. And like mental illness there's a tricky gray area between being really sick and just having a few problems," he said.

The solution that Shiller proposed was a checklist like one that a clinician would use to determine a person's psychological health. The list included the following:

▶ Sharp increases in the price of an asset class or stock shares

▶ Public excitement or euphoria about these increases

▶ Media frenzy

▶ Stories about people earning great sums of money, producing envy in those who haven't yet invested

▶ Growing interest in the asset class among the general public

▶ New theories or paradigms used to justify unprecedented price increases

▶ A decline in lending standards

As an investor, if you can recognize any of these symptoms in a stock or asset class that you are thinking of buying, think again. Also, check your own thoughts (and feelings) for signs of wishful thinking and expansiveness. The market and our perceptions do get "overpriced," and, as we have seen, it is not only a euphoric market that behaves irrationally.

We are hardwired to value the truth and plausibility of a rational self and a rational market, a tidy view to hold of both ourselves and the world around us. Even as we act out quirky intentions or observe the craziness of an overheated market, we quickly search for rational explanations. Nobel laureate and commentator Paul Krugman recently wrote in the *New York Times*, "Why should the reaction to the latest catastrophe be any different? In fact, what I hear from my finance professor friends is that there's a lot less soul-searching under way than you might expect." Krugman suggested, somewhat ironically, that since Wall Street's appetite for complex strategies (the kind that sound clever and are easily sold to credulous investors) survived the Long-Term Capital Management debacle, there was no reason why it couldn't survive the recent crisis.

You will recall that Long-Term Capital Management (LTCM) was the hedge fund that was founded by John Meriwether, the former vice chairman and head of bond trading at Salomon Brothers. Its board of directors included Myron Scholes and Robert C. Merton, who shared the 1997 Nobel Prize in Economics. Employing complex trading strategies such as fixed-income arbitrage and statistical arbitrage combined with high leverage, LTCM failed in the late 1990s, leading to a massive bailout by other major financial institutions, supervised by the Federal Reserve. In 1998, the hedge fund lost $4.6 billion and became the poster child for excessive risk in the hedge fund industry. The fund closed its doors in 2000.

Although it was enormously successful in its early years, with annualized returns of over 40 percent, the spectacular breakdown of LTCM's statistical models resulted in its untimely demise. It was the context of LTCM's failure and the markets' general return to business as usual that explains Krugman's comment, "My guess is that the myth of the rational market—a myth that is beautiful, comforting and, above all, lucrative—isn't going away anytime soon."

THE BIG BANG

Writing about the fallibility of Wall Street's mathematical models, Columbia professor Joseph Stiglitz said that, based on statistics, the 1987 stock market crash "could have occurred only once in every 20 billion years, a length of time longer than the life of the universe." Stiglitz was awarded the Nobel Prize in Economics in 2001 for his work on the economics of information and was on the climate change panel that shared the Nobel Peace Prize in 2008. In response to the recent financial meltdown, which

Stiglitz blames on bankers and other financial professionals who misused mathematical models to justify risky ventures, he said, "September 15, 2008, the date that Lehman Brothers collapsed, may be to market fundamentalism (the notion that unfettered markets, all by themselves, can ensure economic prosperity and growth) what the fall of the Berlin Wall was to communism." He has also called the financial industry's call for self-regulation an oxymoron.

Stiglitz asserts that major financial institutions, high on the excesses of foolish risk taking and expansive thinking, systematically devastated the global economy. He compares the outcome to a near-death experience. Stiglitz said, "At the center of blame must be the financial institutions themselves. They—and even more, their executives—had incentives that were not well aligned with the needs of our economy and our society. They were amply rewarded, presumably for managing risk and allocating capital, which was supposed to improve the efficiency of the economy so much that it justified their generous compensation. But they misallocated capital; they mismanaged risk—they created risk."

According to Stiglitz, the culpability lay with incentive structures that were designed to reward short-term profits and encourage excessive risk taking. His proposal for reform was the following:

▶ Mitigate the incentives for excessive risk taking and alter the short-term focus by requiring bonuses to be paid on the basis of five-year returns, rather than annual returns.

▶ Create a financial product safety commission, to make sure that the products bought and sold by banks are safe.

▶ Establish a financial systems stability commission that would "take an overview of the entire financial system, recognizing the interrelations among the various parts, and . . . prevent the excessive systemic leveraging that we have just experienced."

▶ Impose additional regulations to improve the safety and soundness of the financial system, such as "speed bumps" to limit borrowing.

▶ Pass better consumer protection laws, especially laws that prevent predatory lending.

▶ Enact better competition laws. Stiglitz maintains that financial institutions have been able to prey on consumers through credit cards partly because of the absence of competition.

▶ Disallow institutions that are too big to fail. Stiglitz states, "If it is that big, it should be broken up."

THE MYTH OF
THE RATIONAL MARKET

Markets will never operate by the same laws as physics, nor will one model explain them. Far from the rational trader depicted in textbooks is the often conflicted, loss-averse, given to expansive thinking investor, namely, you and me, who makes mistakes. We plan poorly, hesitate at decisive moments, or fall prey to crowd behavior and groupthink. It is not that we want to, but, as we have seen, it is the way that our minds work. Neuroeconomics fills in many of the gaps left by those who still subscribe to the efficient market hypothesis and demonstrates convincingly that irrationality is both a macroeconomic and a microeconomic phenomenon.

There are many mind games that we engage in to maintain our sense of self, or to delude ourselves that our thinking is rational. This plays out at both the individual and the institutional level, with complicity on both sides. Why else would investors continue to turn over their money to the same institutions that have been shown in the past to have been guilty of mismanagement, excessive risk taking, conflicts of interest, and a lack of transparency, and that, after achieving front-page headlines and offering the requisite apologies, have predictably resumed business as usual? There is more than great marketing and public relations at work here.

Is it a collective amnesia that makes us not remember Adelphia, Tyco, WorldCom, and Enron? Have we forgotten the celebrity analysts who had recommended these companies as "buys" and the brokerage firms that unhesitatingly charged commissions for stocks that some of their brokers knew had no chance of going anywhere but down? Has the name Arthur Andersen completely vanished from memory? It is a fact that in the same year that the analyst scandal broke, investors handed over more money than before to Citigroup and Merrill Lynch, which were accused as major offenders.

One explanation is that greed allows us to forget or persuades us to reinterpret the past. Our desire for instant gratification or our need to chase losses—that is, to make up for previous ones—causes us to selectively delete crucial information. George Loewenstein, a Carnegie-Mellon economist and director of its Center for Behavioral Decision Research, has demonstrated in numerous studies that we irrationally discount revealed conflicts of interest and, in general, underestimate their importance. Neuroeconomics has also shown that when beliefs come into conflict with reality, we create explanations and narratives to make reality conform to our beliefs rather than reshape our beliefs to conform to reality.

EUPHORIC INVESTING

Over the years, many professional investors have mentioned to me their tendency from time to time to trade in a euphoric state of mind, usually defined as feeling absolutely confident, even invincible. We forget that our investing is often more than just a financial event. As we have seen, feelings and attitudes affect decisions, based on irrational psychology fueled by biology that implicates both the body and the brain. We know from neuroeconomics that our mind, on both the physiological and the behavioral level, often makes decisions based on expectations, and that anticipating rewards (i.e., profits) and receiving them are experienced in totally different areas of the brain. Neuroeconomics has also shown that, after two repetitions of a stimulus, the brain automatically expects a third. It is no wonder that after two profitable trades, we take it for granted that the next investment will be a sure winner.

The neuroeconomic finding that the neural activity of someone who is making money in the market is identical to that of someone who is high on drugs or having sex has been described to me anecdotally many times in interesting ways. In an interview with Leo Melamed, the chairman emeritus of the CME told me that sometimes his trading was "a huge high. It's indescribable." He then added, "As a matter of fact, it is sexual. I think it physically drains you. It's very much like an orgasm that you have in a physical sense. It is comparable to making love. So, it's an enormous high. The danger is not to allow it to affect other aspects of your life. I was always very careful that it shouldn't."

Another professional investor, David Lansburgh, told me when he was still a floor trader, specializing in foreign currencies and S&P futures, that when it came to trading, "There's nothing in the world like it. When you're busy and the adrenaline is rushing: Give me one place in the world where I want to be and it is right here." Other professional investors have told me that, from their perspective, trading in the market was better than sex. As one professional who wanted to remain anonymous put it, "It is as physically and emotionally satisfying without the muss and fuss."

Given the complicated emotions that we attach to love and sex, it is not surprising that our investment decisions, with their strong psychological and physical associations, can make us feel overconfident in the pursuit of unrealistic and unachievable goals. This phenomenon is further complicated by the fact that many investors cling to sacred cows and strange superstitions when it comes to their investing. On the trading floor, traders carry lucky charms and medals and wear favorite items of clothing, such as colorful custom-made trading coats or ties and shoes that have never set foot off the trading floor's hallowed ground. They also follow a special, sometimes elaborate, pattern of ritual meant to guarantee a successful result, and often chart a carefully designed route to and from work where a slight deviation or roadblock changes everything. Years ago, I was asked by an older, venerable member of the exchange in the members' bathroom to move down, as I was using his lucky urinal. It is also not unusual to see a member in the break room who is silently uttering a prayer, psyching himself up, or preparing like a bullfighter to enter the ring.

When I interviewed Jeffrey L. Silverman at his trading desk, with financial graphs and indicators flickering across computer screens, we spoke about the relationship between superstition and expansive thinking, risk taking, and money management. Silverman stated that when an investor focuses on the noise in the market, that is, the superficial day-to-day data that most investors get lost in, rather than the signal, the underlying fundamentals of a market, fear and greed influence psychology. He said, "Greed comes in because when you've got the market going your way, you have a tendency toward increasing the size of your position to the limits of your money." Silverman's solution was to follow a disciplined approach that keeps the margined equity ratio low to avoid those emotions. Low leverage equals low emotions.

This idea works both for individual investors and for large financial institutions as well. If the big banks and mortgage institutions had not freed up money and dispensed cash to almost anyone who reached out a hand, and if once-venerable investment houses had not overindulged in credit default swaps and mortgage-backed securities, there would have been a lot less emotion in the global economy.

On a personal level, Silverman had an interesting story to tell about his own irrational exuberance and superstitions as a professional investor. He said that earlier in his career, when he was "swinging for the fences," he used to have this theory that when he felt good about one of his positions, he felt compelled to listen to market analysis on the radio. But he also thought that the act of listening to the radio made the market turn against him!

"What I failed to recognize, until I spent five years in therapy, is that listening to the radio was a statement that my mind was becoming so supremely confident that everybody else in the same position was equally overconfident and everybody in the opposite position was throwing in the towel, that was the moment to get out. Invariably, within a day or two of my deciding to listen to the radio on the way to or from work, I'd get creamed."

There was also another indicator, one with which many investors can identify, that Silverman realized meant that he was overtrading or overstaying his welcome in a market: the purchase of big-ticket luxury goods. "I'm the person who owned a hundred thousand dollar Toyota or a million dollar Ferrari and we're not talking that it cost a million. It cost me a million dollars! I quickly learned that the first sign of expansive thinking for me was when I started thinking about buying a car or a vacation home." Silverman said that in those moments of euphoria, the appropriate response was not to pat yourself on the back for being so smart by enticing your brain with high-end goods and services. He learned the hard way that this was the signal to reach for the phone and tell your broker to get you out.

THE ESSENTIAL PSYCHOLOGICAL BARRIERS TO SOUND INVESTING

In my experience, there are other common mistakes that investors make that challenge our rationality and need to be regularly addressed. The following is a list of what I consider to be the essential psychological barriers to sound investing, all of which I have personally fallen victim to over a long career in the market.

Although I originally developed this list to train proprietary traders who were mostly short-term traders, the concepts are equally compelling to investors who focus on a longer time horizon. Once these psychological barriers are viscerally understood in thoughts and feelings, investments often cease falling apart.

▶ Not defining a loss

▶ Not taking a loss or a profit

▶ Losing control of your investment

▶ Getting locked into a belief

▶ Revenge investing

▶ Wishful thinking

▶ Not seizing an opportunity

▶ Being more invested in being right than in making money

▶ Confusing the noise with the signal

▶ Not applying your investment method consistently

▶ Not having a well-defined money management plan

▶ Not investing in the right state of mind

Not Defining a Loss

Aside from Max Bialystock, the fictional character in Mel Brooks's 1968 movie *The Producers* who concocted an implausible musical, *Springtime for Hitler*, that was designed to flop at the box office, the reason that most people invest is to make money. No one buys the market assuming that it has topped out. Conversely, no one sells expecting the market to rally to new highs. However, this happens all too often. For this reason, it is vital to have a defined risk before, not after, you enter the market. If you are afraid to take a (defined) loss, don't invest.

Not Taking a Loss or a Profit

There is an old investment saying that states, "Your first loss is your best loss." Often, it is true, because, as we have learned from neuroeconomics, loss aversion prevents us from ridding ourselves of a failing investment, as we are hoping against hope that our money will come back. Knowing how to take a loss is integral to the investment process. So is its opposite, taking a profit.

When the market has reached a defined objective, it is time, as they say on the trading floor, "to ring the register." Many times, the market will not give you a second chance. There is a body of sayings that I have heard over the years from professional investors that make this point in a colorful way. One such saying is, "When the ducks are quacking, you have to feed them," which was explained to me to mean that when other investors are screaming in the market that they have to have the position that you own, you have to think of them as a bunch of ducks that need to be fed. Until you feed the ducks, you haven't made any money.

Another similar saying is attributable to a trader who was a co-owner of a large Chicago investment firm that specialized in trading agricultural commodities. A major force in the market, he said, "When the circus is in town, you have to sell peanuts." I always found this particular saying intriguing because it conveys not only the idea that you have to sell when the time is right, but additionally that you have to do it in a timely way. Once the tents are folded and the wagons roll out of town, there is no one around to sell to.

Losing Control of Your Investment

There is an old Borscht Belt joke told by the comedian Henny Youngman involving the once terrifying serial killer known as "the Boston strangler." A man is sitting in his living room, reading the evening paper, when he hears a knock at the front door. Approaching the entrance he asks, "Who is it?"

The psychopath on the other side of the door answers, "It's the Boston strangler."

The man walks down the hall past the living room and into the kitchen, turns to his wife, and says, "It's for you, dear!"

Aside from its obvious misogyny, this anecdote conveys a memorable reminder of what happens to an investor who takes a trade from someone else that he has no control over. In other words, taking a tip is tantamount to getting strangled. This is a door that you don't want to open. In actuality, we never have control of our investments; macro events can quickly alter the best-laid investment plan. You do, however, have the ability to manage yourself and what you invest in and why.

Getting Locked into a Belief

That is exactly what it is—prison. The fact that you believe that a particular stock is going up or that the global economy is going to hell in a handbasket is irrelevant. As we have seen, the tendency of the brain is to reshape reality to conform to its view of the market. A sound investment plan provides an objective view based on intellectual skepticism, research, method, and evidence. The ideal is to perceive the market with a clear mind that has considered opposing points of view. As traders say, the mind is like a parachute, best used when open.

Revenge Investing

It is not uncommon for investors to trade angry after a series of losses, or to bring angry feelings from unrelated events to their investments. In response to negative stimuli, many traders whom I have supervised have told me that they felt "pissed off," betrayed, or disappointed by the market, often in terms that suggested that, to their irrational way of thinking, it was all thought out from above and very personal. Overtrading often derives from an illogical need to get even, or to chase losses that the trader is "owed." In such cases, I would refer to this kind of behavior as kamikaze trading, as it is, by its very nature, destined to crash-land.

Wishful Thinking

In a classic example of wishful thinking, economist Irving Fisher asserted that "stock prices have reached what looks like a permanently high plateau" a few weeks before the stock market crash of 1929, which was followed by the Great Depression. Wishful thinking is the irrational formation of beliefs that result in decisions that are psychologically pleasing, but are not based on evidence, rationality, or objective reality. Also referred to as the valence effect of prediction, it is the tendency of people to overestimate the likelihood of good things happening. Valence refers to the positive or negative psychological charge that something has.

Neuroeconomic findings have consistently demonstrated that, holding all else equal, investors have a positive outcome bias. In one study, participants assigned a higher probability to picking a card that had a smiling face on its reverse side than to picking one that had a frowning face. In addition, some studies have shown a valence effect in attribution when we overpredict the likelihood of positive events happening to ourselves relative to others. Wishful thinking is related to magical thinking, feelings of invincibility, and irrational exuberance.

Not Seizing an Opportunity

As a consequence of loss aversion, investors have a tendency to hesitate at decisive moments when it comes to executing trades. Among professional traders, this is called "being gun-shy" or "failing to pull the trigger." The experience ranges from psychological distraction to paralytic hesitation at critical moments of financial decision making. It is like going to the airport and watching the planes take off. Wouldn't it be better to be on board and arrive at a desired destination? It is amazing how many full-time traders spend hours and hours working on daily, weekly, and monthly price charts, honing their skills to employ a host of technical studies and indicators, but when the market approaches their buy point, they can't buy it!

Being More Invested in Being Right than in Making Money

Over the years, I have witnessed a common phenomenon among professionals. It occurs on Wall Street, in Chicago's commodity pits, at the options exchange, and in large and small hedge funds around the globe. In almost every trading room, there are individuals who run around and announce to their colleagues that their system, method, or technical analytic work predicted the high or low of some significant market move. But what they don't possess are profits because their main investment was not in making money, but rather in being right. Investing is a bottom-line activity. The name of the game is to make money.

Confusing the Noise with the Signal

There is a constant, unending stream of distractions in the market, whether you are a value investor in search of an undervalued asset or a long/short trader intent on capturing the next price tick. The challenge for the investor is to have a focus that is laser-straight. Too often our investment plan or methodology is ambushed by external snakes and hairpins and internal head fakes and blind alleys.

The difficulty for many investors is that they choose an investment approach that does not suit their personality or comfort level. As a consequence, they get lost in the noise when their real focus should be the signal. You cannot be a long-term value investor if you don't have the patience and discipline to watch an underappreciated asset slowly go up in value, or if your tendency is to take the first small profit or retreat after an inevitable short-term loss. It is critical that you adopt a method consistent with your personality that allows you to have a unique perspective on the market that you can exploit.

Not Applying Your Investment Method Consistently

If your approach to the market has merit, you must use it consistently. If not, your investment becomes an intellectual, rather than a profitable, exercise. *Webster's New World College Dictionary* defines *invest* as "to put (money) into business, real estate, stocks, bonds, etc. for the purpose of obtaining an income or profit." I think this pretty much says it all.

Not Having a Well-Defined Money Management Plan

The purpose of a well-defined money management plan is to preserve capital. Professional traders understand that addressing risk is the most important aspect of the investment process, in the face of our brain's natural response of acting irrationally when the market moves against us or provides us with a tempting small profit. As with the trading plan, money management is an ongoing process that requires consistency and regular evaluation. It is not uncommon for professional investors who consistently perform profitably to give up a month or a year of earnings because of a lapse in their money management. Seasoned traders know intuitively the need to psychologically guard oneself from the deleterious effects of a single or series of impulsive trades that can throw an investment account out of whack.

Not Investing in the Right State of Mind

Just like the psychologically successful survivor in the *Army Field Manual*, many professionals have developed their own version of "jungle eye," which, you will remember, is the ability to look beyond what our innate perceptual biases and debilitating emotions would have us focus on. In the jungle, it is a matter of life and death to stay strong and to have the presence of mind to see beyond the immediate pattern of bushes and trees that are before us. It is only when you learn to look further out that you can find natural breaks in the foliage. In the financial jungle, many of the same rules apply. Survival depends on our ability to adapt and compete by virtue of our reason and mental strength. The challenge is to be psychologically fierce: alert, disciplined, patient, and anxiety-free in an unforgiving environment.

In Chapter 7, I will discuss the importance of establishing realistic investment goals that suit your personality and identifying the critical factors that determine the edge that makes the difference.

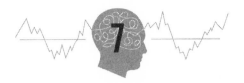

Defining the Big Picture

T he solution to overcoming our natural inclination toward irrational investment decisions begins with an
understanding of what causes them. Contrary to the
neoclassical model, neuroeconomic research has convincingly
demonstrated that our irrational choices are driven by emotion,
cognitive biases, faulty reasoning, and subconscious psychological and perceptual inferences. Because the brain reacts more often
than it reflects when it comes to money, we are wise to heed Daniel
Kahneman's admonition: "The most natural way to think about a
decision is not always the best way to make the decision."

Regardless of whether you invest in individual stocks, are
a quant who trades for a billion-dollar hedge fund, or just have
some money in a 401(k) or some other retirement plan, your decision making needs to be governed by rules and the ability to
see broadly. Kahneman calls this "taking the global view." It all
begins with knowing what you want from the market and then
developing a specific set of rules and an investment plan to set
your trading goals in motion. When asked what it takes to be
a successful investor, Benjamin Graham replied, "People don't

need extraordinary insight or intelligence. What they need most is the character to adopt simple rules and stick to them."

LONG-TERM GROWTH AND FINANCIAL STABILITY

Even if you are a short-term trader, you will be well advised to invest with a focus on your long-term growth and financial stability. Establishing goals is a key factor in enhancing performance that allows for the creation of a benchmark based on success over time and not on the near-term fluctuations of the market. Concentrating on the day-to-day dollars—made or lost—in your trading account is a sure recipe for slash-and-burn investing. Neuroscientist Peter Kirsch stated, "Even though money cannot satisfy any primary needs—you can't eat it or mate with it—the association between money and reward is very strong." Add to this the fact that research has shown that the thrill of an anticipated profit activates the brain with greater excitement than the actual gain itself does, and it becomes clear why we need a go-to set of rules and a firm understanding of our investment goals.

Using Benjamin Graham's basic principles of investment as a broad outline, you can develop a list of investment rules, to be operationally defined, that work for you. For those who consider themselves active investors, or who are quants trading for a bank or some other financial institution, the reference to *The Intelligent Investor* may seem odd, as its focus is on the long-term appreciation of undervalued assets. The choice is meant only to provide one example of how to develop a personal list of investment rules to govern your decisions.

My point is that the process of developing a system of rules, one that is consistent with your risk tolerance and fits your personality, and establishing goals that will allow you to follow them is the same, no matter what the time frame. One of the most successful traders I have ever known was a competitor on the trading floor who was an in-and-out of the market agricultural commodity trader and whose investment model was Warren Buffett. He had read everything that Buffett had written about investing, including Berkshire Hathaway annual reports going back more than 30 years. When I asked him how he used that information for the swing trading of commodities, he said that he had figured out a number of things from the literature that he referred to as his "kernels of truth," and he utilized them in his trading. He said, "Somehow my subconscious is programmed with all of these things and, at appropriate times, they come to me automatically."

THE INTELLIGENT INVESTOR

In *The Intelligent Investor*, Graham summed up his investment philosophy by saying that an intelligent investor must be businesslike in his approach and guided by specific principles. Put simply, value investing focuses on buying a stock, business, or other asset at less than its intrinsic value, with these stipulations:

▶ Know the business.

▶ Know who runs the business.

▶ Invest for profit.

▶ Have confidence.

It is clear to me that, whether an investor is engaged in purchasing an undervalued company or a single S&P futures contract, the need for research and sound judgment is critical. In both instances, following a hunch or taking a tip is poison. Graham said, "You are neither right nor wrong because the crowd disagrees. You are right because your data and reasoning are right."

Value investing requires the investor to be knowledgeable about the business in which she is investing, even if buying only a single share of stock. The intelligent investor views herself as a stakeholder who understands the operations and the competitive environment in which the business operates. Also, she knows what it sells and what the external threats and opportunities are, and also its internal strengths and weaknesses. She asks herself, is the company well run? Are the managers honest and efficient? Most important, she knows that research and analysis serve a greater purpose: investor profit.

Active trading also requires knowledge and the ability to act on it. It is vital to have a comprehensive understanding of the contract or equity that is being traded and to have a plan with well-defined risk, as well as a bottom-line orientation that keeps any single loss from getting out of hand. This will act as protection against impulsive trades that destroy trading accounts and allow you to invest consistent with Graham's advice, "not on optimism, but on arithmetic."

In the end, however, you will need to have optimism, but of a different sort. It is not the blind optimism of the wishful thinker or the irrationally exuberant. On the contrary, it is the confident optimism of the well-researched investor who understands his investment and the motivation behind it. Through practiced discipline, he patiently waits to take profit, not for the thrill of it, but as the logical dividend from hard work, based on adherence to rules and achievable, realistic goals.

In *The New Market Wizards*, author Jack Schwager asked hedge fund owner Monroe Trout what were the investment rules that he lived by. Schwager seemed particularly curious to hear Trout's response, considering that, of all those he interviewed, no other market wizard had a system that could even remotely approach Trout's performance in terms of risk/return measurements. Emphasizing the need for an approach to be totally consistent with an individual's personality, Trout said that, even if he gave his trading system away, many professional investors wouldn't be able to make money with it. His point was that to be successful, you need to have an edge in the market and the ability to consistently execute from that vantage point with strict risk control. Too often, investors adopt methods or systems that are not suited for their investment style, and these soon compromise any attempts at strict money management.

Feeling out of control when you are attempting to adopt someone else's trading method or system leads to irrational decisions. Trout said, "Basically, when you get down to it, to make money, you need to have an edge and employ good money management." He was categorical that money management alone was not enough to increase an edge, but that if an investor had a demonstrated profitable approach, strict money management made the difference between success and failure.

SETTING GOALS

As you think about your own investment goals, it is important that you fully appreciate your motivation. Ask yourself, what attracts you to investing? I have worked with many individuals over the years who thought that they wanted to trade, only to discover that they really didn't. Of course, the psychological demands of being an active investor are quite different from those of contributing to a 401(k) or some other retirement plan, so it is important that you know from the outset what kind of investor you are and what will sustain your interest and dedication to be successful. Investing, contrary to popular belief, is not a good recreational activity.

When I was raising my family on Lake Shore Drive in Chicago, I shared a private elevator in my building with a surgeon who lived in the same tier. Most days we would meet in or near the elevator by chance. I would be going off to or returning from the exchange; he would be doing the same from the hospital that he worked in. It was after a particularly hellish trading session one day that my neighbor asked if he could have a word with me.

He told me how interested he had recently become in the stock market and that, whenever he was free, he turned on the financial news or took a sneak peek at CNBC in between operations. I listened, not saying a word.

"Could you teach me how to trade?" he asked, adding matter-of-factly that he was free all of next Saturday morning.

"Sure," I said, and then added how pleased I was that he had approached me because I too had an interest that I was hoping to pursue.

"What is it?" he asked.

I said, with restrained sarcasm, that I had recently seen an old Dr. Kildare movie on the classic film channel that had revived my lifelong interest in medicine. I then told him I was free Saturday afternoon and wondered if he could teach me everything I would have to know to perform surgery. Needless to say, he never asked again.

I am not saying that you have to be a professional investor to be successful, but you certainly have to understand that investing requires a lot of hard work, knowledge, and finely honed skills. After you think that you know everything, I have found, there is still more to know about the market and yourself, or, as John Wooden, the former basketball coach, said, "It's what you learn after you know it all that counts."

Returning to your investment goals, ask yourself if your motive for investing or trading is strong enough to achieve your objectives. There is a direct correlation between your motive and the intent and intensity of any course of action that you take in the market. My work with traders is clear on this subject: your reason for investing dictates how and on what you focus, the approach that you adopt, the efficacy or limitation of your personal beliefs about the market, and the degree to which your state of mind is positive and resourceful. In other words, it dictates all the necessary ingredients for a profitable outcome.

Some might think that this point is so basic as not to be worth mentioning. I believe it is so essential that it requires acknowledgment as a precondition for any market actions. Jack Schwager also echoed this perspective after conducting interviews with some of the world's best traders. He said, "First, be sure that you really want to trade." He said that it is far too common that people invest for the wrong reasons. They think they want to trade when they really don't. As we have seen, the irrationality of our minds leads us to make choices based on unconscious preferences of which we are often unaware.

Rules and Regulations

Now that you have given the matter some thought, I would like to pose a few additional questions to help you sort out your goals and adopt a workable list of investment rules. To begin with, what are your long-term and short-term investment goals? Why is it important for you to achieve these goals? What is preventing you from achieving these goals now? And what specific steps can you take to accomplish your goals?

Here is a partial list of responses to this exercise from a group of hedge fund traders that I supervised who managed hundreds of millions of dollars, trading equities, debt, foreign exchange, and futures. Their time frames ranged from quick in-and-out trading, also called scalping, to long-range, value-oriented investments. The trading styles were in most cases discretionary, but in the case of one trader, the style was completely computerized.

- ▶ To be consistently profitable
- ▶ To be disciplined
- ▶ To focus on opportunities
- ▶ To catch market breakouts and take all my signals
- ▶ To have control over my investments
- ▶ To have a high level of self-esteem when I trade
- ▶ To have more confidence in myself after taking a loss or experiencing a drawdown in my account
- ▶ To have a better understanding of my emotions when I trade

▶ To develop an approach that I can trust and apply it effortlessly

▶ To define my losses and not dwell on them

▶ To trade from the perspective that trading is a process and not merely a series of independent trades

▶ To establish limited risk and limitless profit potential

▶ To become a better investor by constantly learning more about myself

▶ To operate completely in the here and now

In my experience, what prevents most investors from accomplishing their goals are poorly conceived trading rules; an investment plan that is operationally unviable, either because it is inherently faulty or because it does not suit their personality; and an investment psychology that suffers from self-limiting beliefs, poor focus, and an unresourceful state of mind.

Developing good trading rules and a viable investment plan is the easier part of the equation. As we have seen, there is a great deal of market knowledge available, from both the past and the present, in the form of rules and axioms, and also from neuroeconomic studies, to help guide you. The essential point is that trading rules and investment plans need to be regarded more as custom tailoring than as a suit that is off the rack. You will have to determine a time frame and an investment style that fits only you. Also, keep in mind the importance of taking the "global view" and not missing the forest for the trees. It is all very subjective, requiring a great deal of introspection. This is as true for actively trading your own account as it is for trading for a hedge fund, buying individual stocks, or purchasing a mutual fund. You will need to do a lot of research, and when you think you are through, do even more. There are no shortcuts, although your mind will constantly be trying to search them out. If you are investing with someone else, always ask for a track record. If it is incomplete or doesn't comport with a standard benchmark, move on. In my experience, there is no such thing as "a once-in-a-lifetime opportunity."

A track record alone is no safe harbor. Remember the stellar returns of Long-Term Capital Management before it blew up. The past is not a prologue, which is why investment disclosure documents state that past results do not guarantee future returns. For this reason, intelligent investing suggests an investigative approach that is intellectually skeptical, as well as one that values the importance of diversification rather than placing all your eggs in a single basket. Also, commissions and other fees can be real killers, so it is important to shop around and set up a cost structure that won't eat up your profits. Last, and perhaps most important, even when every aspect of an investment looks perfectly right, assume as a given that everything can go hopelessly wrong. Why? Because things happen, which is the reason that you should be investing only discretionary income that you and your family can afford to lose. Much of this may sound basic, but if it is adhered to, it will help you save a bundle and protect you from acting irrationally in the market.

THE PSYCHOLOGICAL FACTORS
THAT STAND IN THE WAY

The really difficult part of accomplishing investment goals is the psychological part, which, predictably, prevents investors from succeeding in the market. The main reasons are self-limiting beliefs, poor focus, and an unresourceful state of mind.

Self-limiting beliefs are inhibiting beliefs that investors possess about themselves and about the market. They are internally represented with the following sort of thoughts: "I don't have enough conviction." "I'm never quite sure I know what I'm doing." "How can I be sure?" "I can't trust my judgment." "I don't believe in myself." "It's impossible to make money in these markets."

Poor focus when investments are made results from confused judgment or distracted concentration. Some investors lack the "vision" to zero in on the essentials, instead being sidetracked by the market's noise. Investors report the following thoughts: "I'm so distracted by procedures that I don't have time to see what is really important." "Taking a loss gets in the way of my next trade." "I'm always thinking about something else just at a decisive moment of decision making." "I can't see the big picture."

An unresourceful state of mind is characterized by fear, anxiety, and confusion. Investors feel angry, frustrated, mixed up, or stupid, and this clouds their judgment. They replay old tapes in their brain that inhibit them from accomplishing their objectives. Characteristic thoughts are the following: "Why am I such an idiot?" "These markets are so frustrating. I can't stand it." "This loss really makes me mad." Individuals also report a lack of physical and psychological energy because of high levels of tension.

Sources of Investor Anxiety

These are some of the major examples of investor anxiety and how they are experienced in the market.

▶ *Fear of failure.* The investor feels intense pressure to perform, ties her self-worth to trading or investing, and seeks perfection. The investor is also concerned about what others think.

▶ *Fear of success.* The investor feels euphoric, with a thought process characterized by wishful or magical thinking. The investor also doubts himself.

▶ *Fear of inadequacy.* The investor experiences a loss of self-esteem, feeling a lack of direction and confidence.

▶ *Loss of control.* The investor experiences a lack of personal responsibility for her decisions and feels that the market is out to get her.

OVERCOMING THE PSYCHOLOGICAL FACTORS THAT HOLD INVESTORS BACK

In my experience, the best way to overcome these psychological challenges is to obtain what professional traders call an "edge." An edge is the investor's leg up on the competition, a particular point of focus that provides a subjective advantage and point of entry into the market. In *The New Market Wizards*, Jack Schwager states that it is absolutely essential to have an edge, and that if you don't know what your edge is, you don't have one. He says, "You can't win without an edge, even with the world's greatest discipline and money management skills. If you could, then it would be possible to win at roulette over the long run using perfect discipline and risk control." The way I see it, your edge derives not only from your investment style and game plan, but, most important, from your psychology.

The Edge That Makes the Difference

The edge that makes the difference, illustrated in Table 7.1, indicates how to eliminate the irrational thinking that can all too

TABLE 7.1

TRADER RESPONSE	HAVING THE EDGE	LOSING THE EDGE
PATIENCE	Waits for opportunities to materialize based on a well-thought-out game plan	Little planning: reacts according to personal whim, irrational bias, fallacy, or illusion
DISCIPLINE	Sees the big picture; responds deliberately	Emotional, anxious; often confused about what to do
STRATEGY	Highly planned; limits losses and lets profits run	Little planning, inconsistent method
EXPERTISE	Well prepared, researched	Unprepared, little market knowledge
MOTIVE	Long-term motive that fits personality	Not clearly defined; wants instant gratification
GOALS	Clearly defined	Ill-defined
RISK MANAGEMENT	Highly controlled risk	Poor risk control
STATE OF MIND	Resourceful, confident	Anxious, distracted

easily intrude on analytical judgment. It also shows the critical importance of investing motives, allowing the investor to focus on what is essential in order to execute a trading plan that is consistent with his personality and feels right. Seasoned investors enjoy what they are doing and feel that their actions are effortless. Once an edge has been developed, a feeling of confidence ensues. Needless to say, discipline, patience, personal responsibility, and repeated success make this a lot easier.

In my interview with Hawksbill Capital Management's Tom Shanks, our conversation focused on his philosophy of markets and how psychology affects trading decisions. He said, "Emotion, and therefore psychology, plays a significant role in the behavior of markets. Sometimes that role is relatively minor; other times it can overwhelm reason and create chaotic conditions." Shanks added that every investor needs to be aware, at a minimum, of the potential for such situations, and have some idea in advance of how to deal with them. He described how some investors are more comfortable with a systematic approach, while others will want to "take the wheel" in hopes of using their experience and situational awareness to guide their decisions through turbulent times. "Good cases can be made for both approaches; a particular investor's approach is a very personal matter," he said.

In either style, Shanks pointed out, danger is presented when ego intrudes. He explained, "No one likes to be wrong, and the aversion to accept that you are wrong leads to several pitfalls: a refusal to admit mistakes, a reluctance to reexamine options, the harboring of market vendettas, an impaired ability to be objective. Regret is an emotional cousin to this antipathy to being wrong; both can work to impair good decision making." He added as an afterthought, "As is the case with all psychological issues, being aware of their presence, and their influence, is the first step in combating their harmful effects."

In Chapter 8, we look at some of the common cognitive biases that intrude on our investment decisions.

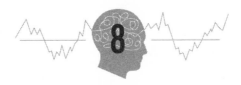

Cognitive Biases

T he very nature of investing subjects us to the dangers of mental pitfalls, which is why we need to have a well-defined and viable process. Our trading rules and investment goals are a first line of defense, guiding us in the direction of disciplined market behavior and preventing us from slipping into irrational modes of thought. Behavioral finance has shown that in situations involving decisions where information is poorly structured, contradictory, and ambiguous and stress is high because of time constraints and social pressure, *things* happen. One reason that we make faulty decisions is that our observations and actions are prone to cognitive biases.

PSYCHOLOGICAL FACTORS AND RULES OF THUMB

A bias is the tendency to draw incorrect conclusions from psychological factors, based on heuristics, or rules of thumb, rather than on evidence. The origin and meaning of the term "rule of thumb" is itself instructive. Thought to have originated with woodworkers, who used the width of their thumbs in place of rulers for measuring things, the principle is intended as a shorthand for understanding, not a strictly accurate or reliable metric. Its key feature is that a rule of thumb is easily learned and applied for approximating the calculation of some measure, or for making a decision.

In "A Voyage to Lilliput," Part 1 of his satirical novel *Gulliver's Travels*, Jonathan Swift describes the fictionalized Tailors' Rule of Thumb: "Then they measured my right Thumb, and desired no more; for by a mathematical Computation, that twice round the Thumb is once around the Wrist, and so on to the Neck and Waist, and by the help of my old Shirt, which I displayed on the Ground before them for a Pattern, they fitted me exactly." The essential point is that, although rules of thumb help to solidify our decisions, they are always approximate and enable our biased thinking. Reliance on their use can lead to errors in statistical judgment, attribution, and memory, skewing the reliability of observed and reported information.

Kahneman and Tversky introduced the concept of cognitive biases in 1972, growing out of their studies of innumeracy, or the inability of individuals to reason intuitively with greater orders of magnitude. They demonstrated that as a consequence of biased thinking, the judgments and decisions of individuals differed markedly from neoclassical theory, which is predicated on a rational decision maker. They explained these anomalies in terms of heuristics resulting in systematic errors. These experiments grew into the *heuristics and biases research program*, which has had a far-reaching influence beyond the discipline of psychology. It was a major factor in the development of behavioral economics and earned Kahneman the Nobel Prize in 2002.

DEVIATIONS OF JUDGMENT

My intention here is not to list all the biases to which humans are prone, but to describe those deviations of judgment that I have experienced and have observed in the behavior of other traders and institutional clients. In my market activities, I have found that these are the biases that most frequently intrude on our investing and trading decisions. Many of them have been empirically verified in the fields of behavioral finance and neuro-economics, such as the ones already discussed:

▶ *Confirmation bias.* The tendency to seek information or to interpret information in a way that confirms one's pre-conceptions. In the market, investors demonstrate a predisposition to favor information that confirms their position or hypotheses, regardless of whether it is true. They also reinforce their existing beliefs by selectively collecting new evidence and by interpreting existing data in a biased way, or by selectively recalling confirming information from memory. Empirical studies have also shown that individuals test hypotheses in a one-sided way, focusing on one possibility and neglecting alternatives. Moreover, research has demonstrated that in situations involving great emotion, or when established beliefs that shape expectations are challenged, confirmation bias is pronounced and contributes to overconfidence.

▶ *Loss aversion.* The valuing of a loss more than a gain, usually about twice as much. Kahneman and Tversky, who coined the term, said, "The disutility of giving up an object

is greater than the utility associated with acquiring it."
In response to the desire to avoid loss, we exhibit ever-
increasing and imaginative modes of systematic and predictable irrationality.

▶ *Herd behavior.* The conforming tendency to follow the
opinions and behaviors of the majority in order to feel safe
and avoid conflict. This is also related to the bandwagon
effect, or the tendency to believe something, or choose a
course of action, because many others do.

▶ *Groupthink.* As defined by Irving Janis, a research psychologist at Yale who is famous for his theory of groupthink,
"a mode of thinking that people engage in when they are
deeply involved in a cohesive in-group, when the members'
strivings for unanimity override their motivation to realistically appraise alternative courses of action." Individual
creativity and independent thinking are lost in the pursuit
of group cohesiveness. Janis came up with eight symptoms
that characterize the phenomenon. Many of these can be
frequently observed on trading floors, in investment banks,
on hedge fund trading desks, and in financial policy-making
organizations. They are:

1. Illusions of invulnerability, which create excessive
   optimism and encourage risk taking

2. Rationalizing warnings that challenge the group's
   assumptions

3. An unquestioned belief in the morality of the group,
   causing members to ignore the consequences of their
   actions

4. Stereotyping those who are opposed to the group as weak, biased, spiteful, or stupid

5. Direct pressure on members who question the group to conform, couched in terms of disloyalty

6. Self-censorship of ideas that deviate from the group consensus

7. Illusions of unanimity among group members: silence is perceived as consensus

8. Mind guards, the self-appointed members who shield the group from dissent or challenging information

▶ *Wishful thinking.* The formation of beliefs and the adoption of behaviors based on what is pleasing to imagine instead of making decisions based on evidence and rationality. This is also related to positive-outcome bias, the tendency to overestimate the probability of good things happening, and magical thinking.

As you think about how these cognitive biases influence your own market behavior, keep in mind their influence on your research, that is, the way you search for information to confirm or disprove an investment idea. Also, look at their influence on how you interpret the data. Ask yourself if you are being objective or if you are skewing the information to confirm a subjective belief that is not sustained by the evidence. In addition, consider the possible effects of biased thinking on memory and the way you report your investment ideas to others. It is only through awareness and an intellectual and emotional commitment to change that we can begin to overcome the potential pernicious effects of our individual biases.

THE ENDOWMENT EFFECT

Anyone who has found himself on the losing side of a market position, which in reality is anyone who has ever invested, has experienced the *endowment effect*, a term coined by behavioral economist Richard Thaler. The endowment effect, also known as *divestiture aversion*, is that individuals value assets more once those assets become their property. To illustrate this point, Thaler brought a group of University of Chicago Business School graduate students into a room and asked them how much they would bid for a coffee mug. A consensus was reached whereby individuals said that they would pay $10 each for the cup. Unbeknownst to them, all along the plan was to give them the mug for free. The students were handed their gift and asked to wait in the hall. After a short time, they were brought back into the room and asked how much they would want to receive for selling their cups. Again a consensus was reached; however, this time the students would not part with *their* mugs for less than $13!

This experiment and other neuroeconomic studies reveal that people irrationally place a higher value on objects that they own than they do on objects that are not theirs. Although the endowment effect differs from loss aversion, the two biases reinforce each other in situations where the asset price has fallen compared to the owner's purchasing price. When it comes to investing, the endowment effect can be insidious.

There has been more than one occasion in my career supervising traders on the exchange floor and on trading desks when I have had to divest them of losing positions. Of course, this is not my desired first course of action. For most traders, establishing strict risk management guidelines with explicit consequences for going outside of carefully monitored trading behavior is sufficient. But sometimes the volatility of the market, or the irrationality of a particular trader's thought process, makes a more aggressive posture necessary. I understand, firsthand, how irrationally controlling an established position in the market, however wrong, can be. I have made this mistake too many times, and I only hope that I have learned something. What is really interesting, and what never ceases to amaze me, is how self-destructively attached we become to our losing positions, wrongly believing that they are ours and we own them. I have seen men the size of NFL fullbacks cry at my insistence that they clear the books, get out of the market, and start over fresh. I have known others who looked at me with scorn, or with catatonic eyes. Still others have tried to make me feel as if I were asking them to undergo the amputation of a limb. All this irrationality derives from our strong feeling of ownership, even if it is only of a sinking ship that is headed for a financial underwater graveyard.

MISSING OUT

Related to this aversion to divesting ourselves of our positions is our fear of *missing out*. Many times traders have used this explanation with me as a justification for staying in a losing position. In their minds, the logic made perfect sense: if they were out of the market, how could they catch the next move? Of course, the fact that their current loss was the reason that they had to divest themselves hardly entered into the equation. The best way to stay in the market is to have a strategy that allows you to enter and exit on your terms, consistent with your plan, and that does not lock you into a system of belief where there is no way out. Any investment that falls outside of those parameters is not worth *your* pursuit. Your investment process needs to allow you to return to a position once the market has clearly demonstrated, based on evidence and not bias, that it has turned.

Interestingly, no matter how much emotion these exercises of authority have engendered, whenever I have had to get a trader out of the market, invariably, days later, I have always been thanked. Traders have often told me that they were "blind" or "couldn't see the light." Several have asked me quite candidly, "Was I out of my mind?" or words to that effect. The point is that even when they knew they were acting irrationally—and some did understand that, even as they tried to convince me that they were making sense—later they would realize that the psychological forces that had overtaken them were within their control.

One of the ways in which we run into trouble as investors is a result of the framing effect. We draw different conclusions depending on how information is presented to us. Experiments by Kahneman and Tversky have demonstrated that framing influences the choices one makes, contrary to the classic axioms of rational choice theory. These studies led to the development of prospect theory. It is important to keep in mind that framing results both from the external manipulation of decision-making options and from subjective factors based on the investors' beliefs, habits, and state of mind. Interestingly, consistent with the results of the wine tasting and master sommelier studies discussed earlier, neuroscientists have linked the framing effect to neural activity in the amygdala, and have identified the role of the orbital and medial prefrontal cortex (OMPFC) in moderating emotion on decisions. Using functional magnetic resonance imaging (fMRI) to monitor brain activity during a financial decision-making task, they observed greater activity in the OMPFC of those research subjects who were less susceptible to framing effects. Once again, we can observe the need to monitor the frames that each of us internalizes in the form of research, anecdotes, stereotypes, and rules of thumb that provide the analytical and emotional filters that we rely on to understand and respond to events.

SELF-SERVING AND BETTER THAN AVERAGE

Also related is the *self-serving bias*, which occurs when investors attribute their gains to personal factors of their own making, but attribute their failures to external factors that are beyond their control. The self-serving bias is observed in the all-too-familiar human tendency to take credit for one's successes, but to abdicate responsibility for one's failures. It is also demonstrated in the predisposition to evaluate ambiguous information in a way that benefits one's interests.

Empirical studies have verified the presence of the self-serving bias in conjunction with what is often referred to as the better-than-average effect. Also known as "illusory superiority," individuals are biased to believe that they perform better than the average person in areas that are essential to their self-esteem. One of many positive illusions relating to the self, the self-serving bias is a phenomenon that has been heavily studied in social psychology. It is generally defined in psychology texts as a cognitive bias that causes people to overestimate their positive qualities and abilities and to underestimate their negative ones, relative to those of others. The self-serving bias is evident in areas of individual perception that include intelligence, performance on tests, and the possession of desirable characteristics or personality traits.

I have observed the self-serving bias firsthand in working with a variety of traders and investors of greatly varying abilities. I don't think that in any trading room that I have ever visited, a trader has introduced himself as being submean. It is not only in Lake Wobegon that "all the children are above average." Although this phenomenon of illusory superiority can be widely observed in the general population—after all, it would be a rare occurrence to encounter anyone anywhere who introduced himself as being below average—exaggerated competence in the mind of someone who is managing a financial institution or trading billion-dollar portfolios is downright frightening.

THE FOCUSING EFFECT

Another well-researched bias that causes deviations in judgment is the *focusing effect*, or *focusing illusion*, which occurs when people place too much importance on a particular aspect of an event. In one study, participants were asked how much happier they believed Californians are compared to Midwesterners. Both Californians and Midwesterners said that Californians must be considerably happier, when, in fact, there was no difference in the actual happiness ratings of the two groups. The bias is the result of the fact that most people focused on and overweighed the sunny weather and the supposed easygoing lifestyle of California. They also devalued and underrated other aspects of life and markers of happiness, such as low crime rates and safety from natural disasters such as earthquakes.

Investors are predisposed to make a similar mistake, as indicated by the recent financial meltdown. We focus on notable differences when making predictions or financial decisions in the market and exclude those that are less conspicuous. Kahneman has proposed that the focusing illusion is also observed in the behavior of people who consistently overestimate the role of income on overall well-being, when in reality, a rise in income has only a small and transient effect on happiness.

As we have seen, it is a natural and predictable tendency to overestimate specific values to which we attach subjective importance, as well as to demonstrate an overreliance on conventional measures. A relevant example of this is how individuals often enter into a trade. Obsessing on an anecdotal report or news item, they purchase a stock or asset class on a whim, rather than weighing meaningful data that are more informative and predictive of future earnings.

Recently, I have noticed that gold is being aggressively hawked on late-night TV infomercials by actors posing as glitzy millionaires or as a disingenuous adman's notion of well-tailored investors. It is clear to me that the intention is solely to exploit cognitive biases: to distract critical faculties in order to capture the viewers' focus, provoking an irrational reaction.

ESCALATION OF COMMITMENT

Another mental trap that can influence our investment decisions is called *escalation of commitment*, first described by behavioral

psychologist Barry M. Staw. The phenomenon occurs when people use prior investment to rationalize increased investments of
time or money in a decision, despite new evidence suggesting
that the decision is probably wrong. It is also known as the *sunk
cost fallacy*. The bias has been used to explain and characterize the U.S. commitment to military conflicts in Vietnam and in
Iraq, where treasure spent and lives lost served to justify continued involvement.

Irrational escalation of commitment refers to a situation
in which people make irrational decisions based upon rational
choices in the past. Examples of irrational escalation of commitment are frequently seen when individuals engage in a bidding
war, continuing their bids to reinforce a subjective notion of commitment. In the stock market, an investor may consider himself
committed to his position—he has bet so much of his stake that he
refuses to exit—even with new information that sheds doubt on
his decision. Traders often irrationally state their level of commitment to bad trades as if they were pledging allegiance to the flag.

The dollar auction is a frequently employed experiment
that demonstrates this concept. Designed by economist Martin
Shubik, the game illustrates how players with perfect information are compelled to make an irrational decision based completely on a sequence of rational choices. The game begins when
an auctioneer (usually a behavioral economist or neuroeconomist) volunteers to sell off a dollar bill with the following rule:
the dollar goes to the highest bidder, who pays the amount that
he bids; however, the second-highest bidder also must pay the
highest amount that he bid, but he gets nothing in return.

The bidding begins with one of the players bidding 1 cent,
hoping to make a 99-cent profit. She will quickly be outbid by

another player bidding 2 cents, as a 98-cent profit is still desirable. Similarly, another bidder may bid 3 cents, making a 97-cent profit. In this way, a series of bids is maintained. However, a problem becomes evident as soon as the bidding reaches 99 cents, when the player who has bid 98 cents now has the choice of losing the 98 cents or bidding a dollar, which would make his profit zero. After that, the competing player has a choice of either losing 99 cents or bidding $1.01 and losing only 1 cent. After this point, the two players continue to bid the value up well beyond the dollar, so that neither stands to profit. What the game exhibits is the irrational lengths to which players will go to maintain their commitment. By the end of the game, although both players stand to lose money, they nevertheless continue to bid feverishly, fueled by their past investment.

THE POWER OF BELIEF

Another bias that is relevant for investors is the *belief bias*. Related to confirmation bias, it occurs when a person's evaluation of the logical strength of an argument is biased by his belief in the truth or falsity of the conclusion. Belief bias has been verified, independent of analytical ability, in psychological experiments.

In a series of studies, participants were presented with deductive arguments in which each was offered a series of premises and a conclusion and asked to indicate whether the conclusion necessarily followed from the premises given. Researchers observed that individuals rejected valid arguments with unbelievable conclusions, and endorsed invalid arguments with believable conclusions. They concluded, validated by fMRI scans, that instead of following directions and assessing logical validity, the subjects based their assessments on personal beliefs. "In the belief-neutral trials, activation was seen in the upper parietal lobe, a region involved in mathematical reasoning and spatial representation. In the belief-laden trials, the additional activation of the front left temporal lobe was observed, a region involved in the retrieval and selecting of facts from long term memory. This indicated that in belief-laden reasoning, people also drew upon memory in addition to abstract reasoning." Over the years, I have heard traders strenuously argue the merits and validity of investment ideas whose logical validity could be explained only in the context of their subjective beliefs.

When you are investing, it is not so difficult to find yourself lost in a belief system of your own making. There have been many times in my own career when I have had to learn this lesson the hard way, digging myself out of a hemorrhaging trade only when the pain of fighting the market was so great as to bluntly slap into me the irrationality of my belief in an unsustainable position. Selective perception is a fierce enemy, and we are predisposed to succumb to it in what we erroneously believe to be in our best interests. Relevant to this discussion is the *pseudocertainty effect*, first described by Kahneman and Tversky in prospect theory. The concept refers to empirically studied behavior in which individuals make risk-averse choices if the expected outcome is positive, but risk-seeking choices to avoid negative outcomes. Decisions are affected by simply reframing the descriptions of the outcomes without changing the actual outcomes.

We are proficient at providing ourselves with reasoned explanations as to why our judgment, though faulty, is correct. Sometimes we also fall prey to what is termed an information bias.

Because of cognitive dissonance, or the anxiety caused by holding contradictory ideas simultaneously, we embark on an expedition to gain more information, which we irrationally believe we need in order to compensate for a losing position, even when that extra information is irrelevant to the investment that we are in.

POSTPURCHASE RATIONALIZATION
AND THE NEGLECT
OF PROBABILITY

Another heavily studied psychological bias, related to the endowment effect, is what is usually called *postpurchase rationalization*, the flip side of buyer's remorse. This common phenomenon occurs after individuals have invested a significant amount of time, money, or effort in something, and they need to convince themselves that it must have been worth it. For investors, purchase of a particular stock or asset class is often rationalized retrospectively in an attempt to justify the choice and stay consistent with the original intention.

A particularly pernicious bias, known to be efficient at destroying investment accounts, is what is referred to as the *neglect of probability bias*. It is the tendency to completely disregard probability when making a decision in an emotionally charged situation. As we have seen, there are many ways in which someone's judgment can deviate from rational decision making with regard to probability or to the use of other sources of information. This bias, however, is markedly different because the investor completely disregards probability when deciding, instead of employing probability incorrectly or distorting its significance.

REACTANCE

Reactance occurs when an individual has an emotional reaction, such as denial, that is in direct contradiction to an external threat, the market, which is irrationally interpreted to be the source of eliminating specific behavioral freedoms, making a profit. It sounds crazy, but, after all, we are speaking about the irrationality of our investment behaviors!

Typically, reactance is exhibited when someone is pressured to accept a threatening view or attitude. Reactance, which causes individuals to adopt or strengthen a perspective that is contrary to what was intended, also increases resistance to rational persuasion. An example of such behavior can be observed when an individual engages in a self-destructive or prohibited activity in order to deliberately flout authority. I have observed traders curse the market, abandoning all logic and resisting clear judgment, when their deeply held beliefs and self-esteem are under attack. Threatening to get even, they refused to let the market (or the longs or the shorts) chase them out of their position.

ANCHORING

Anchoring is a cognitive bias that describes our natural tendency to rely too heavily, or "anchor," on one trait or piece of information in decision making. In an often-cited example of anchoring, a person is looking to buy a used car. The individual focuses excessively on the odometer reading as a basis for evaluating the value of the car, rather than judging how well the engine runs, or the vehicle's make and model. In our investment decisions, we become easily susceptible to this bias by anchoring on specific pieces of information that may have little, if anything, to do with our investment criteria. A classic example of anchoring was demonstrated in an experiment conducted by Richard Thaler at the University of Chicago, the citadel of rational economics. Volunteers were invited to participate in a wine auction where the winning bottle would go to the highest bidder. Before people bid, however, they were asked to fill out a slip of paper with the last two digits of their social security number. In almost every case, the highest bidders had the highest social security numbers.

BLIND SPOTS

The last bias that we will discuss is the *bias blind spot*. As you think about some of the factors that cause distortions in your investment decisions, it is particularly important to know about this one. Bias blind spots occur when investors fail to compensate for their subjectively known cognitive biases. The term was coined by social psychologist Emily Pronin and her colleagues at Princeton University's Department of Psychology.

Pronin explained to subjects the better-than-average effect, the self-serving bias, and many other cognitive biases. As described earlier, according to the better-than-average bias, specifically, people tend to see themselves inaccurately as "better than average" for positive traits and as "less than average" for negative traits. When Pronin subsequently asked subjects how biased they themselves were, they rated themselves as being much less subject to the biases that she and her fellow researchers had described than the average person. This finding clearly explains the need for investor vigilance against any potential bias that causes deviations in judgment as well as the constant challenge that our irrational brain poses. No matter how much we know about markets, there is always more to learn about ourselves.

In Chapter 9, we will look at cognitive fallacies, another category of mental traps that lead us astray.

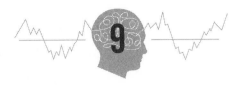

Fallacies

A fallacy is a misconception resulting from incorrect reasoning that often triggers an emotional reaction. Fallacious arguments are structured to exploit rhetorical patterns that obscure logic. Although lacking in validity, these arguments appear seductively persuasive. Some well-known examples are appeals to belief, emotion, fear, and tradition. Other examples include personal attack, generalization, creating a straw man, and begging the question. At the core of the fallacy is a distorted, exaggerated, or misrepresented assertion that leads to a faulty conclusion. Simply stated, it is an error in reasoning rather than one that involves incorrect facts. For the investor, a number of psychological fallacies that impair performance are ready to intrude at any given time.

PLANNING: EASIER SAID THAN DONE

Often underestimated, the *planning fallacy*, or the tendency to misjudge task-completion times, is one whose frequently misunderstood importance cannot be overstated. The original definition of the planning fallacy, expanded below, was the predisposition to underestimate task-completion times. There are numerous real-life examples in public works projects and proposed legislation, and also in corporate management and financial projections, where the effects of this fallacy are all too evident.

In a classic study, psychology students were asked to estimate how long it would take to complete an essential academic assignment. The average estimate was 40 days. The students also estimated how long it would take "if everything went as well as it possibly could," which averaged 27 days, and how long it would take "if everything went as poorly as it possibly could," which averaged 49 days. The average actual completion time was 56 days, with only about 30 percent of the students completing their task in the amount of time that they had predicted.

The researchers also asked participants to estimate when they thought their projects would be 50 percent, 75 percent, and 99 percent completed, with the following results:

▶ Only 13 percent finished their project by the time they had assigned a 50 percent completion.

▶ Only 19 percent finished by the time they had assigned a 75 percent completion.

▶ Only 45 percent finished by the time of their assigned 99 percent completion.

One explanation for the planning fallacy is the focusing effect, the cognitive bias that occurs when individuals place too much importance on one aspect of a decision, causing an error that leads to inaccurately predicting a future outcome. When individuals formulate a plan, they eliminate factors that they perceive as lying outside the specifics of the project. They also have a tendency to discount high-impact risks that they perceive as being unlikely to happen. Business strategy professors Dan Lovallo and Daniel Kahneman have expanded the original definition of the planning fallacy to include the tendency to underestimate the time, costs, and risks of future actions and, simultaneously, to overestimate the benefits of those actions. According to this new definition, the planning fallacy results in both time and cost overruns along with benefit shortfalls.

What happens to the best-laid plans of mice and men is a cliché, but how many times have I observed the results of unrealistic plans and projections of would-be traders, clients, and investors? The answer is, too many. People seriously overestimate their own performance and underestimate the cost in money and time that successful investing requires. In our minds, we discount all the blind alleys and false starts. Being overly optimistic and way above average, we can perceive only our next great success. I am reminded of the famous quote by Thomas Edison, "The reason a lot of people do not recognize opportunity is because it usually goes around wearing overalls looking like hard work."

BLACK SWAN THEORY

The *fallacy of accident* is described in the taxonomy of material fallacies, widely adopted by modern logicians, based on Aristotle's six works on logic. It is a fallacy based on the faulty logic of a generalization that disregards exceptions. An often-cited example is the following argument: Cutting people is a crime. Surgeons cut people. Therefore, surgeons are criminals. The problem is that cutting people is only sometimes against the law. The exception does not either break or define the rule.

The converse fallacy of accident argues from a special case to a general rule. It is illustrated in this argument: every swan I have seen is white, so it must be true that all swans are white. The problem, of course, is that what has been observed is only a subset. One cannot possibly see all swans.

As we discussed earlier, Nassim Taleb described the critical role of Black Swan Events in his 2007 book *The Black Swan*. In his view, all historically consequential events in art, science, and politics exhibited the characteristics of Black Swan Events. They were unplanned and unpredicted, and they had a life-altering effect on society. Examples are the development of the personal computer, the Internet, world wars, and the attack on 9/11. A Black Swan Event has three attributes. First, it is an outlier because it lies outside the realm of expectation, so that nothing in the past can point to its possibility. Second, it has a consequential impact; and third, despite its outlier status, we are predisposed to invent explanations for its occurrence after the fact, making it rational and predictable. Taleb asserts, "A small number of Black Swans explain almost everything in our world, from the success of ideas and religions, to the dynamics of historical events, to elements of our own personal lives."

Explaining his concept, Taleb wrote, "Before the discovery of Australia, people in the old world were convinced that *all* swans were white, an unassailable belief as it seemed completely confirmed by empirical evidence. The sighting of the first black swan might have been an interesting surprise for a few ornithologists (and others extremely concerned with the coloring of birds), but that is not where the significance of the story lies. It illustrates a severe limitation to our learning from observations or experience and the fragility of our knowledge. One single observation can invalidate a general statement derived from millennia of confirmatory sightings of millions of white swans. All you need is one single (and, I am told, quite ugly) black bird."

Taleb believes that financial institutions are particularly vulnerable to Black Swan Events and are exposed to losses beyond what is predicted by current models. One problem, already referred to earlier in Chapter 3, is what he calls the ludic fallacy. *Ludic* comes from the Latin *ludus*, meaning "play, game, sport, pastime," and is understood by Taleb as the misapplication of games to model real-life situations. He describes the fallacy as "basing studies of chance on the narrow world of games and dice." The problem is in the belief that the unpredictable randomness found in life resembles the structured randomness found in games. This stems from the assumption that it is possible to extrapolate accurately from variations in statistics based on past observations, especially when these statistics are presumed to represent samples from a bell-shaped curve.

According to Taleb, statistics work only in those situations, such as casinos, where the odds are visible and defined. Based on platonic forms, a philosophical term relating to the existence of universals, the predictive models gravitate toward mathematical purity and fail to take essential ideas into account. Chief among these are

▶ Possessing all information is impossible.

▶ Small, unknown variations in the data can result in a major impact.

▶ Models based on empirical data are flawed, as events that have yet to take place cannot be accurately predicted and accounted for.

These concerns are highly relevant in financial markets, where banks and investment institutions employ value-at-risk models based on normal statistical distributions. The reason is that many high-impact events are simply without precedent, undercutting the basis of this kind of modeling. A primary concern of Taleb's is not to attempt to predict Black Swan Events, but to build systems that are robust, that is, stress-tested for the impact of these events should they occur. He also argues for the use of counterfactual, or "what-if," reasoning when taking on risk.

Taleb has recently offered the following principles as an effective response to Black Swan Events:

▶ What is fragile should break early, while it is still small. Nothing should ever become too big to fail.

▶ There should be no socialization of losses and privatization of gains.

▶ People who were driving a school bus blindfolded (and crashed it) should never be given a new bus.

▶ Do not let someone making an "incentive" bonus manage a nuclear plant—or your financial risks.

▶ Counterbalance complexity with simplicity.

▶ Do not give children sticks of dynamite, even if they come with a warning.

▶ Only Ponzi schemes should depend on confidence. Governments should never need to "restore confidence."

▶ Do not give an addict more drugs if he has withdrawal pains.

▶ Citizens should not depend on financial assets or fallible "expert" advice for their retirement.

▶ Make an omelet with the broken eggs.

Explaining his rather elliptical last point, Taleb said, "This crisis cannot be fixed with makeshift repairs, no more than a boat with a rotten hull can be fixed with ad-hoc patches. We need to rebuild the hull with new (stronger) materials; we will have to remake the system before it does so itself. Let us move voluntarily into Capitalism 2.0 by helping what needs to be broken break on its own, converting debt into equity, marginalizing the economics and business school establishments, shutting down the 'Nobel' in economics, banning leveraged buyouts, putting bankers where they belong, clawing back the bonuses of those who got us here, and teaching people to navigate a world with fewer certainties. . . . In other words, a place more resistant to black swans."

The main point here is that Black Swan Events are often misunderstood in the financial arena, conceived of as being extreme outliers. This is significant and worrisome, because, as we have experienced in the recent global meltdown, these events play a vastly larger role than regular occurrences. More generally, traditional decision theory, based on a fixed universe or a model of possible outcomes, ignores and minimizes the effect of events that are outside the model: it considers the "known unknowns," but ignores the "unknown unknowns," which underscores the need for counterfactual reasoning when considering risk.

GAMBLER'S FALLACY

The *gambler's fallacy*, also called the *fallacy of the maturity of chances*, is the mistaken belief that if deviations from expected outcomes are observed in repeated trials of a random process, then these deviations are likely to be corrected in the future. Simply put, it is the predisposition to think that future probabilities are affected by past events, when in reality they are unchanged. For example, if a coin is tossed repeatedly and heads comes up a greater number of times than is expected, a gambler may incorrectly believe that this means that tails is more likely to turn up on the next coin toss. Such an expectation is irrationally thought to be owed, as if the universe is somehow aware that a flip on the tail side is due. The fallacy results from a faulty understanding of the law of large numbers. In probability theory, the law of large numbers describes the outcome of performing the same trial a large number of times. According to the law, the average results from a large number of experiments should be close to the expected value, and will tend to become closer as more trials are performed.

The gambler's fallacy is also known by a more colorful name, the *Monte Carlo fallacy*, because of an astonishing event that occurred at a roulette table in Monaco's luxurious Beaux Arts casino. On August 18, 1913, "black" came up on the roulette wheel an unprecedented number of times in succession. As one observer described it, there was a near-panicky rush to bet on red, beginning when black appeared for the fifteenth time in a row. Falling victim to the fallacy, players doubled and tripled their stakes, believing that there was hardly a chance that black would continue to turn up. After the twentieth spin of the wheel, the betting and the accrued losses were tremendous, but in the end, after black appeared a phenomenal twenty-six times, it was only the casino that grew wealthier by millions of francs.

Investors and traders often make this mistake, believing that a market needs to rally or sell off as a result of a prior day's, week's, or month's performance. They irrationally argue that the market is overbought or oversold, is above or below a significant moving average, or has shown an unusual price movement for a short period of time. I have seen groups of traders on hedge fund desks and on the exchange floor commiserating with each other, having suffered large losses after adopting failed contrarian positions in response to a sudden and steep short-term price move. Not unlike a roulette wheel that demonstrates an ability to frustrate people and prove a "sure bet" wrong, the market is the perfect catalyst for the gambler's fallacy.

The *inverse gambler's fallacy* is a term coined by philosopher Ian Hacking to refer to a deviation in judgment that is similar to the gambler's fallacy. It is the erroneous belief that an unlikely outcome of a random process, such as rolling double sixes on a pair of dice, implies that the process is likely to have occurred many times before reaching that result. Predicting the bottom or top of a market based on a particular chart pattern spike and misinterpreting the significance of a market event are also examples of false logic, just as after observing the roll of double sixes, it is wrong to suppose that the dice have been rolled before.

The *reverse gambler's fallacy* is also an interesting example of irrational thought. It is the mistaken belief that heads or tails—or the market rallying or breaking—is the result of some mystical preconception of fate that has allowed for consistent results. The individual asks himself, why change now if the odds favor the position? The fallacy is the erroneous conviction that the universe magically possesses a memory of past results that tends to favor or disfavor a future result.

Kahneman and Tversky proposed that the gambler's fallacy is produced by a psychological bias called the *representativeness heuristic*, a rule of thumb that individuals use to judge the probability or frequency of a hypothesis by considering how much it resembles commonsense data, as opposed to using a formal calculation. According to this view, people expect that a short run of random outcomes should share the properties of a longer run—specifically, that deviations from the mean should balance out. That is why, after observing a long run of red on a roulette wheel, most individuals erroneously believe that black will result, rather than another red. When Kahneman and Tversky asked subjects to make up a random-looking sequence of coin tosses, they tended to arrive at sequences in which the proportion of heads to tails stayed close to even in any short segment, more so than would occur by chance. They interpreted this to mean that people mistakenly believe that short sequences of random events are representative of longer ones.

HISTORIAN'S FALLACY

The *historian's fallacy*, first described in 1970 by Brandeis University professor David Hackett Fischer, occurs when a person assumes that decision makers from the past viewed events from the same perspective as the historian who subsequently analyzed their decision, as if both were in possession of the same information. It is different from *presentism*, a mode of historical analysis in which present-day ideas are projected into the past.

Fischer cautioned historians that their subjects were not able to see into the future. As an example, he cited the well-known argument that Japan's surprise attack on Pearl Harbor should have been avoidable because of the many previous warnings that an attack was imminent. What this argument overlooks, said Fischer, is that there were innumerable conflicting signs that suggested possibilities other than a surprise military attack. Only in retrospect are the indications of war obvious. This kind of thinking is related to *hindsight bias*, the tendency to perceive past events as having been more predictable in retrospect than they were before they took place. Hindsight bias has been experimentally validated in games, politics, and medicine. In psychological studies of hindsight bias, subjects also tend to remember their predictions of future events as having been stronger than they actually were, particularly in cases where these predictions turned out to be correct. One explanation for this is the *availability heuristic*, a phenomenon in which people predict the frequency of an event based on how easily an example can be brought to mind. It was first reported by Kahneman and Tversky.

An example that they cite is the case of someone being asked to estimate the proportion of words that begin with the letter *R* or *K* relative to words that have the letter *R* or *K* in the third position. Most English-speaking people immediately think of words that begin with the letters *R* (ranch, rusty, ring) and *K* (kitchen, kite, key), but it requires more concentrated effort to think of any words where *R* or *K* is the third letter (street, borrow, acknowledge);

thus, the immediate answer would probably be that words that begin with *R* or *K* are more common. In reality, words that have the letter *R* or *K* in the third position are more common. In fact, three times as many words have the letter *K* in the third position. The availability heuristic works on the psychological principle that information that comes to mind readily must be significant.

As investors, we easily fall prey to tapping into data that are closest at hand. Media coverage helps fuel this bias with widespread attention to spectacular events, such as Enron-like bankruptcies, and less coverage of more routine, less sensational events, like the daily operations of well-functioning companies. In psychological experiments, when asked to rate the probability of a variety of causes of death, subjects tend to rate "newsworthy" events as more likely because they are easily recalled from memory. Accordingly, people falsely rate the chance of mortality from plane disasters higher than that from car crashes, and death from natural disasters such as hurricanes, shark attacks, major storms, and earthquakes as being more probable than death from less dramatic and more common causes, such as medical errors. We must vigilantly guard the clarity of our financial decisions from both the inherent drama of big fish and the electric charge of lightning and thunder.

An interesting finding in a scientific experiment that studied the availability heuristic involved imagination. When people were asked to imagine an outcome, they tended to immediately view it as more likely than people who were not asked to imagine the same result did. In one study that occurred before the 1976 presidential election, undecided individuals were asked simply to imagine Gerald Ford or Jimmy Carter winning the upcoming election. Subsequently, they reported the candidate that they had imagined as president as being significantly more likely to win the upcoming election, demonstrating both the psychological power of this heuristic and the predisposition allowing it to serve as a basis for logic.

Returning to the historian's fallacy, as investors, we tend to rely on these same heuristics to aid us in collecting data and evaluating the risks and rewards of our financial decisions. We make faulty assumptions predicated on past experiences or historical data that cause deviations in judgment. Like the historian who wrongly attributes motives and intentions to earlier decision makers, we too are predisposed to analyze past market events using the benefits from later insights. We allow history to peek into the future, leading to projections, based on poor evidence, that may never materialize.

According to Fischer, historians sometimes employ the "fog of war technique" in an effort to avoid the trap of the historian's fallacy. I think it is one that would work for investors as well. In this approach, the actions and decisions of significant actors, such as presidents or military commanders, are evaluated primarily on the basis of what they knew at the time, and not on future developments. According to Fischer, this method was pioneered by the American historian Douglas Southall Freeman in his biographies of George Washington and Robert E. Lee. As investors, we are always subject to fog. It is our mission to make it out profitably.

PSYCHOLOGIST'S FALLACY

Analogous to the historian's fallacy is the *psychologist's fallacy*, first described by William James in *Principles of Psychology* in

1890. James wrote, "The great snare of the psychologist is the confusion of his own standpoint with that of the mental fact about which he is making his report." The fallacy occurs when an observer assumes the objectivity of his own perspective when analyzing a behavioral event. As investors, we are often predisposed to interpreting market actions based only on what we know about ourselves. Such a bias leads the observer to presuppose that others possess or lack knowledge or skills. Too often, investors ascribe behavioral meanings to events that, in reality, are only mirror reflections of their own motivations and values.

TEXAS SHARPSHOOTER FALLACY

The last fallacy that I will discuss goes by a highly descriptive name: the *Texas sharpshooter fallacy*. It occurs when data that have no relationship are interpreted or manipulated until they appear to show correlation. The name is derived from a hotshot who fires at the side of a barn, then paints a target around a cluster of hits and claims to be a sharpshooter. In essence, why this fallacy resonates with traders and investors is that it's not such an infrequent occurrence for individuals to believe that they have discovered a silver bullet system for exploiting market action. The mistake is that you can't use the same information to construct and test the same hypothesis; to do so is to be guilty of the Texas sharpshooter fallacy. The fallacy is related to the clustering illusion, which will be discussed in the next chapter, or the psychological tendency to identify and interpret patterns in randomness where none exist. It may also be related to the experience of seeing connections in meaningless data, such as pareidolia.

Pareidolia is a psychological phenomenon involving a vague image or sound that is perceived as being significant. Familiar examples include seeing images of animals in clouds, seeing the man in the moon, and hearing hidden messages on records. It can also involve the subjective perception of instructions embedded in price charts when no such information is really there. Many times traders have said to me in exasperated disbelief when I could not confirm their perspective, "What's the matter with you? Don't you see it; this chart is just begging you to sell!" There have also been instances when, at the very same time, other traders insisted that the identical chart was begging *them* to buy. Chapter 10 concentrates on this phenomenon, and other illusions that distort our view of the market.

Illusions

An illusion is characterized by perceptions that differ from objective reality. Simply stated, it is a distortion of the senses, revealing how the brain normally organizes and interprets sensory stimuli. In a visual illusion, the information gathered by the eye is processed by the brain to give an imprecise mental impression, or percept. Media theorist Marshall McLuhan famously declared that he was more interested in percepts than in concepts—that is, the way people experience the world rather than how they think about it.

There are three types of visual illusions: literal, physiological, and cognitive. Literal illusions create images that are different from the objects that make them; physiological illusions are the effects on the eyes and the brain of excessive stimulation by brightness, color, and other such factors; and cognitive optical illusions occur when the eye and the brain make unconscious inferences. Illusions also occur with other senses. For example, a ventriloquist creates the auditory illusion that the voice we hear comes from the dummy. As we see Edgar Bergen's sidekick mouthing words, we hear Charlie McCarthy speaking.

Mimes also create a repertoire of illusions that fool the brain, exploiting the way we unconsciously infer the physical world. We marvel at Marcel Marceau, the internationally acclaimed French actor and mime, in the persona of Bip the clown, running into imaginary walls, climbing fake stairs, leaning on make-believe shelves, and frustrating himself in a phantom game of tug of war.

COGNITIVE DISTORTIONS
OF REALITY

For the investor, illusions appear in the guise of cognitive distortions: exaggerated and irrational thoughts that taint our financial decisions. The theory of cognitive distortions was first proposed by David D. Burns, a pioneer in the development of cognitive-behavioral therapy and a professor in the Department of Psychiatry and Behavioral Sciences at the Stanford University School of Medicine. Here are some of the most common cognitive distortions.

All-or-Nothing Thinking

This involves making decisions and experiencing their effects in absolute terms. This illusion is related to the logical fallacy of the *false dilemma*, also called the *false dichotomy*, and the *either-or fallacy*, which occurs when two alternative statements are held to be the only possible options, although in reality there are more. In financial decision making, it may involve a situation in which only two investment choices are considered, although in fact there are others from which to choose. Closely related is the tendency to think in extremes, also known as *black-and-white thinking*. Many investors routinely engage in black-and-white thinking, as in the experience of boundless optimism when a trade is going well and then suddenly switching to abject despair at a setback. Another example is creating position sizing based on an all-or-nothing perspective, adopting a boom-or-bust mentality.

Overgeneralization

This involves taking isolated cases and using them to make far-reaching generalizations. This illusion is also known as the *fallacy of insufficient statistics* and the *fallacy of the lonely fact*. No matter what you call it, this distortion of reality comes from reaching a faulty conclusion based on insufficient evidence. It commonly involves a broad statement based upon the statistics of a small sample that fails to sufficiently represent the whole population. Bulls and bears fall prey equally to this distortion.

The opposite of hasty generalization, known as *slothful induction*, denies the logical conclusion of an inductive argument, viewing it instead as mere coincidence. Despite its name, this resistance to following the evidence is based not on sloth, but on ignorance, entrenched belief, and vested interest. As scientific evidence linking lung cancer to smoking mounted, tobacco companies consistently resisted and repudiated the evidence. Brown & Williamson went so far as to state, "It is our opinion that the repeated assertion without conclusive proof that cigarettes cause disease—however well-intentioned—constitutes a disservice to the public."

Loki's wager is a related form of logical fallacy that relies on the unreasonable insistence that a concept that cannot be defined cannot be discussed. The fallacy's focus on overspecification relates to the cognitive distortion of overgeneralization. Loki, the trickster god of Norse mythology, wagered his head in a bet with the dwarf Brokkr. Loki lost the bet, but managed to keep his head because he argued that his neck was never included in the bargain. Since Loki and Brokkr were unable to reach a consensus as to where his neck ended and his head began, the dispute remained forever unresolved. This kind of argument is made not only about heads and necks, but also about bulls and bears and where to buy and sell the stock market.

Mental Filter

This involves focusing almost exclusively on certain minute aspects of a financial event while ignoring other, more global aspects—for example, focusing on the intraday fluctuations of a stock rather than on its long-term growth. It is easy to get caught up in this pattern. The market is an endless inkblot of subjective interpretation, which is exactly why it is so critical that you focus on what really matters: your plan, its execution, investment discipline, and patience.

Misleading vividness is a term that is applied to the communication of anecdotal evidence. It occurs when someone explains something in vivid detail to try to make it appear more important than it really is, even when it is an exceptional occurrence. Its intent is to create a hasty generalization by convincing a listener that an isolated event is a widespread problem. Turn on your local TV news tonight, and you will see several examples. Kahneman and Tversky have shown in experiments that, although misleading vividness does little to support an argument logically, it exerts a strong psychological effect because of the availability heuristic.

Misleading vividness is a particularly pernicious distortion because it causes the investor to irrationally latch onto a small number of dramatic events and internalize them in such a way that they outweigh statistical evidence. This sort of reasoning takes the following form:

1. "The last time I bought Microsoft, Morningstar issued an unfavorable rating, and I got my head cut off" (unlike Loki).

2. "Therefore I never trade technology stocks where big point drops are likely to happen."

People often reach decisions employing this fallacious logic because vivid events make a very strong impression on the mind. An individual who bought Enron shares might be inclined to believe that the stock market is more dangerous than other forms of investment. After all, losing a large part of one's retirement fund will have a greater impact on the brain than will statistics about the long-term growth of a balanced stock portfolio.

Jumping to Conclusions

This means drawing conclusions from little, if any, evidence. There are two forms of this distortion that are usually identified: mind reading, or assuming that one has special knowledge of the thoughts or intentions of others, and fortune telling, or exaggerating one's knowledge of how things will turn out before they happen. This mode of irrational thinking is related to the *slippery-slope fallacy*, which states that a relatively small first step inevitably leads to a chain of events culminating in some significant outcome, much like a boulder being pushed over the edge of a slope.

This distortion suggests that making a move in a particular direction starts something down a path, and it will continue to slide in the same direction. Impatient investors often create these sorts of arguments in their minds to justify getting out of a position that is profitable, but that has not yet fulfilled its potential. In response to a news item, special knowledge, or a crystal ball, they wrongly persuade themselves that, should they fail to act, an inevitable chain of events will lead to a "certain" loss.

So embedded is this idea in our collective psyches that we continually draw on a number of metaphors and expressions that convey the idea that small missteps can lead to tremendous events that have undesirable or unexpected consequences. To name but a few: foot in the door, domino effect, and boiling a frog (that is, slowly, so that it won't perceive the danger when it is being cooked to death). The last is a compelling metaphor for the inability of people to react to important changes that occur gradually. My favorite, however, is the camel's nose, a metaphor with a similar meaning.

According to linguist Geoffrey Nunberg, the image entered the language in the nineteenth century by way of a fable about an Arab who allows a camel to stick its nose into his tent, then other parts of its body, and so on, until the camel is fully inside and refuses to leave. The message is clear: a small, undesirable situation—no bigger than a nose—will gradually result in unavoidable worsening. Banks and brokerages, aware of our susceptibility to this message, repeatedly warn that a small monetary misstep may result in a calamitous effect. It is no wonder that this type of thinking intrudes on our financial decisions. There is a positive side to this idea as well, embedded in the ancient Chinese proverb, "A journey of a thousand miles begins with a single step." It is a good place to start when it comes to undoing the many illusions that undermine financial decisions.

Disqualifying the Positive

This involves rejecting positive experiences or outcomes, believing that they really don't count for subjective reasons. As a result, individuals maintain a negative belief that is contradicted by objective reality. An example may take the form of an investor's harboring the irrational belief that if she makes a profitable trade, it is the result of luck, but if she makes an unprofitable trade, it is because she is a failure. Many times an individual reaches this unfortunate conclusion about herself, even though everything about the investment was in agreement with a thoughtful plan. It may have been well researched, executed, and risk managed—all positives—but the investor nevertheless blames herself. She feels that she is at fault, and her brain argues that the loss was symptomatic of personal inadequacy when, in reality, the investment may not have worked out for myriad reasons that were outside her control.

Related to disqualifying the positive is another form of spurious reasoning known as *special pleading*, which introduces favorable details or excludes unfavorable details by alleging "special" considerations without proper qualification. It is an abrogation of the rational assumption that in an argument, wherever a distinction is claimed, a relevant basis for that distinction needs to be identified and substantiated. Simply put, special pleading is no more than an attempt to gain an exemption from a generally accepted rule or principle without justifying the exception. In philosophy, it is assumed that special pleading is a subversion of logical reasoning. As investors, we often plead with ourselves that a particular investment in stocks, bonds, or real estate is special. Our minds persuade us to move forward without verifying, even though our decision is outside the bounds of prudent risk parameters or the established rules of a trading plan.

MAGNIFICATION AND MINIMIZATION

This means distorting aspects of an event or a memory by magnifying or minimizing its importance in a way that fails to correspond to objective reality. This is a familiar enough practice to most of us, embedded in such popular expressions as "make a mountain out of a molehill." The idiom, of course, captures the fact that people often react disproportionately to situations. An earlier metaphor conveying the same insight was offered by Lucian of Samosata, a second-century Assyrian rhetorician and satirist who wrote in the Greek language. Known for his wit and bite, he spoke of the tendency to make elephants of flies. Investors need to be aware of our commonplace tendency to magnify and minimize the psychological significance of market occurrences.

When I was still a principal in an investment firm that specialized in proprietary trading, I would often take new traders on a cook's tour of the exchange floor, illustrating some of the same points that are being made here. I would describe many of my own investment shortcomings, punctuated by conversations with elite traders, who would personalize their own experiences resulting from falling prey to cognitive biases, fallacies, and illusions.

The trading floor is a psychological petri dish, the perfect place, if one is so inclined, to interact with and study a vibrant and thriving culture of traders. They are largely a high-performing and profitable group, and their behavior provides a diorama of how the human brain works in situations of risk taking under stress. Like Olympians, the best traders demonstrate great physicality, mental toughness, and critical decision making, as well as grace under fire.

The professional trader's job description is more easily stated than accomplished: managing finances and emotions at the exact moment of putting one's money where one's mouth is. The challenge is further complicated by the nature of the workplace in which the trader performs: a ruthless environment in which colleagues and competitors note every monetary and psychological blunder, reviewing them publicly in the most explicit terms.

One of the more popular stops on my tour with novices was the members' break room, a laboratory for magnifying and minimizing market events, where one could overhear stories that were as rich in detail as a Balzac novel. The names and dates changed, but the content of the aggrieved was always the same: legendary trades that got away, and investment mistakes by the innocent that were someone else's fault.

One particularly destructive type of magnification is called *catastrophizing*, an irrational mode of thinking that assumes the worst possible outcome, focusing on every negative possibility, however unlikely. A subtle example of this cognitive distortion can come into play when investors find themselves in volatile markets. As ambiguity and stress levels rise, our minds tell us that the situation is unbearable and force us to get out, when, in reality, the market that we are experiencing is just uncomfortable. These markets are rife with opportunity and often highly profitable, but few investors have the inner strength to capitalize on their psychologically distorting gyrations. It is at these times that investors believe that the sky is falling, and sheepish stockbrokers refuse to answer their phones.

Emotional Reasoning

This is making decisions based on feelings rather than on objective evidence. It is the irrational belief that what we are feeling at any moment is a true assessment of ourselves. Feeling stupid or boring does not mean that we are these things. Likewise, feeling guilty when taking a loss does not mean that we did something wrong. Emotions constantly intrude on the thinking process, distorting thoughts and beliefs that influence actions.

Related to emotional reasoning is the issue of *personalization*, or assuming personal responsibility for situations that are beyond the investor's control. It is a deviation in judgment that personalizes everything. An example is thinking that whatever happens in the market, from research to execution, is a reaction to you personally. The investor may also compare himself unfavorably to others, trying to determine who is smarter, quicker, a better trader, and so on. The underlying assumption is that the individual's self-worth is in question. Those who fall prey to this type of thinking are continually setting up arbitrary tests in which they evaluate themselves against subjective measures of their own making. When the investor "measures up," there is a temporary reprieve from inwardly directed harsh feelings, but when she falls short, the person experiences a loss of self-worth, believing that her "real" value has been revealed. Both emotional reasoning and personalization result from the same shortcomings: making decisions on the basis of feelings without thinking, and reacting to a psychologically challenging environment without the benefits of evidence and reasoned analysis.

Holding Oneself to an Impossible Standard

This involves engaging in a style of thinking that insists on the way things "should be" or "ought to be" rather than negotiating the difficult emotional and intellectual terrain that one is faced with; it also involves adopting rigid rules that, the individual argues, always apply. Psychologist Albert Ellis, who is generally considered one of the originators of the cognitive paradigm shift in psychotherapy, termed this type of thinking *mental masturbation*.

In addition to their application in mental health, Ellis's insights have been adapted to nonclinical settings by counselors, consultants, and coaches to address a range of issues that include increased performance, social skills, career changes, balancing finances, weight control, and stress management.

One of the fundamental premises of Ellis's approach is that psychological disturbance is a function of how people construct their view of the world through language, belief, meaning, and philosophy. Describing the role of cognitive, emotional, and behavioral processes, Ellis explained that rational emotive behavior therapy assumes that thinking, emotion, and action are interrelated processes, each of which is rarely experienced in a pure state. He said, "Much of what we call emotion is nothing more nor less than a certain kind—a biased, prejudiced, or strongly evaluative kind—of thought." Adding that both feelings and behaviors have a significant impact on thinking in the same way that thinking has an influence on emotions and behaviors, Ellis also observed, "Evaluating is a fundamental characteristic of human organisms and seems to work in a kind of closed circuit with a feedback mechanism: Because perception biases response and then response tends to bias subsequent perception. Also, prior perceptions appear to bias subsequent perceptions, and prior responses appear to bias subsequent responses. What we call feelings almost always have a pronounced evaluating or appraisal element."

The distortions of thought and emotion that are triggered in the financial arena occur in a similar way and are experienced at a gut level. The results, as we have seen, are misunderstandings of risk, errors in execution, overconfidence in one's ability, and compromised decisions. The goal is to break free from the closed psychological circuitry of a faulty feedback mechanism that reinforces biases, fallacies, and illusions. The solution begins with awareness, leading to cognitive and emotional strategies that reinterpret our market experience through language, belief, feelings, meaning, and action.

Labeling

This involves naming behaviors and events using negative, highly colored, or emotionally loaded terms. An extreme form of overgeneralization, labeling merely provides branding, rather than seeking to understand or explain behavior. Investors who engage in this irrational mode of thinking perceive themselves and their actions in absolute and unalterable terms instead of attempting to examine specific decisions in the context of particular market conditions. I have heard traders many times, both seriously and in jest, refer to themselves as losers after a misstep in their investing. Reflecting on their experience, most would agree that it is far more constructive to analyze what went wrong in order to determine how to improve in the future.

ILLUSIONS OF CONTROL
AND CORRELATION

There are several other empirically verified illusions, more akin to cognitive biases, that intrude on investors' decisions. They are the illusion of control, illusory correlation, clustering illusion, illusion of asymmetric insight, and money illusion.

Let's take a look at each and consider its implication for our financial decisions.

Illusion of Control

This is adopting the belief that an individual can control, or significantly affect, outcomes that in fact we have little or no influence over. The illusion of control has been demonstrated in a number of studies, and researchers have suggested that it is tied to self-esteem: an individual's belief that he has a certain level of control over his success motivates him to work harder to achieve his goal.

In a series of experiments by psychologists Herbert M. Jenkins, William C. Ward, and L. G. Allan that involved subjects determining their control over switches that illuminated lights marked "score" and "no score," the results were startling. The connections for the lights were arranged so that each attempt switched on one light with a specific probability, so that in reality, subjects had either no control over which light was on or a variable amount of control determined by the researchers. Amazingly, the participants' estimates of control revealed no correlation with how much actual control they had, even when they were told that there might not be a causal effect between the lights going on and their actions. The finding suggested that the experience of being in control was directly related to how often the "score" light lit up, even when there was no correlation with which button was pressed. In each instance, subjects reported exerting control over the lights.

In another series of experiments, Harvard professor of psychology Ellen Langer has demonstrated the prevalence of the illusion of control, which she defined as a person's belief that his probability of success is higher than would be determined by an objective assessment. Langer found that individuals were more likely to behave as if they could exercise control in a chance situation in which specific skills were required and there was some involvement in decisions.

The illusion of control has also been observed in games of chance, such as shooting craps, where players tend to throw harder for high numbers and softer for low numbers. Under some conditions, subjects have even been induced to believe that they could influence the outcome of a random coin toss. Subjects who guessed a series of coin tosses more accurately began to believe that they were in reality better guessers, and to think that their guesses would be less successful when they were distracted.

Studies have also shown the harmful effects of the illusion of control, specifically in the thinking of problem gamblers and investment bank traders, where faulty logic propels risk taking beyond a reasonable degree.

Open University professor of organizational behavior Mark Fenton-O'Creevy has shown that, while the illusion of control can promote motivation, it is not conducive to sound decision making. He has found that it is associated with resistance to feedback and that it impedes learning, as well as predisposes investors to assume greater risk. In a study with professional bank traders, Fenton-O'Creevy showed that individuals who were prone to a high illusion of control had significantly worse performance on analysis, risk management, and contribution to trading desk profits, earning substantially less than their colleagues.

It used to be a rule of thumb among trading executives, when they were looking to hire proprietary traders, to seek out individuals with successful histories in music, tennis, golf, or basketball. In general, these individuals were trained to think in subtleties, allowing themselves to let go and move with the flow. The need for control usually would not intrude on their performance. As a group, they were unlike former hockey players or football stars, who ached for control. Taking the bull by its horns, they were determined to fight on, no matter what the obstacle.

Illusory Correlation

This involves assuming a nonexistent relationship between two variables. This frequently occurs when the link captures one's attention simply because it is novel or distinctive. According to a study conducted by David Hamilton and Terrence Rose, illusory correlation is one of the ways in which stereotypes form and are perpetuated. The researchers demonstrated that stereotypes lead people to expect certain groups and traits to fit together, and to overestimate the frequency of these correlations.

University of Toronto medical professor Donald Redelmeier and behavioral psychologist Amos Tversky studied arthritis patients over a 15-month period, while also taking into consideration comprehensive meteorological information. Virtually all of the patients interviewed were certain that their bouts with the illness correlated with the weather. In fact, the actual correlation was close to zero.

In another study examining illusory correlation, clinical psychologists observed its effects in psychodiagnostic testing. The research demonstrated "that although projective testing is not helpful in the diagnosis of mental disorders, some psychologists continue to use such tests because of a perceived, illusory correlation between test results and certain attributes." An example that was cited was a test that asked patients to draw a person on a blank page so that the drawing could be used as an indicator of an underlying mental condition. The researchers found that some psychologists believed that there was a correlation between drawing a person with big eyes and the presence of paranoia, even though no such correlation exists. They also found that when deliberately uncorrelated data were presented to college students, students asserted a correlation that did not exist.

As investors, we often mistakenly assume that two variables are linked when, in fact, they are not. To avoid making this mistake, it is important to ask whether the evidence indicates an actual correlation. If it does not, as we have seen, our mind is all too eager to be persuaded that there is an illusory relationship. This also means that when a correlation is asserted, insist on hard data as evidence. Too often, when brokers and pitchmen promote correlations, what they are really banking on (pun intended) is the manipulation of your expectations.

Clustering Illusion

The clustering illusion is believing in the existence of patterns where none are present. The clustering illusion was widely reported in a study that examined the shooting performance of professional basketball players. Cornell University professor of psychology Thomas Gilovich and colleagues found that the suggestion that basketball players shoot in "streaks," sometimes referred to as having a "hot hand," was largely false. In the data they collected, the success of a previous basket very slightly predicted a subsequent miss over another successful shot. Kahneman and Tversky explained the clustering illusion as being caused by the representativeness heuristic, a rule of thumb whereby people judge the probability of a hypothesis based on a comparable known. Investors are famously susceptible to this illusion, which is why reliance on evidence and verification is so crucial.

Illusion of Asymmetric Insight

This illusion means believing that an individual's knowledge of her peers surpasses her peers' knowledge of her. In a study titled "You Don't Know Me, but I Know You: The Illusion of Asymmetric Insight," Princeton University psychologist Emily Pronin demonstrated that individuals revealed asymmetry in assessing their own interpersonal and intrapersonal knowledge relative to that of their peers.

Traders and investors commonly believe that they understand others (e.g., the market) better than others understand them. The logic behind this illusion stems from a fallacious viewpoint that assumes that other investors possess a significant blind self, while we possess far greater insight. The same effect can be observed on trading desks and in investment groups, where the in-group believes that it understands better.

Related to this is the scientifically explored introspection illusion, coined by Emily Pronin: a cognitive bias in which "people wrongly think they have direct insight into the origins of their mental states, while treating others' introspections as unreliable. In certain situations, this illusion leads people to make confident, but false, explanations of their own behavior or predictions about their future mental states."

Money Illusion

The money illusion involves focusing on the nominal value of money rather than on the value that is derived from its purchasing power. The term *money illusion* was coined by John Maynard Keynes, who described the tendency of people to think of money in numerical terms, rather than in terms of its real value. Princeton's Eldar Shafir, with colleagues Peter Diamond and Amos Tversky, has provided compelling empirical evidence for the existence of the money illusion and how it affects financial behavior in a variety of experimental and real-life situations. For traders and investors, it is critically important to be aware of the money illusion and to recognize that any funds used for investment must be understood in the context of money's real value: its purchasing power.

Awareness alone will not allow you to overcome this or any other cognitive distortion. Although it is a critical first step, commitment to improve and repeated trial and error are the ultimate recipe for overcoming illusions' undesirable effects.

In Chapter 11, I will discuss the central but not always discussed issue in all investment decisions: our deep-seated fear of losing.

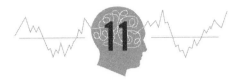

Taking a Loss

At the heart of all our financial decisions is an aversion to loss. Kahneman and Tversky convincingly demonstrated this phenomenon in prospect theory, which described the natural predisposition of individuals to prefer avoiding a loss to achieving a profit. It is for this reason that individuals are quick to show a gain and, paradoxically, against all that we know about sound investing, slow to cut their losses. "If I just hold on, the market may turn around" is something that I've heard from traders and clients numerous times. Individuals have even justified their failure to get out of bleeding trades under the guise of exercising patience. The faulty logic goes like this: "discipline" dictated a wait-and-see approach, to be "patient" and not register a loss. Unfortunately, in these instances, it is wise to obey the trading axiom that the first loss is the best loss, and the Keynesian observation of irrationality outlasting solvency is a near sure bet.

Investors need to be aware of how they personally feel about risk in a literal sense. Only then can they fully comprehend the problems and opportunities that are associated with it. This is by no means an abstract topic. Knowing where you are on the continuum, from very cautious to aggressively embracing risk, will determine the success or failure of your performance.

Based on conversations and interviews that I have had with some of the country's best traders, I have found that profitable investing often comes down to the response to a question that I received from a seasoned pro. In the study of his richly appointed apartment, with an expansive view of the city, the trader spoke candidly about his long career in finance. Punctuating the conversation with descriptions of some of the many floor-to-ceiling trophies of his success, he admitted that his fortune had been built on three things: knowledge, nerve, and the ability to lose money. He said with an impish smile, "Everybody has the ability to lose money, but it takes nerve to lose and then choose to stay in the game."

CONFIDENCE, NOT OVERCONFIDENCE

The trader's point was that after sustaining a loss or a string of losses, it is hard to continue to make trades. It is similar to a batter trying to emerge from a hitting slump, a basketball player maintaining confidence after a series of failed shots, or a writer struggling to get unblocked. He said that market success required "audacity," which he felt was his greatest strength, "to assume that you were smart and quick enough to make a trade and take advantage of opportunities" once you were in a rut. He added, "I found that the psychology of being able to lose money and come back was a big factor. Because it is very easy to lose money and become discouraged." The investor felt that having a great deal of confidence in the face of defeat, even after taking a beating in the market, was key.

The essential point for him, and for the many other highly successful investors whom I have interviewed, was the same: the critical importance of developing internal strategies that allow you to overcome the fear and psychological wounds of loss and trade effectively. It is interesting, perhaps because of loss aversion, how rare it is for financial books to examine investor loss in an in-depth and meaningful way. Why is it, in the many hundreds of books that I have read on trading and investment, that the issue only infrequently rears its ugly head? Not that the subject of loss is entirely absent, but when it does appear, even in recent works on behavioral finance and neuroeconomics, it is handled from a distance, with such headings as "How to Cut Losses," "Expectations versus Experience," and "The Neural Activity of Losses." Perhaps the writers thought that if the blood and sweat of loss is not confronted, the issue will go away quietly. It won't. Its presence is at the center of everything that we do in the market. Like the sun, whose heat and glare are real, loss is here to stay. Stated simply, knowing how to take a loss is the hardest and most important lesson that an investor has to learn.

In *The New Market Wizards*, Jack Schwager states that the great traders realize how intrinsic the element of losing is to being successful in trading. One of the traders he interviewed, Linda Raschke, who was also interviewed by MIT neuroeconomist Andrew Lo for *The Heretics of Finance*, told Schwager that it never bothered her to lose money because she always knew that she would make it right back. Linking loss acceptance to investor confidence, Schwager stated, "Because exceptional traders are confident that they will win over the long run, individual losing trades no longer seem horrible; they simply appear inevitable—which is what they are."

It has been my experience, repeated many times by elite investors, that once these investors have made a trade that is true to their plan, based on effective risk control, they don't even think about the trade in terms of losing money. This is what investors refer to as discipline. Of my many hundreds of interviews with top traders, I don't believe there was ever an instance where discipline was not mentioned. Once it is exercised, there is no need for second-guessing. In a revealing 2010 interview, billionaire Steven Cohen of the $12 billion S.A.C. Capital Advisors hedge fund said, "I think about the risk. I think about the trade. I don't think about the money." Cohen, who is reputed to be an excellent poker player, said that he learned to trade as a result of his understanding of the risks involved and the discipline that is necessary from gambling. He said, "Poker was the biggest determinant in my learning to take risks."

I'm not recommending that you spend more time playing poker or hang around in casinos, but the point is clear: the only way to tame uncertainty is to be aware of its effect within ourselves. Discipline keeps you on your game plan, with a focus on methodology and strict risk control. This shift in focus is important because it reframes the investment process from one of fear to one of problem solving. Trading scared, or not to lose, is a blueprint for failure. Schwager made the same observation when he said, "There is no more certain recipe for losing than having a fear of losing. If you can't stand taking losses, you will either end up taking large losses or missing great trading opportunities—either flaw is sufficient to sink any chances for success."

In the movie *Wall Street*, Gordon Gekko aptly fully captures the phenomenon of loss aversion when he declares, "Nothing ruins my day like losses." The common ways that most investors handle the issue of loss are denial, inaction, confusion, and anger.

Denial and the Ostrich Effect

In the *Tao of Trading*, I asked if it was any wonder that most investors were not getting the results that they wanted from the market. I thought not, because in my experience, most investors trade with their eyes closed, their ears shut, and their nervous systems turned off. I did not pass along this observation to be mean or off-putting, or to spark a nonexistent controversy. Years of working with clients and traders led me to question why investors gamely tolerate growing losses resulting from ill-conceived plans with poor risk assessment. Denial does not help. In the words of Loretta Castorini to her impulsive lover Ronny Cammareri in the movie *Moonstruck*, "Snap out of it!"

In behavioral finance, there is a term that describes this form of denial. It is appropriately termed the *ostrich effect*, or ignoring an obvious negative financial situation by pretending that it does not exist. The name comes from the commonly held, but factually incorrect, belief that ostriches hide their heads in the sand to avoid danger.

In a 2006 article in the *Journal of Business*, Hebrew University of Jerusalem's Dan Galai and NYU's Orly Sade explained differences in returns in the fixed-income market by citing the ostrich effect, attributing the behavior to an aversion to receiving information on potential interim losses. Later research by George Loewenstein, Carnegie Mellon University's Herbert A. Simon

Professor of Psychology and Economics, confirmed the behavior by demonstrating that Scandinavians looked up the value of their investments 50 to 80 percent less often during bad markets.

Inaction

It is not unusual for traders and investors to adopt the counterproductive strategy of deferring action to cope with their fear of losing. Psychologists are familiar with this behavior in individuals as a means of dealing with anxiety. It is a way of postponing or giving up on a task or decision. Related to investor inaction is the psychological phenomenon of procrastination, which psychologists Schraw, Wadkins, and Olafson have characterized as being defined by three criteria: behavior that is counterproductive, needless, and delaying.

Inaction may be triggered by stress, a sense of guilt, diminished self-worth, or social disapproval. Traders have often reported to me that they experienced a feeling that they had not lived up to, or met, a personal commitment or responsibility, as well as fearing how they would be perceived by fellow traders. These feelings create a cycle of irrational thoughts and debilitating emotions that inevitably leads to further inaction.

In essence, investors and traders become sidelined when they fear the prospect of suffering a loss. The issue is further complicated because the anxiety that is experienced, along with thoughts of diminished self-worth, contributes to a defeatist mentality. An additional element that rears its ugly head is the need for perfection, which has been shown to go hand in hand with this type of behavior. Perfectionists expect so much of themselves that they are scared that they cannot meet their own standards to achieve lofty goals.

The important point for traders and investors to understand is that inaction, bluntly stated, guarantees only one thing: failure. When I work with traders, I often quote the familiar saying, "If you sleep on the floor, you can't fall out of bed." Too often, individuals adopt this philosophy when dealing with risk. Traders who are gun-shy and express a fear of "pulling the trigger" realize intuitively that if you don't shoot, you cannot miss the target. Many times, anxiety is stimulated by a genuine lack of knowledge, or a strong insecurity about what exactly should be fired upon.

When the investor has developed an investment approach with a specific focus, and is armed with the psychological understanding that taking a loss—the real fear—is an inevitable part of the process, then, and only then, will the investor have the capability to take part in the fray, seize market opportunities, and not miss out. When missing out becomes more painful than being inactive, triggers get pulled and targets are hit.

One way to begin to change entrenched behaviors of inaction is to stop punishing yourself when you are not sure what to do, and to start rewarding yourself by developing a sound game plan with a specific focus that will allow you to invest competently and with confidence.

Confusion

Confusion about an investment results from not working out a well-defined risk management formula prior to entering a trade. Whether you are betting on the direction of the British pound or drilling for oil for British Petroleum, your chances of minimizing uncertainty and confusion are greatly enhanced by knowing what you are doing. Having a plan, evaluating risk, executing precisely, and preparing for worst-case situations will greatly increase the likelihood of success. Taking these steps will also reduce unproductive emotion and ambiguity, and, importantly, provide clarity in market decisions. When I interviewed Jeffrey Silverman, he stated that for him, the more emotions that could be eliminated, the better his chances of focusing entirely on his trading plan with patience and decision. He said that his investment approach dictated that he avoid being emotional by preparing for multiple outcomes and thoroughly calculating his market exposure. He summed up his philosophy by way of advice: "Be unemotional about getting in, be unemotional about the position, and be unemotional when getting out." In reality, one can never be certain, but one can certainly minimize confusion.

Anger

I used to tell my traders that reacting to the market out of anger is like choosing to hold your breath until the market goes your way. It is an exercise in futility with devastating consequences. In my experience, investing when you are angry will not affect a positive outcome and greatly increases the possibility of turning a small loss into a big one. I should note here that recent research in decision making suggests that understanding the role of anger is more complicated than was originally thought. Despite its reputation as an emotion that inevitably leads to rash behavior, in some instances, with certain individuals, anger appears to promote effective decisions. Nevertheless, I still would not recommend that you get angry the next time you are plagued with financial indecision, despite preliminary findings from recent studies.

THE TRUTH ABOUT TAKING A LOSS

We sometimes forget that investing is a full-blown mind/body experience. In our minds, we breezily plan the intellectually comforting next step in the market, only to experience later, in the midst of a storm of risk and reversals, the all-out assault on our nervous system. Our decisions have consequences that we experience with all our senses.

PHYSICAL SYMPTOMS OF TAKING A LOSS

- Rapid or shallow breathing
- Sweating
- Constriction of muscles
- Upset stomach
- Tension headache
- Feeling of malaise

EMOTIONAL SYMPTOMS OF TAKING A LOSS

- Anger
- Depression
- Disillusionment
- Distraction
- Anxiety
- Irritability
- Frustration
- Low self-worth
- Embarrassment

In *The Intuitive Trader*, I suggested that there is a striking similarity between the discipline that is needed by the professional trader and the discipline that was needed by the fierce warrior of feudal Japan. In the midst of the battle, there was no time for the samurai to think about the proper way to launch an attack or swing a sword; technique had to be integral, without the slightest hesitation. Likewise, the actions adopted by investors need to be reflexive, disciplined, and prerehearsed.

VISUAL IMAGERY THAT INVESTORS SEE WHEN TAKING A LOSS

▶ Sights of past failures

▶ Pictures of investment obstacles and disappointments

▶ Visions of unrelated mishaps of a generalized nature

▶ Planes crashing, oil rigs exploding, wells hemorrhaging on the ocean floor

▶ The sight of money burning

AUDITORY IMAGERY THAT INVESTORS HEAR WHEN TAKING A LOSS

▶ The voice of doom and gloom

▶ Recordings of negative past experiences

▶ Memories involving embarrassing situations or feelings of low self-worth

▶ The sounds of failure

▶ Exploding bank accounts and nest eggs cracking

SENSORY IMAGERY THAT INVESTORS FEEL WHEN TAKING A LOSS

▶ The body feels heavy.

▶ The shoulders droop.

▶ The torso is hunched.

▶ Facial muscles slacken.

▶ Breathing is short.

▶ Eyes are cast downward.

▶ The investor feels slow, weak, and out of energy.

The Book of Five Rings is a text on kenjutsu and other martial arts, written by the samurai Miyamoto Musashi, circa 1645. It is considered a classic treatise on strategy, much like Sun Tzu's *The Art of War*. There have been many translations, and the book enjoys a broad audience for its insights into areas beyond the martial arts: leadership, personal development, and philosophy. Musashi advises, "Think of what is right and true. Learn to see everything accurately. Become aware of what is not obvious. Be careful even in small matters. Do not do anything useless."

BELIEFS THAT INVESTORS POSSESS WHEN TAKING A LOSS

ABOUT THEMSELVES

▶ "I can never make a winning trade."

▶ "I'll never learn; I always make the same mistake."

▶ "I have to be perfect."

▶ "If I take a loss, then I'm a loser."

▶ "I must not know what I am doing."

ABOUT THE MARKET

▶ "The market is rigged."

▶ "It's impossible to have a winning investment."

▶ "The professionals always make money on me."

▶ "You can never get a decent fill."

▶ "My broker's always out to screw me."

The Book of Five Rings is held in high esteem by professional investors for its spare, no-nonsense perspective, which I believe reveals the fundamental truth that everything that you do as an investor matters. From research to execution, it is important to be in a frame of mind such that each effort builds inevitably to an outcome, and this outcome will be a success only if it is the result of thoughtful calculation, implemented with precision.

SELF-DEFEATING ATTITUDES THAT INVESTORS POSSESS WHEN TAKING A LOSS

▶ Holding oneself to an impossible standard

▶ Attempting to please others

▶ Thinking in terms of black or white, all or nothing, total success or total failure

▶ Focusing on negative things

▶ Believing that one's childhood or past experiences have programmed one for failure

▶ Demanding certainty of oneself or the market

▶ Defining investing as being impossible

▶ Representing a bad trade or investment as a catastrophe

▶ Labeling oneself in a globally negative way

I also believe that coping with the fear of loss for the investor is best appreciated when it is considered as an analogue for the warrior's greatest psychological hurdle: overcoming his anxiety about being killed. In *Zen and Japanese Culture*, D. T. Suzuki writes, "Those who are reluctant to give up their lives and embrace death are not true warriors." Of course, for most of us, investing is not a competition that has life-and-death consequences; however, the challenge is a similar one: to overcome ordinary reasoning, habit-driven behaviors, physical symptoms, and self-defeating beliefs.

YOUR PERSONAL EXPERIENCE WITH LOSSES

As you can see, learning to take a loss consistently, without regret, is immensely difficult. Our natural predisposition to avoid all the discomfort that is associated with taking a loss is omnipresent, psychological as well as physical. It is no mere intellectual phenomenon that is easily resolved, or that can be dismissed with firm resolution or willpower. Stating the problem succinctly, the investor needs to find the resources within himself to adhere to a long-term goal of profitability at the very moment he is experiencing the short-term trauma of incurring a loss, with all its conscious and unconscious implications.

As you think about your own experiences with and reactions to incurring loss, ask yourself the following questions:

▶ How does all this relate to me?

▶ How do I personally experience taking a loss?

▶ What physical symptoms do I experience?

▶ What emotions do I have when I take a loss?

▶ What do I see?

▶ What do I hear?

▶ What specific anxieties do I have that are associated with a loss?

▶ What do I believe about myself and the market when taking a loss?

▶ What self-defeating attitudes have I experienced?

If you can answer each of these questions thoughtfully, taking the time to reflect inwardly on your experiences with loss, then you are in a much better position to understand the essential nature of becoming a consistently competent investor. This perception is consistent with insights that are emerging from neuroeconomics.

OVERCOMING THE FEAR
OF LOSING

Denise Shull is the founder and CEO of Trader Psyches, a consultancy that works with individual and institutional traders. I first became aware of her research after observing a presentation that she gave at the Chicago Board of Trade. Shull applies recent findings from behavioral finance, neuroscience, and psychoanalysis to issues involving risk and trading. Her work began at the University of Chicago in 1993, where she was involved in research focusing on the role of the unconscious on behavior.

Over glasses of wine at the Ritz-Carlton, I questioned Shull about her current work and, specifically, about what she felt, based on the latest research, was the most effective way of getting investors to overcome a fear of losing. She restated my question and said that she did not try to overcome a trader's fear of loss, but rather tried to overcome the undesirable behaviors (e.g., being gun-shy) that often lead to a loss. Shull said that her process was to lay a foundation by developing awareness. "From there we work *with*, not against resistances, to become conscious of biases and tendencies. Traditionally that technique is called 'joining.'" She added, "Emotional architectures arising out of one's history come out to play in everything from analysis to final decisions to implementation to recalibrating model-based trading systems. . . . Our work brings the traders to full consciousness of feelings such as wanting to be right or wanting to *have been* right." As traders become more able to see these tendencies—her preferred word for biases—through their conscious and unconscious, social and emotional lenses, they automatically become more "rational."

In the case of losses, this means beginning to see them as an intrinsic, inevitable part of investing and not as disruptive or failed events.

In Chapter 12, we look at the issue of risk management in order to better understand how to develop a conceptual framework for overcoming irrational thoughts, fears, and beliefs in investment decisions.

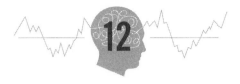

Risky Business

T he key to understanding investment risk is recognizing that it goes far beyond math and strategy, deep into the recesses of human psychology and emotion. Simply stated, notwithstanding quantitative models, the law of probability, game theory, and neoclassical economics' notion of the rational decision maker, when it comes to risk, all too often we merely fly by the seat of our pants.

Investors regularly agonize over when to buy and sell, or whether to buy back after selling. For most of us, our emotions are too involved in our choices to allow us to strictly adhere to a trading system or mathematical model, even if we believe that doing so represents the whole solution. Behavioral finance has clearly shown that rational decision making is the exception, and judgment by emotion and imperfect reasoning the norm.

The concept of risk is central to any discussion of investment and individual performance. Every investor must fully understand when to embrace risk rather than avoid it, and how to circumscribe risk rather than let it get out of control. In investing, one also comes to appreciate that risk and reward are opposite sides of the same coin. In his foreword to Howard Abell's book *Risk Reward*, veteran trader Jeffrey Silverman states one of the critical psychological hurdles that the investor faces. "To succeed at trading you need to be simultaneously humble and superconfident—humble enough to admit you are wrong, humble enough to take personal responsibility for everything that goes awry. Yet you must have the confidence and temperament to take on the world and say, in effect, 'All of you are wrong. I am right!' Believe me, there is a lot of self-analysis, experience, much of it painful, costly, and soul searching that goes into resolving this paradox."

When it comes to risk, we try to quantify, calculate, manage, and control it, but, in the end, what's most important is how we respond to it. Do we gravitate to it, or do we avoid it like the plague? Risk is an integral part of our lives, yet it is only vaguely understood; its psychological implications challenge us to our very core. What we do know is that the way risk is perceived is a very personal matter, that is, individuals make different estimates of the danger and uncertainty that are associated with an investment opportunity.

HEURISTICS AND BIASES

In an effort to understand how people make decisions involving risk, psychologists Daniel Kahneman and Amos Tversky performed a series of gambling experiments to study how we evaluate probabilities. Their findings, as discussed previously, demonstrated that people employ heuristics and other cognitive biases. Chief among those identified were

▶ *Availability heuristic.* Events that are more easily brought to mind are judged as being more likely than events that are less so.

▶ *Anchoring.* Individuals will start with one piece of known information and then adjust it to create an estimate of an unknown risk, but the adjustment will usually not be sufficient.

▶ *Asymmetry between gains and losses.* Investors are risk-averse with respect to gains but risk-seeking when dealing with losses.

▶ *Threshold effect.* Individuals prefer to make choices based on perceived degrees of certainty. They will choose an option that allows for movement from uncertainty to certainty over a similar option that does not produce full certainty.

Kahneman and Tversky also found that investment experts were not necessarily any better at estimating probabilities than the ordinary person. Experts often expressed overconfidence in their estimates and relied too heavily on small data samples.

The Affect Heuristic

Paul Slovic, a professor of psychology at the University of Oregon and president of Decision Research, is a leading theorist on risk perception. Writing extensively about cognitive biases with coauthors Kahneman, Tversky, and Gilovich, he has studied the role of the affect heuristic in choices involving risk. This heuristic explains the influence and importance of feelings in decision making.

The word *cancer* typically generates an affect of dread, while the word *mother* usually generates an affect of warmth and affection. A picture of a gray-haired, nurturing figure beneath ad copy that reads, "Mother said it would be a good investment," produces a very different feeling from copy that suggests, "Buying this stock won't cause cancer, but it is the next worst thing."

In addition to explaining correlations between perceptions of risk and reward, Slovic also found that the affect heuristic accounted for the degree to which a risk is understood and the reasons why risk often evokes a feeling of dread. He also showed that the more a decision engenders feelings of threat, catastrophe, or being out of control, the higher are the perception of risk and the need to have it reduced. To sum up, this research demonstrated that the perception of risk—its characteristics and severity—was subjective: visceral and dependent on intuition, experiential thinking, and emotional judgment.

DRILL, BABY, DRILL!

In the aftermath of BP's *Deepwater Horizon* explosion, *New York Times* columnist David Brooks wrote an incisive op-ed piece about the developing environmental catastrophe in the Gulf of Mexico. He argued that although the public debate was breaking down into familiar political categories—with conservatives calling it Obama's Katrina and liberals offering the incident as proof of the need for greater governmental control over the energy industry—the essential issue was neither political nor partisan. Brooks said, "The real issue has to do with risk assessment.

It has to do with the bloody crossroads where complex technical systems meet human psychology."

His point was that society has come to depend on an ever-expanding array of high-tech systems. These complex systems, which are hard to understand and difficult to control, are the guts of financial markets, energy exploration, space exploration, air travel, defense programs, and modern production plants. Every day, individuals are asked to monitor these networks, weigh the risks of a system failure, and adopt appropriate measures to reduce those risks. "If there is one thing we've learned, it is that humans are not great at measuring and responding to risk when placed in situations too complicated to understand."

In his view, this occurs for a variety of reasons. For one thing, individuals have difficulty imagining how small failings can combine to lead to catastrophic disasters. Second, people are predisposed to become acclimated to risk. "As the physicist Richard Feynman wrote in a report on the Challenger disaster, as years went by, NASA officials got used to living with small failures. If faulty O rings didn't produce a catastrophe last time, they probably won't this time, they figured." Feynman believed that this type of thinking was like playing Russian roulette. As in the financial industry, when things progress without incident, people unconsciously adjust their definition of what constitutes acceptable risk, even though they are informed in almost every investment disclosure document that successful past performance is not a positive indicator of future success.

Third, people place undue faith in backup systems and safety devices. Statistics inform us that more pedestrians die in crosswalks than when jaywalking. We have a false sense of security in crosswalks and are less likely to look both ways. According to recent reports, a Transocean official reminded everybody on the *Deepwater Horizon* oil rig that, in the worst-case scenario, the blowout preventer would save them. The illusion of this fail-safe system encouraged the crew to behave in reckless ways.

Fourth, people match complicated technical systems with complicated chain-of-command structures. The management hierarchy on the *Deepwater Horizon* seems to have been completely confused: officials from BP, Transocean, and Halliburton were tangled in competing lines of authority, with blurred definitions of who had the ultimate responsibility.

Fifth, individuals tend to express good news and repress bad news. A culture of silence settled in when it came to problems. Workers didn't want to lose their jobs, and executives feared saying anything that might affect shareholders' profits.

Finally, as is too often the case, groupthink set in and people began to think alike. In the days leading up to the *Deepwater Horizon* disaster, engineers were compelled to make a series of risk assessments: what sort of well casing to use; how long to circulate and when to remove the heavy drilling fluid from the hole; how to interpret the results of various tests. They made these decisions in an atmosphere that encouraged overconfidence, without any clear sense of the havoc that they were about to unleash on the environment.

Clearly, BP's failure is not just a cautionary tale about oil. Individuals at Bear Stearns, Lehman Brothers, and AIG also fell prey to the same kind of incompetent risk assessment that led to the eventual demise of their businesses: false security, irrational exuberance, failed risk perception, groupthink, and a good-news bias. Right now, smart people in trading rooms, on trading floors, and in their homes and offices around the world are engaging in their own versions of irrationally risky behaviors (although I'm quite sure they don't see it that way). It is not that they are unaware of the basic concepts of how to control risk. For the purposes of this discussion, I'm speaking only of investment risk; far more irrational behaviors are being played out in other no less psychologically challenging activities.

We are all too aware of the need for airbags, seat belts, safety harnesses, circuit breakers, shock absorbers, and blowout preventers. An environmental protestor's sign recently shown on CNN read, "Don't drill if you can't stop the spill." Yet we keep drilling, and investors and traders frequently enter into the market impulsively, motivated by expansive thinking, with insufficient risk control. It is only later, after the shit hits the fan, that we feel regret and ask ourselves, as in the case of the housing bubble, what were we thinking?

HEADING OFF THE NEXT CRISIS

Given that perceptions of risk and desired financial outcomes are as diverse as individual investors, we need to monitor ourselves to become aware of how we experience risk and what actions are consistent with our personality and our investments. Neuroeconomics has clearly demonstrated the anomalies and inconsistencies in our decisions, which assume the need for and desirability of regularly defending ourselves against our natural pattern of investment behavior. Like everything else in life, risk and its determinants cannot be understood in black and white, nor can they be taken for granted or resolved with a one-time solution. For this reason, we must become aware of our conscious and unconscious thoughts, images, and dreams—all irrational, but useful.

On numerous occasions, I have had elite traders tell me that they correctly entered or exited a position based on an image or dream that came to them out of the blue. One such example was related to me by the legendary trader George Segal, who spoke about getting out of a trade that was losing even though it hadn't violated his risk parameters. He explained that he took his dreams and feelings seriously when it came to determining whether he was in the right position. Of course, these feelings were not based on mere hunches. He had a long, proven track record of having made tens of millions of dollars for himself in the market.

Exhibiting his sense of humor, Segal said, "Getting out of a losing trade is an uplifting feeling to me. It's not as uplifting as getting out of a winning trade, but it really takes the burden off your shoulders. When you can't sleep or when it affects your life, you've got to do something about it. It's very easy just to pick up the phone and say 'good-bye!'"

Over the years, I've noticed something very interesting with institutional clients that is related to our earlier discussion of the BP catastrophe and is consistent with the latest neuroeconomic findings. Although many of these investors possessed highly sophisticated risk management systems—which measured market exposure by providing statistical analysis of both individual positions and the entire portfolio, often running shock analysis based on historical crash scenarios—when traders found themselves in a losing position, they would concoct imaginative explanations of why they were right and the risk management system was wrong.

This was the exception rather than the rule, but it does offer insight as to why, in almost every trading room, anywhere that markets are traded, there are empty chairs of individuals whose impulsive behavior was a disaster waiting to happen. Ask their managers how this could have occurred, and you usually get a shrug of the shoulders, followed by some variation of "Who would ever have expected this trader to act that way?"

This same phenomenon can be observed on the macro level. Computerized trading of stocks came to Wall Street in the 1980s and was implicated in exacerbating the market crash of October 1987. Since then, the computers have become considerably more powerful, and the algorithms that control their trading have become vastly more sophisticated. Now called high-frequency trading, computerized trading played a significant role in the giant market plunge of May 6, 2010, also known as the "flash crash."

Stock exchange officials say that more than half of all trades are now executed by just a handful of high-frequency traders, using rapid-fire terminals that essentially force slower investors to give up their profits, and then disappear before anyone knows what happened. High-frequency traders generated about $21 billion in profits in 2008, according to the TABB Group, a research and strategic advisory firm focused on capital markets.

Ever since computerized trading became dominant in the nation's equity markets, experts have warned that the computers' increasing complexity and speed threaten the stability of markets. This happened on May 6, 2010, when stock prices plunged and the Dow fell roughly 600 points in a matter of minutes.

The crash began when several hundred stocks on the Big Board, including the 30 major stocks that make up the Dow, fell sufficiently for the New York Stock Exchange to switch to slow-motion trading, in which traders on the floor tried to arrest the decline by manually seeking out buyers. But that did not work, because trading shifted immediately to broader markets, controlled by computer systems, where the plunge continued.

In the months before the plunge, the SEC had been warned that the lack of coordination between trading platforms, along with the expansion of high-speed trading in alternative markets, had furthered systemic risk and increased opportunities for market manipulation.

"We need to work out a common consensus as to how markets react when stock prices start to plunge in very short time periods," said Richard G. Ketchum, the chief executive of the Financial Industry Regulatory Authority, the industry group that polices brokers and exchanges.

Asked why the exchanges had not already agreed on such rules, Ketchum responded: "I can't say that I have a good answer for that. We should have. And now we must." As of this writing, no coordinated action has been adopted.

HAVEN'T WE HEARD THIS BEFORE?

It is a familiar refrain coming from individuals in positions of regulatory authority who have the task of assessing and managing risk. In response to why no one had predicted the housing bubble, Alan Greenspan, the former chairman of the Federal Reserve, proclaimed to Congress, "Everybody missed it, academia, the Federal Reserve, all regulators." And as the mortgage market was coming apart, home buyers, convinced that real estate prices were destined to stay high, signed on to whatever mortgage put them into the largest home.

Michael J. Burry ran the hedge fund Scion Capital from 2000 until 2008. He is one of the few people who saw the housing bubble developing and profited handsomely from his positions on the right-side of credit default swaps. In a brilliant article titled "I Saw the Crisis Coming. Why Didn't the Fed?" Burry questioned why no one in Washington showed any interest in hearing exactly how he arrived at his conclusions about the housing bubble and its potential for crippling the global economy. Concluding that Greenspan was closed to recognizing the possibility and magnitude of the ensuing systemic risk, he related an incredibly revealing story.

Al Hunt of Bloomberg Television, who had read Michael Lewis's book *The Big Short*, which relates the story of Burry's analysis of the housing market, asked the former chairman directly why the Fed had not recognized the risks in the mortgage market. Greenspan responded that Burry's insights had been a "statistical illusion." Perhaps, he suggested, the hedge fund owner was just a supremely lucky flipper of coins. Greenspan added that he had sat through many meetings at the Fed with "crack economists," and not one of them had warned of the crisis that was to come.

Similarly, another psychologically interesting behavior that I have noticed with institutional clients, who I would have thought would have acted differently, was their total denial of risky behavior. I have witnessed seasoned investors sitting for days on losing positions that I knew from experience, and from observing their past performance, were way outside their risk limits. Averting their eyes from the harsh reality of their situation, they believed that somehow tomorrow would be different. An unexpected event or shift on the economic horizon would end the misery, and once again all would be well. Rarely did that happen.

RISK MANAGEMENT AND SUCCESSFUL INVESTING

As we have seen, the keys to successful investing are hard to obey, even for the most seasoned investor. The following risk management tips will probably seem familiar, since they are simple enough to be told over and over again:

- ▶ Have a well-defined plan that allows you to correctly determine market direction and, if you are a short-term trader, precisely time your entry into and your exit from the market.

- ▶ Employ strict risk control and money management rules, so that no single investment or series of investments will destroy your account.

- ▶ Tolerate the psychologically challenging noise of a position, often referred to by value investors as quotational risk: the temporary capital loss due to a decline in stock price that is not materially indicative of a deterioration of fundamentals.

- ▶ Avoid the psychological pitfalls of cognitive biases and debilitating emotions that negatively influence your actions, and instead employ internal stimuli that positively guide decision making.

The best traders and investors understand both the need for wisdom to guard against emotional content that distracts them from optimum performance and the seemingly contradictory need to embrace emotions and intuitions that will allow them to achieve their goals. They routinely employ thinking and feeling, intuition and analysis to get the most out of themselves, which also means that they are less susceptible to risk blindness.

A seasoned member of the Chicago Board of Trade explained it this way: "I have to know what my little niche is. That's where I have market certainty and control. I am always looking to capture some control over my little territory, when I can manage exactly what it is that I'm doing."

The trader went on to say that he felt that he was a creature of habit who relied on familiar patterns based on price movement and feel, adding that he really believed that when he observed these patterns, he could project what was going to happen next in the market. He said, "I have seen it so many times in the past and have been able to exploit those situations. So I guess, to a degree, it is intuitive." This would seem to be consistent with Malcolm Gladwell's claim in his book *Blink* that "decisions made very quickly can be every bit as good as decisions made cautiously and deliberately."

For this trader, the decision was quick but highly deliberate, based on years of profitable outcomes and a long and successful track record. Since he was completely focused on his plan and his method, risk control was the natural concomitant. He said, "I look to take advantage of analogues that seem reliable based on my previous market experience. I also try to watch out that I'm not being too intense, to stay psychologically relaxed and focused. And additionally, I always keep my stop in."

THE SYSTEMATIC APPROACH

Investors always explain their risk management techniques in very personal terms. Some, like Toby Crabel, a former client, who runs Crabel Capital Management, a global alternative investment firm managing more than $2 billion in assets, opt for a purely mechanized approach. In an interview in my office at Rand Financial, he explained the main measure of risk that he employed in his investing. He said, "I look at the daily standard deviation of the portfolio, which we run at about 35 to 40 basis points." Crabel added that he looks at the monthly average of daily standard deviations and includes peak-to-trough drawdown on a daily and intraday basis in the analysis. To underscore the point, he said, "We look at it every half hour or something like that."

Crabel said that he takes into consideration where the portfolio is relative to the very highest point that it has reached on a daily and intraday basis. He said, "Certainly daily close is what we use for practical purposes, but you know, on a very volatile day, I'll look at intraday stuff as well." Crabel added that he also monitors a move to a new high in the portfolio from the low point. "I look at how long it takes to get back to new highs after the drawdown has begun," he said. "That tells me something about the continuing health of the portfolio."

When asked why risk control was so difficult for most investors, he said that most people do not realize how much risk they are assuming when they become involved in a market. To illustrate the point, he said, "I think the classic example is somebody who trades systematically, but the risk side is subjective. In the final analysis, that ends up being a subjective strategy." He cautioned that if allocation methods and also entry and exit points aren't objective, then the strategy is subject to individual biases. He said, "You have to look at the management of risk within the portfolio. Without doing that, somehow you'll have problems when the markets become extremely volatile."

In Crabel's opinion, investors who don't have every aspect of their trading automated tend not to trade during unnatural events, when the markets are more volatile, but also provide rare opportunity. He explained, "So, in essence, they stop trading," quickly adding, "I've had this experience personally. When the markets would increase in volatility, I would cut back trading or I'd stop altogether. It was a survival mode that I would go into." Crabel said that he resolved the issue by looking over a 20-year database where he could analyze the moves that were possible as he planned the portfolio. Only then did he feel that he was in a position to determine how much risk was acceptable during these periods in order to participate in the market. He also said, "I look at what I think the markets are capable of doing to me in a worst case, a price shock. And what I need to allocate to each market on a strategy-by-strategy basis."

A three-time All-American and professional tennis player, Crabel compared risk management to sports. He said, "When I was playing tennis at my best, when I was tired or a little out of shape or got to feeling overconfident, that's when I would take risks and go for the winner. I would have to do that in order to win. I would have to take added risk. But in the case of markets, when you are not feeling very strong about things, your tendency is going to be to take a few shots that you really shouldn't; you're taking extra risk." That is precisely why he said that all investing needs to be automated, "so the risk is completely and unequivocally managed."

There are many successful approaches and techniques for managing risk. The real difficulty is finding one that works for you. It could be systematic or discretionary, but it needs to suit you in order to protect you from yourself, that is, from your natural biases and your predispositions to act in a self-sabotaging way. The enemy is always there on the micro and macro level, ready to attack in the guise of overconfidence, wishful thinking, groupthink, risk creep, and denial. Just look around. It is only too easy to observe risk blindness in ourselves, in others, and in the financial system.

INMATES RUNNING THE ASYLUM

The trial of Jérôme Kerviel, the man accused of being responsible for billions in losses at the French bank Société Générale, ended in June 2010. After a two-year investigation and three weeks of court hearings, judges and prosecutors could only shake their heads in bewilderment, left no wiser about what caused the former trader to make his enormous, unauthorized bets.

The unwinding of an estimated €50 billion in open positions on Kerviel's trading book cost Société Générale €4.9 billion, the equivalent of about $7 billion. Kerviel admitted that he had falsified documents and entered fake trades to hide his bets, but he maintained that his bosses had turned a blind eye and, in fact, encouraged his activities as long as they were making profits.

"It wasn't me who invented these techniques; others did it, too," Kerviel said. "These practices were known and recognized by management."

Jean-Pierre Mustier, the former chief executive of the investment banking division that employed Kerviel, said, "I can't understand how his nerves could have handled the pressure of that much risk."

Mustier, who had spent six years as a trader, but had left the bank in 2009 amid an unrelated insider trading investigation, argued that rather than having fostered a culture of excessive risk taking, Société Générale had failed by creating an environment in which there was "too much trust."

The way the markets are constructed, the lines between gambling and investing often seem apocryphal and thin. I'm reminded of William F. (Blackie) Sherrod's quip, "If you bet on a horse, that's gambling. If you bet you can pull three spades, that's entertainment. If you bet cotton will go up three cents, that's business. See the difference?" The same question at times may just as well apply to stocks, bonds, and mortgage-backed securities. In *The Big Short*, Michael Lewis describes how, in the wake of the financial meltdown, perhaps the best definition of investing is gambling with the odds in your favor.

I don't believe that his view is entirely correct, but I do believe in the wisdom of "caveat emptor," buyer beware. There used to be a men's outlet store in New York called Syms that would advertise its products under the banner, "An Educated Consumer Is Our Best Customer." That logic also works for your investments.

I will end our discussion of risk with a quotation from *The Big Short* that provides a fundamental insight into the nature of risk as experienced in the recent global meltdown.

"On Wall Street in 2008 the reality finally overwhelmed perceptions: A crowded theater burned down with a lot of people still in their seats. Every major firm on Wall Street was either bank-rupt or fatally intertwined with a bankrupt system. The problem wasn't that Lehman Brothers had been allowed to fail. The prob-lem was that Lehman Brothers had been allowed to succeed."

In Chapter 13, we will take a look at the role of intuition for investors.

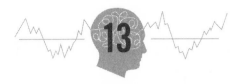

The Power of Intuition

In his groundbreaking book on intuition, *The Intuitive Edge*, author Philip Goldberg writes, "The more we know about intuition, the better equipped we are to use our own; the better our intuition, the more we are in a position to understand it." A prized ideal among traders and investors, true intuition is greatly sought after, but all too often poorly understood. It is variously defined as a premonition, feeling, wish, impulse, hunch, awareness, belief, or state of mind. So what exactly is intuition, and how can investors cultivate it to its fullest potential?

In philosophy, intuition is thought to be a way of knowing that cannot be acquired either by inference or by observation, an original and independent source of knowledge that understands reality as an interconnected whole. The Greeks considered intuition to be the apprehension of universal principles by intelligence rather than by the fleeting impressions of the senses. The distinction used by the Greeks implied the superiority of intellectual intuitions over sensory information.

Christian thinkers made a distinction between intuitive and discursive knowledge: God and angels knew intuitively what humans could comprehend only by reasoning. Descartes insisted that there were not two faculties of intuition, the sensual and the intellectual, but only the faculty of the mind. John Locke and others criticized Descartes's position, and under the influence of such criticism, perception and the intellect came to be regarded as two distinct, intuitive faculties, both of which were necessary for genuine knowledge. Kant took sense perception to be the paradigm of intuition, although pure intuitions of space and time were also basic to his system. For Bergson, intuition was an evolved form of instinct. Russell formulated the conceptual-perceptual distinction as the difference between "knowledge by description" and "knowledge by acquaintance," and also proposed a faculty analogous to sensation that apprehended universals. The logical positivists felt that it was unnecessary to posit such a faculty and explained the apprehension of nonsensory intuitive knowledge as the result of psychological conditioning.

The role that intuition plays in mathematics and ethics has also sparked lively debate. According to mathematical intuitionism, the foundation of mathematical knowledge rests on concepts that are immediately clear and irreducible. Likewise, ethical intuitionism posits the existence of fundamental truths that are known intuitively.

In *The Disciplined Trader*, Mark Douglas observes, "A true intuitive impulse—a deeper level of knowledge and wisdom that will always indicate the next appropriate step to take—that will always be in our best interest, feels very much like wishing and hoping. In other words, it is very difficult to distinguish between the two, making it very easy to mix them up, which is one of the reasons we find it difficult to trust our intuitions."

INTUITION: A RELIABLE SOURCE OF INFORMATION?

There are many wide-ranging reasons why it is difficult for investors to identify and then to rely on their intuition. The individual faces not only the inherent conflicts present in his psychological makeup, but also the limitations of having to work within the constraints of rational empirical biases, where epistemological assumptions have venerated rationalism and objectivity and largely discredited the importance of intuition.

In *Your Money and Your Brain*, the *Wall Street Journal*'s personal finance columnist Jason Zweig takes issue with Malcolm Gladwell's claims that decisions made very quickly can be every bit as good as decisions made cautiously and deliberately. Zweig contends, "Gladwell is a superb writer, but when it comes to investing, his argument is downright dangerous." He goes on to say that intuition can yield accurate results, but only when it is applied under the right conditions, which Zweig defines as situations in which the rules for reaching a good decision are "simple and stable." Acknowledging that this is rarely the case in the world of investment, Zweig said, "In the madhouse of the financial markets, the only rule that appears to apply is Murphy's Law. And even that guideline comes with a devilish twist: Whatever can go wrong will go wrong, but only when you least expect it to," which is why he cautions, "If all you do is 'blink,' your investment results will stink."

Although Zweig's view is common, I think it misunderstands the powerful role and potential of intuition in the life of investors. Tony Saliba, a highly successful options trader whom I interviewed on many occasions and who was featured in *Market Wizards*, had this to say about it: "Intuition is ultimate market wisdom; knowing exactly what to do next, free of internal and external prejudice, having unshakeable self-confidence and self-trust." Top trader George Segal abandons positions when his trades start to bother him and he can't sleep. George Soros, one of the world's leading hedge fund managers, who made $4 billion in 2009, reportedly considers dumping his holdings when he suffers a backache. Untold sums circulate the globe as the result of competent decisions that money managers make based on gut feelings. Obviously, not all of these trades make money, but professional traders do rely on intuition as a vital tool in their arsenal of psychological and strategic skills.

NATURALISTIC DECISION MAKING

Gary Klein is a research psychologist known for his work in the emerging field of naturalistic decision making. Unlike the developers of laboratory models, which fail to consider the harsh realities of how experts arrive at vital choices in the field, Klein created a conceptual framework for studying expert decision making in professions ranging from firefighting to medicine. His research involves studying cognitively complex functions in demanding situations marked by time pressure, vague goals, high stakes, organizational constraints, and uncertainty. Klein discovered a critical difference between experts and novices when they are presented with recurring situations. Experienced people were able to come up with solutions more quickly because the situation matched a prototypical situation that they had encountered before. Novices, lacking this experience, needed to cycle through different scenarios and used trial and error. Klein's model has influenced changes in the ways the Marines and the Army train their officers.

Consistent with my own observations of the role of intuition in *The Intuitive Trader*, Klein's research explains how people make relatively fast effective decisions—in life-and-death situations—without having to compare options. As in the world of investing, where time pressure, high stakes, and changing parameters are the rule, Klein observed that seasoned decision makers employed experience to identify recurring situations and intuitively chose competent solutions. In essence, his model is a blend of intuition and analysis. The intuition is the pattern-matching process that quickly identifies a feasible course of action, and the analysis is the mental simulation, a conscious and deliberate review of the most effective way to accomplish the task. The reliability of intuition depends on focus, past knowledge, and experience.

In an interview at UC Berkeley's Institute of International Studies, Nobel laureate Daniel Kahneman discussed the importance of intuition for individuals who needed to rely on their gut feelings as an essential part of their work, also explaining the debate it has sparked in light of his work on heuristics and other cognitive biases that—unlike true intuition—lead to irrational decisions.

Kahneman said, "One of the important developments in recent years in my life has been that I try to understand controversy and I try to reduce controversy. Amos Tversky and I made our reputation by finding flaws in what people do. It was the method we used. It's not that we ever thought that people are stupid, but this is what we were doing. Many people have responded to that by saying that we're drawing a distorted picture of human nature."

Citing the research conducted by Gary Klein, the leader of the naturalistic decision-making movement, and the seeming contradictions that its findings pose on the role of decision making to Kahneman and Tversky's work on cognitive biases, Kahneman said, "They (the proponents of naturalistic decision making) are very interested in intuition and deliberately skeptical about the kind of work that we've done. I approached Gary Klein because I liked his work, actually, and we've been collaborating on an article, so I was citing in my lecture examples from his work on professional intuitions."

Kahneman cited the example of the captain of a firefighting company combating a blaze on a roof who suddenly yells to his men, "Let's get out of here!" just before the house explodes, and later is not aware of why he gave the order when he shouted the command. Only through careful analysis is it learned that his feet were warm, and that was the cue that triggered the sense that something very dangerous was about to happen.

Reflecting on the role played by intuition in this example, Kahneman said, "That's a beautiful example of a perfect intuition, and that's the kind of thing that has been feeding people who think that all our discussions on biases and mistakes are overstated. So, it sets a very interesting problem that Klein and I have been trying to sort out together. When do intuitions develop and when don't they?"

SOMETIMES YOU REALLY SHOULD JUST DO IT

According to Harvard psychology professor Daniel Gilbert, "One of the ironies of human psychology is that desperately

THE POWER OF INTUITION   211

wanting something can make attaining that thing all the more difficult." As the stakes go up, performance often goes down. In one research study, subjects practiced putting golf balls, and got better as they continued to play. Their game play kept getting better, that is, until they were offered a cash reward for the next shot, at which point their performance fell sharply, as though off of a cliff.

"This is because we pay close attention to what we're doing when what we're doing matters, and though close attention is helpful when our task is novel or complex, it is positively destructive when our task is simple and well practiced." In another study, Gilbert reported that golfers were asked either to take their time and think about their stroke or to step up and swing as quickly as possible. "Although novice golfers did better when they took their time, expert golfers did worse," he said.

The lesson from this research is that thinking about tasks that are already automatic is not just pointless, but outright debilitating. "It may be wise to watch our fingers when we're doing surgery or shaving the family dog, but not when we're driving or typing, because once our brains learn to do something automatically, they don't appreciate interference."

ANTONIO DAMASIO AND THE NEUROBIOLOGY OF THE MIND

What is clear from neuroscience is that our brain, drawing on emotional memory, has the capability to determine when our decisions are good or bad long before we are consciously aware that we have decided anything.

Antonio Damasio, professor of neuroscience at the University of Southern California, conducts research that focuses on the neurobiology of the mind, especially neural systems that influence memory, language, emotion, and decision making. His work has helped to identify the neural basis for emotions in social cognition, creativity, and our choices. Damasio developed the somatic markers hypothesis, which proposes a mechanism by which emotional processes can guide or bias behavior, particularly decision making.

As in the case of emergency room nurses and doctors, firefighters, and traders, Damasio explains how real-life decisions require assessment through cognitive and emotional processes in environments that produce many complex and conflicting alternatives with a high degree of uncertainty. In such situations, cognitive processes often become overloaded, and we are unable to provide an analytically informed option. Somatic markers can aid the decision process. In the environment, reinforcing stimuli induce an associated physiological affective state.

Think of the fire captain's warm feet before he shouts out a warning to his men or George Soros's backache as the presenting signal for exiting the market. These types of associations are stored as somatic markers, possibly in the ventromedial prefrontal cortex, a subsection of the orbitomedial prefrontal cortex. In future situations, these somatic markers are reinstated physiologically and guide cognitive processing. "In cases where complex and uncertain decisions need to be made, the somatic markers from all reward- and punishment-associated experiences with the relevant stimuli are summed to produce a net somatic state. This overall state is used to direct (or bias) the selection of the appropriate action. This process may occur covertly (unconsciously), via the brainstem and ventral striatum, or overtly (consciously), engaging higher cortical cognitive processing. Somatic markers are proposed to direct attention away from the most disadvantageous options, simplifying the decision process."

Damasio's research is quite exciting, and for me particularly, because it establishes a firm biological basis for the critical importance of gut feelings, which could be stated only anecdotally, based on decades of observing the behavior of traders and investors, when I was writing *The Intuitive Trader*. At the time, the prevailing view was that feelings should be ignored or controlled in the belief that emotions and rational thought were separate activities and that emotions were just too difficult to understand biologically. The research of neuroscientists like Damasio has demonstrated that emotional brain circuits are just as tangible as circuits for seeing, hearing, smelling, and touching. The implication is profound: our emotions are largely the brain's interpretation of our visceral response to the world at large.

As we consider the vital role of intuition for the seasoned investor, now verified by neuroscience, we can state the following:

▶ Emotional memories are permanently ingrained in the brain. They can be controlled, but they can never be erased.

▶ The body, as represented in the brain, is our frame of reference for what is experienced as mind.

▶ Emotions are integral to our ability to reason. While too much emotion may impair reasoning, not enough may be equally harmful.

▶ Gut feelings are indispensable tools for rational decision making. Without intuition, individuals would have great

214 INVESTING AND THE IRRATIONAL MIND

difficulty responding effectively in ambiguous and uncertain circumstances, and in thinking about the future.

INTUITION AT WORK

Too many books have been written about intuition as a psychic ability akin to extrasensory perception. Psychologist Gary Klein correctly points out that intuition is not about how Luke Skywalker gets in touch with "the Force." It is important to keep this distinction in mind, because, once intuition's real value for investing is understood, attempting to either suppress or inhibit it as a form of bias no longer makes sense. Not that everyone should entirely rely on intuition, however.

As investors, it is important for us to appreciate the critical role that intuition plays in making better decisions. The essential point is that intuitions should not be blindly followed by novices, but rather should be understood as vital to our decision making in a way that cannot be replaced by analysis or procedure. The challenge is threefold: building intuition, applying it, and safeguarding it against the obstacles that often get in the way.

In *The Power of Intuition*, psychologist Gary Klein offers a good definition of intuition that is useful for investors, "the way that we translate our experience into action." Stated simply, this establishes the fundamental truth about intuition, which is that it is built through discipline, focus, preparation, and experience, and is not a form of magical thinking. Klein's research has established that intuition is gained on the basis of accumulated and compiled experiences in situations in which professionals are swimming in a sea of ambiguity and facts. "There are too many facts and too many combinations of facts. The more complex the decisions, the faster the complications add up."

Evidence shows that when individuals ignore intuition, their performance goes down, and that attempts to promote analysis over intuition are often futile and counterproductive is also growing. For those who do not or cannot trust their intuition, less effective decisions are inevitable. There is a dilemma for most investors, although in my view an artificial one, that may be stated this way: because we know from behavioral science that our rationality is limited and is subject to biases, fallacies, and illusions, intuition is conventionally regarded as a mode of unreliable and impulsive thinking.

Herbert Simon won the Nobel Prize in 1978 for his work on decision making and problem solving, and introduced the concept of "bounded rationality" to explain the problems inherent in decisions made merely by gathering all the facts. But the current research is clear: for seasoned professionals, intuition permits effective, competent, and reliable decisions.

Based on his findings, Klein concluded, "What enables us to make good decisions is intuition, in the form of very large repertoires of patterns acquired over years and years of practice." Without these patterns and experience, decision makers would be stymied in their choices. Formal methods of analysis alone are insufficient, even with supercomputers crunching all the numbers. They can match experienced decision makers only in limited gamelike tasks, such as chess, and then only after a great amount of work. "Formal analyses can be valuable to supplement intuition, but they can't substitute for intuition" when it comes to expert decisions.

It should be obvious that just because one has learned the value of intuitive decision making does not mean that one should immediately begin to rely on this form of decision making as a dominant skill. This caution should be particularly adhered to by individuals who are new to investing. I mention it because, based on my experience with proprietary traders and beginning investors who have written letters after reading my books, some people are all too eager to put their gut feelings to practical use. Intuition is the result of years of hard work and battle-tested experience in which investors had to size up market situations accurately and respond competently.

INTUITION AND THEORY OF MIND

A research team at Caltech authored an influential paper entitled "Exploring the Nature of Trader Intuition." The team consisted of an electrical engineer, Antoine Bruguier, whose research focuses on computational lithography, which is the set of mathematical and algorithmic approaches designed to improve the resolution attainable through photolithography, a process used in microfabrication; associate professor of philosophy Steve Quartz, who employs neuroscience to probe fundamental problems of the mind, ranging from how the mind emerges from the developing brain to how we make decisions; and Peter Bossaerts, the William D. Hacker Professor of Economics and Management.

The study focused on a stock market situation in which the success of traders was attributable to an approach based on social cognition rather than on the use of mathematical models. They found that

"Contrary to what standard finance theory predicts, we hypothesize that the brain does not use mathematical models but instead heuristically uses a social cognition approach. Specifically, we posit that humans understand stock markets by using Theory of Mind (ToM), the ability to attribute to others mental states different from one's own. Here we show that humans engage brain structures related to ToM (paracingulate cortex, anterior cingulate cortex, insula, and amygdala). Subsequent behavioral tests show that ToM, rather than mathematical, abilities are better predictors of success in forecasting stock markets."

In our interview at the Ritz-Carlton, I discussed the Caltech study with Denise Shull, who is known for her expertise in the application of research findings from neuroeconomics and emotional and behavioral finance. I specifically asked her about the study's value to traders, given its emphasis on the importance of theory of mind, as well as feelings and emotions, in making investment decisions. The conversation took off when I asked Shull what, in her opinion, was the current most interesting research in neuroeconomics. Without any hesitation, she said, "The single most exciting study published to date—in my opinion—was done by an electrical engineering Ph.D. at Caltech, Antoine Bruguier, and it is called 'Exploring the Nature of Trader Intuition.'"

Citing the difficulty in getting the research published, "I have to wonder," she said, "if what they really didn't like was the implication—which is that what is known as 'theory of mind' is more important than probability skills in predicting markets."

Shull went on to underscore the importance of theory of mind (ToM), an essential ability, for understanding the psychological position of other people, and the practical way in which we use it in our suppositions about what others are thinking, feeling, or intending to do. "When I first read it, my reaction was that the essential finding turns traditional finance on its head! If the skill required is fundamentally predicting other people's behavior, maybe we ought to be studying social networks more than we study financial engineering!"

Shull went on to say that forthcoming research out of Europe suggests that we may even have certain neurons for interpreting ToM when we can see people and different types of neurons for when we don't have "a visual" on the person—for example, interpreting through symbols, as we do when we are watching markets and charts. She added, "In my opinion, ToM explains 'natural' traders."

In the interim, I spoke and e-mailed at length with the study's lead researcher, Antoine Bruguier, about the findings. I put a no-nonsense question to him to get at the study's real-world ramifications. I asked him specifically, in light of "Exploring the Nature of Trading Intuition," what he felt were the practical implications for traders and financial firms that were given the task of managing risk.

He said, "If the results of this paper are confirmed, they would have very important implications to traders. They are a reminder that trading is essentially a social activity and that, while it may be possible one day to model the behavior of the markets, the current simple models are not sufficient to capture all the effects." Bruguier also told me to be aware that he was not saying that all mathematical models were junk, just that they have to be taken as approximate.

As a final reminder of the preliminary nature of his findings on trader intuition and theory of mind, he underscored the need for additional research furthering one of his study's findings. He said, "I don't have any data on this, though, so please note that so many hypotheses and models break down when tested with real-life data. But that is essentially my point: one should not get carried away by elegant mathematical descriptions; they have to be tested when humans are in the mix."

After I met Shull in Chicago, I shared with her my conversation with Bruguier and his preliminary take on the findings about which both of us had been so excited. I e-mailed her a follow-up question that I needed to have answered in order to refine my own thinking about the mutually interactive roles of intuition and theory of mind. I asked her, from a practical standpoint, what, in her opinion, was the relationship between intuition and ToM for helping investors improve performance.

I found her answer to be thoughtful and exactly to the point. She said, "Explicit ToM seems to occur literally more in your brain, while intuition occurs more in your body. In other words, ToM can be worked on directly through understanding trading volume, for example. Intuition, however, needs to be worked on like a sport, gaining muscle memory for the experience of unconscious pattern recognition."

In either case, the crucial step, Shull said, is to reassess thinking and emotions, a process that she employs in her work consulting with individual investors and trading groups. She added, "Begin to use feelings and emotions first and foremost as data."

INTUITION AND ANALYSIS

For the purposes of investing, it must be remembered that neither intuition nor analysis alone is sufficient for effective decision making. The issue is one of emphasis, and here I would argue for using analysis to support intuition, as opposed to the other way around. The point is to allow our intuition to drive our analysis or our investment plan so that it guides our comprehension of circumstances. Used in this way, intuition allows us to identify opportunities and helps us decide how to react. Our trading plan verifies our intuition to make sure that we are not going astray. Again, we are not looking for our intuition to get us in touch with "the Force," but rather to capitalize on the work that is dictated by our experience.

An example straight from the trading floor occurs when a market goes into a steep decline and then, for no apparent reason, quickly reverses. You have seen it on the tape or on the evening news focusing on the "inexplicable" volatility in the market. In these situations, something very interesting usually happens. After a period of free fall, there is a sudden and unexpected moment of exhaustion that comes over the floor. It is just for an instant, after all the buyers have given up on dumping their long positions that were showing a loss, and all the sellers who had added to their short positions run out of additional offers. Despite the intensity and mass confusion, seasoned traders who look to buy at these moments, staying true to the trading axioms "buy low" and "don't follow the crowd," feel the bottom intuitively long before they have time to analyze it as a buying opportunity. They are not, of course, always right, but more times than not they are. Personally, I would experience these moments in the pit of my stomach or as an electric prod in the back of my neck. Some traders have told me that they would feel their mouths go dry or even lose their breath. A 30-year veteran once told me that he would always feel fast markets coming to an end "as if a wooden spoon was being shoved up my ass," which forced him to buy the bottom.

The trader's inelegant description conveys the essential elements of intuition at work:

▶ Physical cues allow us to recognize familiar patterns.

▶ Patterns activate action scripts.

▶ Action scripts are assessed through mental simulation.

▶ Mental simulation is driven by mental models.

Psychologist Gary Klein refers to the process of pattern matching and mental simulation as the recognition-primed decision model that explains how professionals reach fast and effective decisions without the need to generate or compare a set of options. He said, "Pattern recognition primes the decision making process, but it needs to be tested through mental simulation." Mental simulation is employed to evaluate decisions and imagine what to expect before we act so that we know later whether the decision is having the desired effect. Other researchers have reported similar findings with a variety of experts, including commercial pilots, British Army officers, commodity and stock traders, and U.S. Navy electronic warfare specialists. These findings make a convincing argument for the significant reliance on intuition for competent decisions and the importance of learning to use it effectively.

INTUITION AND INVESTING

For the investor, true intuition is the dividend from years of hard work, discipline, focus, and goal setting. It is not to be confused with mere gut feelings or wishful thinking. It is supported by analysis and a solid trading plan. Intuition is not infallible or a magical solution, but it can significantly assist us in making good decisions, if it is employed effectively: to create expectations, catch inconsistencies, and connect the dots.

There is a particular mindset that I wrote about in *The Intuitive Trader* that helps foster intuition for the short-term trader. Its characteristics also apply to the long-term investor.

▶ Mentally relaxed and physically calm (even in the heat of battle or when you are developing your investment plan)

▶ Confident (but not overconfident)

▶ Optimistic (but not a wishful thinker)

▶ Focused on the market, the plan, analysis, and emotional cues

▶ Energized demeanor and high awareness, so that you are ready to act

It is also imperative that the investor learn to let go. This is not a passive, but rather an active process, in which trust is developed to allow subconscious processes to perform at their optimum. It involves relinquishing conscious controls, such as second-guessing, that inhibit intuitive decisions. Letting go is the outgrowth of commitment, discipline, and practice of mind-body skills. Its opposite is trying too hard; feeling tight; worrying about past errors; becoming anxious, cautious, or mechanical; worrying about others; or being obsessed with doing only what's "right."

I'd like to end this chapter with a quote from *The Power of Intuition* that expresses the challenge facing us: "The longer we wait to defend our intuitions, the less we will have to defend. We are more than the sum of our software programs and analytical methods, more than the databases we can access, more than the procedures we have been asked to memorize. The choice is whether we are going to shrink into those artifacts or expand beyond them."

In Chapter 14, we will look at ways to overcome adversity and achieve resilience, whatever the market throws at us.

Adversity and Resilience

M ost professional investors will readily admit that their work is often characterized by turbulence, complications, and heavy blows. In my many interviews with traders and investors, I have been extraordinarily impressed by the various individuals who take part in financial markets. Whether they concentrate on stocks or bonds, futures or options, talented investors are strikingly similar. They are smart, focused, full of ingenuity, and open to new ideas. Many of them have backgrounds in, or at least a strong appreciation of, logic and math, and a facility for solving problems. Among the traders I have written about are accomplished musicians, screenwriters, a former magician, a chef, a professional blackjack player, philanthropists, and an owner of a breeding farm of winning racehorses. There are also others who have a wide and unexpected range of interests that complement their desire to understand markets. All are fiercely competitive, with some who have won championships in boxing, basketball, tennis, racquetball, chess, and even ballroom dancing. Interestingly, at crucial points in their careers, virtually all had failed.

226 INVESTING AND THE IRRATIONAL MIND

These investors did not quit or retreat to the sidelines. For a few, it was merely a matter of reestablishing themselves after a series of losses or prioritizing goals in the wake of an extended period of drawdown that gave them the opportunity to reassess their investment plan or trading method. For others, who went down in a truly spectacular fashion, losing virtually everything, what was called for involved much more than simply rethinking their business approach. Their solution was nothing short of a complete reappraisal of their life and ambition, and the revaluing of their personal sense of self-worth.

One trader hit rock bottom after years of success for reasons that were to be clear to him only after harrowing loss and humiliation. He described his pain as being the result of egocentrism and a stubborn obsession that drove him to subordinate everything in life to a desire to beat the market and prove himself right. Eventually, it cost him his family and friends, and he was forced to declare bankruptcy. He related the stress that he felt at being alienated and alone: "I was divorced, lost all my material possessions, and then woke up one morning and asked myself, 'What happened?'" The trader, who had returned to the exchange floor as an active market maker, added in our interview that he had also wrestled with another question: "What did I do wrong?" He stated, "Everything collapsed on me. I had to come up with answers to change my life, to improve my condition."

Stories like this, although seemingly extreme, are not uncommon and illustrate a fundamental truth about the potential psychological costs of trading and investing. For those who are wondering if they have what it takes to compete with professional investors, it is best to understand that coping effectively with adversity is an essential skill.

THE TWO CHAIRMEN
OF THE BOARD

Early in his career, after a series of reckless losses, a young Pat Arbor, who would go on to become chairman of the Chicago Board of Trade, suffered the ultimate shame for a trader: "busting out." At six foot one, with the lean, taut body of a long-distance runner, Arbor spent 18 months welding I beams 45 stories above LaSalle Street on one of Chicago's Loop skyscrapers in order to put a stake together to get back to trading on the exchange floor. It was from this vantage point that he discovered strengths within himself that he hadn't known he possessed, and he vowed never to fail at trading again. He came to realize that what had taken him down, like many before him, was a volatile mix of wishful thinking and greed. Committed to learning the psychology necessary to becoming a profitable trader, Arbor dedicated himself to a rigorous routine of personal discipline. He developed rules for not only the way he invested, but the way he walked, talked, ate, and stood. In the pit, he disciplined himself with rituals such as forcing himself to balance on his toes for hours at a time as he traded, just to see how much pain he could endure, as a means of achieving self-control. He wouldn't smoke, drink alcohol, or even ingest caffeine.

In the mid-1990s, just a few blocks away from Pat Arbor's office at the Board of Trade, Jack Sandner was busy building his own financial institution, the Chicago Mercantile Exchange (CME), which one day would be the largest financial futures and options exchange in the world. A former top-notch amateur boxer with an impressive 58 and 2 record, at five feet four with a Peter Pan face and strawberry-blond hair, Sandner had been a wiry and fast-moving featherweight in his youth, with a Golden Gloves trophy to prove it. The twists and turns in Sandner's life are truly remarkable: high school, class valedictorian, Las Vegas blackjack dealer, professional dancer, law review editor, and chairman of the board.

Like Arbor, Sandner had had his own brush with near financial ruin midway in his career, after years of success as a professional investor. He told me in a series of interviews that, as far as he was concerned, the distinguishing characteristic of the successful investor was the ability to overcome adversity. He said that people who have suffered reversals many times, and have come through successfully, are prime candidates to become good traders because they have learned how to focus and maintain discipline in situations of psychological hardship. He said, "I think when you grow up and have a lot of life experiences with adversity and learn ways to overcome them, you are confident that no matter how bad the situation is, you tell yourself, 'I can survive.' I can think of numerous times in my trading where things were adverse, but if I didn't have the right attitude, I would have crumbled and walked away and never have been able to come back."

Successful investors know that the next psychological challenge is as close at hand as the next trade, even if they are prepared, are disciplined, and are doing everything right. The mental tenacity exemplified by Arbor and Sandner is a real-life illustration of what it takes to cope with the hurdles that the market perpetually has in store for us.

Whether in Chicago, New York, London, or Tokyo, the most competent investors identify ways within themselves to succeed and, when they get derailed, discover new paths to get back. As one trader said to me, "Our job is to never get psychologically locked in. We are paid to find another window to climb through." All of this is to say that investors need to be able to overcome whatever obstacles stand in their way, relying implicitly on their powers of resilience.

PSYCHOLOGICAL RESILIENCE

Resilience is people's positive capacity to cope with stress and crises. It includes the ability to bounce back after a disruption and to learn how to adapt effectively to future experiences of adversity. Research in the emerging field of positive psychology has shown what common sense would dictate. Resilience does not emerge in people by accident. It is the result of cultivating particular attitudes, cognitive and emotional skills, and the commitment to overcome serious challenges. The American Psychological Association (APA) states, "Being resilient does not mean that a person doesn't experience difficulty or distress. Emotional pain and sadness are common in people who have suffered major adversity or trauma in their lives. In fact, the road to resilience is likely to involve considerable emotional distress." The essential point is that building resilience involves adopting the behaviors, thoughts, and actions that can help us weather adverse conditions. Specifically, we can develop the following psychological skills:

▸ Making realistic plans and taking the necessary steps to carry them out

▸ Adopting a positive view of ourselves

▸ Having confidence in our strengths and abilities

▶ Solving problems rather than engaging in wishful thinking

▶ Managing strong feelings and impulses

Developing resilience is a deeply personal experience. Individuals do not all react the same way to traumatic events. An approach that successfully builds resilience for one person might not work for another. People adopt varying strategies based on both psychological and cultural factors. An individual's cultural orientation affects how she communicates feelings and deals with adversity. As you read some of the following strategies for building psychological resilience, choose the ones that are most appropriate for you.

Consider the observation of the famed psychiatrist Karl Menninger, who said that what distinguishes people is not the events of their lives, but how they react to those events. Inherent in this observation is the idea that we are also distinguished by how we internalize the meaning of events and what action we take that is positive and moves us closer to our goals.

▶ *Take care of yourself.* First and foremost, pay attention to your own needs. Appreciate and learn from your thoughts and feelings, and come to understand—by allowing yourself to experience and feel their presence—what a valuable source of information they are. Also, engage in activities that you enjoy. Caring for yourself helps to keep your mind and body primed to deal with situations that require resilience and will help keep you from falling prey to debilitating thoughts and irrational actions.

▶ *Avoid internalizing adversity as an insurmountable problem.* You can't change the fact that stressful events and crises happen, but you can alter how you interpret and respond to these situations. One strategy is to look beyond the present to see how future circumstances may be better. Another is to note any subtle ways in which you feel better as you deal with difficult situations and build on those feelings.

▶ *Consider adversity as an opportunity for self-discovery.* Psychological resilience provides a great dividend of self-awareness and unexpected insights. Investors who have crashed and burned and have found the resilience to bounce back get to learn something vital about themselves. They may discover that they have grown in some respect as a result of their failure. Studies have shown that many people who have experienced adversity have reported better relationships, a greater sense of strength even while feeling vulnerable, increased self-worth, and a heightened appreciation for life.

▶ *Accept change.* Accepting conditions that cannot be changed can help you focus on circumstances that are within your control to alter.

▶ *Set goals.* Previous goals may no longer be attainable as a result of adverse conditions, and this will provide you with the opportunity to set new ones. Be realistic and keep moving forward. Do something every day—even if it seems like a small accomplishment—that will allow you to get closer to your goals. Avoid goals that are unachievable, or

232 INVESTING AND THE IRRATIONAL MIND

are based on irrational thoughts and wishful thinking. Ask yourself, "What can I accomplish right now that will help me move in the direction in which I want to go?"

▶ *Take decisive action.* Act on adverse situations as much as you can rather than detaching from your problems. Wishing that problems would go away is not an effective strategy and only prolongs the misery.

▶ *Build a positive view of yourself.* Gaining confidence from your ability to solve problems and trusting your intuition helps you develop resilience.

▶ *Keep things in perspective.* Even when facing adverse events, try to consider the reversal in a broader context. Avoid blowing things out of proportion.

▶ *Nurture a hopeful outlook.* An optimistic perspective enables you to have positive expectations. Try visualizing your goals, rather than worrying about and seeing what you fear.

▶ *Maintain personal connections.* Staying close to family, friends, and colleagues is important. Accepting support from those who care about you strengthens your resilience.

There are several other ways to help build psychological resilience, including writing out your deepest thoughts and feelings; speaking with a psychiatrist, psychologist, or counselor; meditation and spiritual practices; and assisting others in their time of need, which offers a double reward. The essential point is to identify ways that are likely to work for you as part of your own strategy for maintaining flexibility and balance in your life as you deal with adverse events.

Complexities of Resilience

Resilience also involves certain seeming contradictions and subtleties, such as the following:

- ▶ Allowing yourself to experience strong emotions, but also realizing that you may need to avoid experiencing these emotions at times in order to continue to function effectively

- ▶ Stepping forward decisively to deal with your problems and meet the obligations of daily living, but also stepping back to relax and reenergize yourself

- ▶ Spending time with others to receive support, but also spending time alone to nurture yourself

- ▶ Relying on your own independence and ingenuity, but also allowing yourself to rely on others

Resiliency Checklist

The APA provides a list of questions for individuals that can help them foster resilience by focusing on past experiences and sources of personal strength, designed to aid in the development of personal strategies. By examining your answers, you may discover how you can respond effectively in times of adversity.

- ▶ What kinds of events have been most stressful for me?

▶ How have those events typically affected me?

▶ Have I found it helpful to think of important people in my life when I am distressed?

▶ To whom have I reached out for support in working through a traumatic or stressful experience?

▶ What have I learned about myself and my interactions with others during difficult times?

▶ Has it been helpful for me to assist someone else who is going through a similar experience?

▶ Have I been able to overcome obstacles, and if so, how?

▶ What has helped make me feel more hopeful about the future?

Taking the time to think deeply about these issues can enhance individuals' sense of self and fortify their complement of trading and investment skills. When I asked a veteran fund manager whom I have known for more than 20 years to respond to many of these same questions recently, she said, "I really enjoyed thinking about these issues. In a busy day of scrolling through patterns of numbers, wiggles, and lines, it's essential to pause and reflect on one's own process."

POSITIVE PSYCHOLOGY

Positive psychology is a recent branch of psychology that concentrates on the scientific study of positive emotions, character strengths, and institutions that promote well-being. Its purpose is the empirical validation of the strengths and virtues that enable individuals and communities to thrive. Positive psychologists seek to identify and "nurture genius and talent," and to explore ways of making normal life more rewarding. The field is founded on the idea that people desire to lead meaningful and fulfilling lives, to cultivate emotions and thoughts within themselves that enhance their experiences of love, work, and play.

Current research has demonstrated many findings that have broad and profound implications. The key point is that these studies have clearly shown that it is possible for individuals to lead more satisfied lives—to be happier and more engaged with life, find deeper meaning, and have higher hopes—regardless of their circumstances. Positive psychology interventions have also been found to "lastingly decrease depression symptoms."

Some of the relevant findings from positive psychology that have been published in leading psychological journals are summarized and listed here:

▶ Wealth is only weakly related to happiness, both within and across nations, particularly when income is above the poverty level (Diener & Diener, 1996).

▶ Engaging in an experience that produces "flow" is so gratifying that people are willing to do it for its own sake, rather than for what they will get out of it. The activity is its own reward. Flow is experienced when one's skills are sufficient for a challenging activity, in the pursuit of a clear goal, with immediate feedback on one's progress toward the goal. In such an activity, concentration is fully engaged in the moment, self-awareness disappears, and sense of time is distorted (Csikszentmihalyi, 1990).

▶ Individuals who are optimistic have better performance in work, school, and sports; are less depressed; have fewer physical health problems; and have better relationships with other people. Optimism can be measured, and it can be learned (Seligman, 1991; Lyubomirsky, King & Diener, 2005).

▶ Physicians who are experiencing positive emotion tend to make more accurate diagnoses (Isen, 1993).

▶ People are unable to predict how long they will be happy or sad following an important event (Gilbert, Pinel, Wilson, Blumberg & Wheatley, 1998; Wilson, Meyers & Gilbert, 2001). The researchers found that people typically overestimate how long they will be sad following an adverse event, yet fail to learn from repeated experiences that their predictions are wrong.

LEARNED OPTIMISM

Martin Seligman is the director of the University of Pennsylvania's Positive Psychology Center. Known as the father of this new field of psychology, he draws on more than 20 years of clinical research to demonstrate how optimism improves and enriches quality of life, and how people can learn to practice it. In his book *Learned Optimism*, he explores techniques for interpreting behavior and experiencing the benefits of a positive interior dialogue.

In a 2010 interview, Seligman said that optimists generally lead healthier, more successful lives. Unlike pessimists, who see problems as "permanent and pervasive" and their own fault, optimists internalize adversity as impermanent, isolated, and impersonal, the result of external factors beyond their control. Seligman stated that individuals can be taught to experience situations in a more psychologically constructive and positive light.

In *The Intuitive Trader*, I examined the internal dialogue of winning and losing traders based on Seligman's work. In the context of almost universal agreement among top traders that a feeling of optimism is central to implementing effective trading strategies, I proposed a peek into the brains of the optimistic and pessimistic investor to contrast the way each internalizes a trade.

▶ The *optimist* experiences a "good trade" as being permanent, pervasive, and personal. A "bad trade" is experienced as impermanent, isolated, and impersonal.

▶ The *pessimist* experiences a "good trade" as being impermanent, isolated, and impersonal. A "bad trade" is experienced as permanent, pervasive, and personal.

I argued that it was exactly the optimist's frame of mind—based on a proven methodology and sound investment plan—that allowed traders to maintain a laserlike focus and to automatically execute the often-repeated axiom, "Let your profits run and cut your losses short." Optimism, based on a competent understanding of and approach to the market, solidified a positive feeling of one's abilities, the conviction and reliability of the trading method, and the existing opportunities in the market to reward the trader for making good decisions.

Seligman is now employing the concepts of learned optimism with the Army, teaching military personnel to think differently about both good and bad events and to appreciate that there is more than one path to an emotionally satisfying life. In the summer of 2009, Seligman explained to a group of sergeants in fatigues the Comprehensive Soldier Fitness program that their generals had just decided to adopt. Ultimately, more than a million soldiers will receive training based on positive psychology. The goal is to foster psychological resilience, which, it is hoped, will make officers and recruits less prone to suicide and post-traumatic stress disorder.

Seligman said that he began his academic career as a pessimist researching dogs in a laboratory. He observed that some dogs, after enduring repeated electric shocks to teach them to perform a task, realized that there was no escape and simply gave up or stopped trying. He speculated that they had learned that their actions were to no effect, behaving much as depressed humans do. This observation later became a model for understanding learned helplessness, a seminal insight in psychology.

As a result of these studies, Seligman grew curious about the dogs that did not quit, no matter what was done to them. He asked himself, what was it about these dogs—and their human counterparts—that gave them the strength and the will to go on?

FLOW

In his groundbreaking book *Flow: The Psychology of Optimal Experience*, psychologist Mihaly Csikszentmihalyi proposed his theory that people are happiest when they are in a state of relaxed and focused concentration, characterized by complete absorption in the activity. The concept of flow is identical to the feeling of being "in sync," "in the groove," or "in the zone." It is an optimal performance state, not unfamiliar to traders and investors, where the individual is fully engaged and has an overwhelming feeling of satisfaction, demonstrating great skill and losing all sense of time.

Csikszentmihalyi described flow as "being completely involved in an activity for its own sake. The ego falls away. Time flies. Every action, movement, and thought follows inevitably from the previous one, like playing jazz. Your whole being is involved, and you're using your skills to the utmost."

In Chapter 15, we will discuss the constant psychological challenges that investors face.

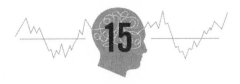

The Psychological
Challenge

I n a career that has included decades of daily engagement
with the market's hard right edge, the part of a price chart
that literally forms before your eyes, I have discovered that
there is a lot to be learned about the world and yourself in investing. Early on, as a participant at the center of constantly breaking news, my task was to compete with colleagues and traders
around the globe to wrestle profits from the market's ever-elusive
and volatile tops and bottoms, flags and channels, spikes and
gaps. What was called for was learning and then implementing
an array of mechanical skills, tactics, maneuvers, strategies, and
mental toughness. In the beginning, I had no real plan. I was
often intellectually and emotionally flat-footed, inventing feeble
solutions and operating on the fly. But I was determined.

TOUGH TIMES AND FERRARIS

Barely managing to survive, I was confronted with ambiguity, anxiety, and hesitation. My mind was bombarded by a host of sensory stimuli and irrational thoughts that often made me question whether I was really up to becoming a professional trader. For me, cognitive dissonance was no abstract concept.

Cognitive dissonance is the uncomfortable feeling caused by internalizing two contradictory ideas simultaneously. The theory behind it assumes that people are motivated to reduce dissonance either by changing their attitudes, beliefs, and actions or by merely rationalizing them. Dissonance occurs when an individual perceives an inconsistency with his beliefs, or when an idea or attitude implies the opposite of another. It is experienced as guilt, anger, frustration, or embarrassment. The "sour grapes" made famous by Aesop in his fable *The Fox and the Grapes* is an example of this phenomenon that is often cited by social psychologists. Unable to reach the grapes, and experiencing dissonance, the fox reduces his anxiety by irrationally concluding that the grapes are sour and, therefore, would not be worth eating.

As a novice, day after day, I became expert at generating psychologically comforting but flawed reasons for my inability to make money and figure out how to trade competently. My failure led to dissonance that expressed itself in the form of confirmation bias, the tendency for someone to favor information that confirms a preconception, independent of whether the information is true. I also drew on anger, inaction, and confusion, as well as self-justifying explanations and other ego defense mechanisms.

Baseball's Branch Rickey, nicknamed "the Mahatma," known for breaking Major League Baseball's color barrier by signing Jackie Robinson, was fond of saying to his players, "Luck is the residue of opportunity and design." My luck started to change when I put my trading on ice—and came up with a plan.

I couldn't afford to wait any longer. I needed to make money. My plan was simple: to learn from the best and the brightest— what were they doing? After all, I could see the tangible results of their success. In the 1980s, Lamborghinis and Ferraris and the mini-châteaus on Chicago's Gold Coast had a way of gaining one's attention. Every day I made a point of speaking to the market's elite traders to find out what they thought about their investing. I observed how they behaved in the market, studying their subtle modes of thought and feeling that were counterintuitive to the way most people perceive events and make decisions. Their choices, while initially appearing irrational, were in fact highly structured and had been well thought out, analyzed, strategic, and risk-managed.

I could see strong commonalities in their approaches, although their methods were extraordinarily different. Some were pure fundamentalists, while others relied entirely on technical indicators. Still others used a combination of the two. There were those whose trades were generated by a system. Other traders seemed to move into and out of the market on a whim. All of them acted effortlessly on the basis of internal and external cues. Initially, it seemed to me that they were tuned into their own radio frequency. When I asked one trader, then among the largest independent investors in the country, why he got into or out of a position, he used a single word to explain: "feel," which I understood firsthand only later. Others told me that the only way to go was to have my buys and sells quantified, and to have a computer generate decisions.

Some, called scalpers, traded quickly, darting into and out of positions in a matter of minutes, or even seconds, activated by something that only they saw that had allowed them to buy fast cars and luxury homes with the profits gained from acute perception. Others waited patiently on the sidelines for trades to develop and accumulated positions that they would hold for years. Yet, despite all the differences in style, there was a syntax of successful trading that applied to all of them.

All these years later, I have come to realize that what is most appreciated by the professional investor is not the monetary rewards, although that certainly is a significant part of it. The real appeal—what motivates hard work, directs strong focus, and sustains the desire to overcome our brains' biases, fallacies, and illusions—is that, if you really commit yourself, there is the potential of reaching the maximum level of your abilities. But none of what success requires is easy. There are no shortcuts, simple answers, or turnkey solutions. In addition, you come to understand that experimentation and investigating blind alleys is also an often exhaustive, but necessary, means of maintaining a competitive edge.

The best traders, who exhibit consistency and who have experienced the benefits of a long career, are tough and smart, although not infrequently gruff, arrogant, and self-absorbed. Where there is longevity, there is often great intelligence, learning from experience, planning, and problem solving. I have also observed in the description and execution of trades a collective capacity for exceptional abstract thought and reasoning. Many traders also possess the unusual skill—like an idiot savant's ability to instantaneously calculate fallen matchsticks—of being able to read the minds and emotions of others.

EMOTIONAL INTELLIGENCE

When the market heats up and the crowd positions itself to rush in a particular direction, these traders profit handsomely from a hypertrophic capacity to perceive and capitalize on emotions. They possess what is called *emotional intelligence*, the ability to detect and decipher emotions in the faces, voices, and actions of others, as well as an ability to identify their own emotions. Perceiving emotions is a basic component of emotional intelligence that permits other processing of affective information: the ability to harness emotions in order to facilitate cognitive activities, such as thinking and problem solving. Emotionally intelligent investors can profit fully from their changing moods in order to capitalize on the markets' emotional fluctuations.

Understanding emotions encompasses the ability to tune in to subtle variations in the way we feel, and the capacity to recognize how emotions evolve over time. This leads to the managing of emotion: the ability to regulate feelings in ourselves and others to achieve our investment goals.

CHESS AND THE BIG BOARD

On the exchange floor, trading is often referred to as high-stakes chess. In the board game, strategy consists of establishing and achieving long-term goals, while at the same time focusing on where to place the various pieces when implementing tactics and maneuvering. Investing also requires a game plan and long-term goals, with strategic and tactical know-how to capitalize on game-play.

A game of chess is usually divided into three phases: the opening, consisting of the first 10 to 25 moves, when players establish positions for the coming battle; the middle game, which is often the fiercest part of the game; and the endgame, when most of the pieces are gone. Kings typically take a more active part in the final struggle, and pawn promotion is decisive. In both chess and investing, there is both an inner and an outer aspect to the activity that needs to be mastered.

In chess, there is an extensive scientific literature on psychology. French psychologist Alfred Binet demonstrated that cognitive rather than visuospatial ability lies at the core of expertise. Adriaan de Groot, a Dutch psychologist and chess master, conducted extensive research in the decades just before and after the end of World War II. His studies involved individuals at all levels of play, from amateurs to masters, exploring the cognitive requirements and the thought processes involved in moving a chess piece. Subjects were required to solve a chess problem under the supervision of a researcher and explain their thought processes.

De Groot showed that chess masters can rapidly perceive the key features of a position. According to de Groot, this perception, developed as a result of years of practice and study, is more important than the sheer ability to anticipate moves. De Groot demonstrated that chess masters could memorize positions shown for a few seconds almost perfectly, but that this ability alone did not account for their skill, since masters and novices, when faced with random arrangements of chess pieces, had equivalent recall—about half a dozen positions in each case. Instead, it was the ability to recognize patterns, which were then committed to memory, that distinguished the skilled players from the novices. When the positions of the pieces were taken from an actual game, the masters had almost total positional recall.

It is not uncommon for veteran traders to make hundreds of trades in a single day, and then, when later asked about a particular trade by a clerk or a supervisor, to remember every aspect of the trade—the time, with whom it was placed, the circumstances of its execution—to a fault. A 2005 brain imaging study of memory in chess players demonstrated that when a grandmaster and an international chess master were compared to a group of novices in a memory task that introduced various stimuli, the pattern of brain activity in the masters was dissimilar from that in the novices. The two masters showed no differences between themselves in brain activity when compared; however, novices did show differences in brain activity in such contrasts. As with the master sommeliers, these results strengthen the hypothesis that, when performing a specific task, experts and novices activate different brain systems.

INVESTOR VERSUS TRADER

Although psychology is almost universally acknowledged as a critical factor in one's success as an investor, its application is as varied as the individuals who trade markets. Psychology can also mean something quite different to traders from what it means to investors. Technical analyst Robin Mesch brought this point into high relief in our interview. She said that, in her experience, she has encountered a pronounced difference in perception and tolerance of risk between those of her clients who are investors and those who consider themselves strictly traders. "With investors,

I have observed that their dominant psychology revolves less around absolute returns and more around returns relative to the overall market." The psychology of a client is far more disturbed by a missed opportunity than by a loss—provided that loss is in line with the performance of the market. She continued, "I was a hero for a brief period when I went to 100 percent cash in July of 2008 and avoided a large part of the market decline, but I was a rogue agent when I hadn't gotten back in off the lows in 2009 and missed the bulk of the 2009 rally." Mesch explained that she too experienced her own psychology of dismay, even though her absolute returns were not at issue. She eventually reached the conclusion that "sharing the misery is somehow different from not sharing in the bliss," an observation that would seem to be completely consistent with the observations by Kahneman and Tversky in prospect theory.

VOLATILITY ANYONE?

How an individual arrives at a particular psychological approach to the market is also fascinating. Toby Crabel has built a career and a business on the consistency of returns that his fund achieves on nearly $2 billion in client assets, based on remarkably low volatility. Why he chose to focus specifically on this issue is a psychologically interesting and revealing story.

In our interview, which focused on his trading process, I questioned the three-time All-American about tennis to see if his approach to the game bore any similarities to his approach to investing. I asked him how he would characterize his game. He said that he was an extremely conservative player. "When I was playing my best, I tended not to miss. I would keep hitting the ball back, always keeping it in play." I asked Crabel if that meant that he was more interested in consistency than in the big shot. He said that he had been doing some soul-searching on this very point, working on "insecurities that I had growing up as a result of an erratic family life." He said that he was always searching for security and stability. He added, "Volatility is something that I just can't stand in a business, or in any other part of my life."

TURTLE SEE, TURTLE DO

Tom Shanks told me that, when he learned to trade as part of the Turtle program under Richard Dennis and William Eckhardt, fully half of their training was devoted to psychology. "That says pretty clearly how important those two legendary traders thought psychology was," he said.

Shanks, who has been running a fund successfully for more than two decades, is a systems trader who, admittedly, also at times relies on his intuition to make decisions. I was interested to speak with him about the role that psychology played in his investing. He said that for human beings with emotions, psychology is inescapable. Even purely systematic traders are influenced by psychology as they design their systems. That influence may be as simple as affecting the decision on the degree of leverage to employ, but it is still present. He said that a case might be made for the claims of quants or other "algo" traders—individuals who employ trading algorithms that essentially trade against other computer-driven systems—who contend that their approach is purely mathematical and free of emotional components, but that approach would be the closest thing that he could think of to emotionless trading.

Shanks added that from his viewpoint, "Psychology is something to be wary of in systems design, as opposed to being something that can be harnessed." He mentioned that he knew traders who employed game theory to try to capitalize on investor psychology, but that was not part of his approach. "Fear, greed, and hope are the enemies," he said.

Shanks is convinced that overtrading is arguably the most dangerous of trading sins. Naïve systems' designers could easily be fooled by the psychology of greed or hope into thinking that they should be more aggressive than would be wise. Fear could lead them into designing systems that exit a position too quickly or that don't trade often enough. In his opinion, regarding the role that psychology played in Hawksbill's analysis for discretionary trading, there were two components: their own psychology, and the psychology that they perceive operating in the markets.

Quoting Socrates, Shanks said that "know thyself" is the paramount principle in the first instance. It is critical to be aware of the influences that emotions exert on your own state of mind at any moment. He continued, "As Bill Eckhardt observed, the markets operate so as to inflict the greatest amount of pain on the largest number of participants. There are lots of trading maxims that address this element: 'When you're yellin', you should be sellin'; when you're cryin', you should be buyin'.' Intense emotions are antithetical to good decision making. Those who can reason well in emotionally charged situations are said to be 'cool under fire.' This is certainly a desirable quality in an investor."

VALUE AND CONSENSUS

Not surprisingly, psychology has a different meaning for Robin Mesch. She explained to me that in her view, the market could best be understood as a pool of participants engaged in a process of determining value and building consensus. An individual enters the market and becomes part of a network. "They merge into a 'mass mindset' that moves as a single body toward consensus as to what is fair value." This process occurs in stages on both an individual and a collective basis.

The time necessary to build consensus depends on how disparate the opinions of the individuals in the collective mindset are at the outset of the negotiation. Mesch explains, "Markets in which the collective psychology is in strong concurrence will take on a trend and look directional. In markets where participants have strong opposing views of value, a long period of negotiation is required before arriving at agreement." In these situations, the market's back-and-forth fluctuations (negotiations) resemble random activity. "Usually, once the market does reach consensus out of prolonged periods of negotiation, an extremely large-scale directional move will ensue," Mesch said.

The first step in this auction process begins with a dramatic directional move that is halted by a feeling of sticker shock on the part of participants. "I call this stage 'shock,'" she said. Stage 2, Mesch calls "anger." Investors say to themselves, "I won't buy or sell it. I'll invest my money elsewhere." At this point, trading slows down as participants search for alternatives, triggering a move counter to the initial direction. Stage 3 is the bargaining phase, which Mesch sees as the market's search to explore value and create consensus. It is during this phase that participants grow used to the price as the shock and anger start to wear off.

Finally, Stage 4 arrives. It is during this stage, according to Mesch, that there is either acceptance or rejection of value. "As participants move through these mindsets of the four stages, the market naturally organizes itself into a bell curve. The bell curve shows me where investors have been willing and unwilling to use price throughout their negotiation process. This is extremely useful when reading market psychology and creating a trading strategy."

For Mesch, the beginning of the formation of the bell curve represents a determination of value; its completion, the acceptance of value, which naturally leads to the market starting the process all over again. From this perspective, "psychology can best be read on price charts on the horizontal axis, which indicates how people perceive and are willing to use price. Quantitative analysis often relies too heavily on price as a critical measurement of information. In my mind, price is really just the messenger—a distribution vehicle of order flows." Mesch is convinced that if a system is going to be successful, it must tap into the underlying force that drives the market. "This force is order flow, and the force behind that is market psychology."

THE BIG SHAGGY

In one of his big-themed op-ed columns, *New York Times* writer David Brooks sought to explain why the various systems created over the past century by economics, political science, game theory, and psychology to help in better understanding human beings always come up short. He said, "None completely explain behavior because deep down people have passions and drives that don't lend themselves to systemic modeling. They have yearnings and fears that reside in an inner beast you could call The Big Shaggy."

Brooks explained that you could see The Big Shaggy at work in a governor of South Carolina who suddenly chucked it all for the "Appalachian Trail," or in the self-destructive overconfidence of oil engineers in the Gulf of Mexico, or in the irrational exuberance that intoxicated investment bankers on Wall Street.

Those were the destructive sides of The Big Shaggy. "But this tender beast is also responsible for the mysterious but fierce determination that drives Kobe Bryant, the graceful bemusement the Detroit Tigers pitcher Armando Galarraga showed when his perfect game slipped away in the summer of 2010, the selfless courage soldiers in Afghanistan show when they risk death for buddies or a family they may never see again," said Brooks.

The intelligent observer goes through life asking: Where did that come from? Why did he act that way? What really happened? The answers are not easy to come by because the behavior emanates from somewhere deep within The Big Shaggy.

INVESTING IS A MICROCOSM OF LIFE

In my introduction, I said that, over time, I have come to believe that the market is truly a Rorschach test. The more I look, the more I see myself. The market is a mirror of complexity, inconsistency, irony, and paradox. Now, as validated by behavioral economics and neuroscience, investing is recognized as having less to do with the science of computation and more to do with the art of managing one's outlook, emotions, and consciousness. It involves invention, imagination, and know-how, and the mettle to exploit the hard right edge of the price chart, which reveals the stock market's next unexpected move.

At the outset, I also said something else that warrants repeating. Investing is a microcosm of life. Within it, we experience joy, uncertainty, frustration, and struggle. It requires courage, optimism, humility, and the desire to succeed. Our challenge is made all the more difficult because our decisions are under assault from our brains. The good news, as we have learned, is that through commitment, diligence, practice, and respect for our intellect and emotions, we can train our brains to serve us, to triumph as investors and, more important, to triumph as human beings.

Notes

PREFACE

1. Paul Slovic and Amos Tversky, "Who Accepts Savage's Axiom?" *Behavioral Science* 19 (1974): pp. 368–373.
2. http://www.whitehouse.gov/omb/inforeg_default.

INTRODUCTION

1. Theory of Mind: Anthony J. Bruguier et al., "Exploring the Nature of Trader Intuition," Swiss Finance Institute, no.10:02.
2. Ming Hsu et al., "Neural Systems Responding to Degrees of Uncertainty in Human Decision-Making," *Science* 310, no. 5754 (2005). See also John Cassidy, "Mind Games: What Neuroeconomics Tells Us about Money and the Brain, Interviews with Peter Sokol-Hessner and Colin Camerer," *New Yorker*, September 18, 2006. Also Peter Sokol-Hessner, Ming Hsu, Nina G. Curley, Mauricio R. Delgado, Colin F. Camerer, and Elizabeth A. Phelps, "Thinking like a Trader Reduces Individuals' Loss Aversion," *Proceedings of the National Academy of Sciences, USA* 106, no. 3 (2009).
3. Paul Glimcher, *Decisions, Uncertainty, and the Brain: The Science of Neuroeconomics* (Cambridge, Mass.: MIT Press, 2003).
4. Dan Ariely, *Predictably Irrational: The Hidden Forces That Shape Our Decisions* (New York: Harper, 2008).
5. David Cartwright, *Schopenhauer: A Biography* (Cambridge, U.K.: Cambridge University Press, 2010).
6. Paul Krugman quote: *New York Times* blog, July 19, 2009.

CHAPTER 1

1. My intention in this chapter is to offer a subjective history of investor psychology in order to provide a context for understanding how my thinking about markets and financial decision making evolved, not to give an exhaustive treatise on the many persons—traders, academics, and psychologists—who have contributed to the field. The individuals and ideas that were cited have been the basis for my own activities in the market and my work with

traders and investors. However, I must acknowledge two additional thinkers who merit attention, the financial historian and economist Peter L. Bernstein for his articles and books, particularly *Against the Gods: The Remarkable Story of Risk* (New York: Wiley, 1996), about the history of risk analysis, and Nassim Taleb for his brilliant books, *Fooled by Randomness: The Hidden Role of Chance in Life and in Market* (New York: Random House, 2001) and *The Black Swan: The Impact of the Highly Improbable* (New York: Random House, 2007). Taleb asserts that scientists, economists, investors, and policy makers are victims of an illusion of pattern. We overestimate the value of rational explanations of past data and underestimate the prevalence of unexplainable randomness.

2. Andrew Ross Sorkin, "A Wish List for Fixing Wall Street," *New York Times* DealBook, May 13, 2008.

3. Scott Patterson, *The Quants: How a New Breed of Math Whizzes Conquered Wall Street and Nearly Destroyed It* (New York: Crown, 2010), pp. 1–12. See also pp. 242–261.

4. Dickson G. Watts, *Speculation as a Fine Art and Thoughts on Life* (reprint Burlington, Vt.: Fraser Publishing Library, 1979).

5. Edwin Lefèvre, *Reminiscences of a Stock Operator* (1923). One of my favorite Livermore quotes: "Nowhere does history indulge in repetitions so often or so uniformly as in Wall Street. When you read contemporary accounts of booms or panics the one thing that strikes you most forcibly is how little either stock speculation or stock speculators today differ from yesterday. The game does not change and neither does human nature." Annotated edition by Jon D. Markman (Newark, N.J.: Wiley, 2010), p. 165.

6. Richard Smitten, *Jesse Livermore: The World's Greatest Stock Trader* (New York: Wiley, 2001), pp. 248–282.

7. Bernard Baruch, *Baruch: My Own Story* (New York: Pocket Books, 1958). See the ten rules of successful investing. Also see James Grant, *Bernard M. Baruch: The Adventures of a Wall Street Legend* (New York: Wiley, 1997).

8. Benjamin Graham and David Dodd, *Security Analysis*, 6th ed., with a foreword by Warren Buffett (New York: McGraw-Hill, 2008). See also Seth A. Klarman of the Baupost Group; Bruce Greenwald, Robert Heilbrunn Professor of Finance and Asset Management, Columbia Business School; and David Abrams, Managing Member, Abrams Capital.

9. Jack D. Schwager, *Market Wizards: Interviews with Top Traders* (New York: Collins, 1993). See also *The New Market Wizards: Conversations with America's Top Traders* (New York: HarperBusiness, 1992) and *Stock Market Wizards: Interviews with America's Top Stock Traders* (New York: HarperBusiness, 2001).

10. Robert Koppel and Howard Abell, *The Outer Game of Trading* (New York: McGraw-Hill, 1995), pp. 92–111.

11. Mark Douglas, *The Disciplined Trader: Developing Winning Attitudes* (Englewood Cliffs, N.J.: Prentice Hall, 1990). See also *Trading in the Zone* (New York: New York Academy of Finance, 2000).

CHAPTER 2

1. Robert Koppel and Howard Abell, *The Inner Game of Trading* (New York: McGraw-Hill, 1997). See also Koppel, *Bulls, Bears, and Millionaires* (Chicago: Dearborn Financial Publishing, 1997), *The Intuitive Trader* (New York: Wiley, 1996), and *The Tao of Trading* (Chicago: Dearborn Financial Publishing, 1998).
2. Ibid., "Syntax of Successful Trading," pp. 37–41.
3. Benjamin Graham and David Dodd, *Security Analysis*, 6th ed., with a foreword by Warren Buffett (New York: McGraw-Hill, 2008).
4. George Soros, *The Soros Lectures: At the Central European University* (New York: Public Affairs, 2010). The lectures can be viewed online at www.georgesoros.com. Also see *The Alchemy of Finance* (Hoboken, N.J.: Wiley, 2003), *Soros on Soros* (New York: Wiley, 1995), and *The New Paradigm for Financial Markets: The Crash of 2008 and What it Means* (New York: Public Affairs, 2008).
5. Daniel Kahneman and Amos Tversky, "Prospect Theory: An Analysis of Decisions under Risk," *Econometrica* 47 (1979): pp. 313–327. See also Amos Tversky and Daniel Kahneman, "Belief in the Law of Small Numbers," *Psychological Bulletin*, 76 (1971): pp. 105–110; Daniel Kahneman and Amos Tversky, "Subjective Probability: A Judgment of Representativeness," *Cognitive Psychology* 3 (1972): pp. 430–454; Daniel Kahneman, *Attention and Effort* (Englewood Cliffs, N.J.: Prentice-Hall, 1973); Daniel Kahneman and Amos Tversky, "On the Psychology of Prediction," *Psychological Review* 80 (1973): pp. 237–251; Amos Tversky and Daniel Kahneman, "Availability: A Heuristic for Judging Frequency and Probability," *Cognitive Psychology* 5 (1973): pp. 207–232; and Amos Tversky and Daniel Kahneman, "Judgment under Uncertainty: Heuristics and Biases," *Science* 185, no. 4157 (1974): pp. 1124–1131.
6. Richard H. Thaler and Cass R. Sunstein, *Nudge: Improving Decisions about Health, Wealth, and Happiness* (New York: Penguin, 2009).
7. John M. Keynes, *The General Theory of Employment, Interest and Money* (London: Macmillan, 1936), pp. 161–162.
8. George A. Akerlof and Robert J. Shiller, *Animal Spirits: How Human Psychology Drives the Economy, and Why It Matters for Global Capitalism* (Princeton, N.J.: Princeton University Press, 2009).

CHAPTER 3

1. Daniel Kahneman and Amos Tversky, "Prospect Theory: An Analysis of Decisions under Risk," *Econometrica* 47 (1979): pp. 313–327.
2. *New York Times* article, "The Behavioral Revolution," Oct. 10, 2008.
3. Thaler wrote a regular column in the *Journal of Economic Perspectives* from 1987 to 1990 titled *Anomalies* in which he documented individual instances of economic behavior that violate traditional microeconomic theory. See "The Ultimatum Game," Fall 1988; "The Winners Curse," Winter 1988; "Saving, Fungibility, and Mental Accounts," Winter 1990; "Preference

Reversals," with Amos Tversky, Spring 1990; and "The Endowment Effect, Loss Aversion, and Status Quo Bias," with Daniel Kahneman and Jack Knetsch, Winter 1991.

4. Described in the journal *Proceedings of the National Academy of Sciences* (February 2010), the research team consisted of Benedetto De Martino, a Caltech visiting researcher from University College London; Colin Camerer, professor of behavioral economics; and Ralph Adolphs, professor of psychology, neuroscience, and biology.

5. Hilke Plassmann, John O'Doherty, Baba Shiv, and Antonio Rangel, "Marketing Actions Can Modulate Neural Representations of Experienced Pleasantness," *Proceedings of the National Academy of Sciences, USA* 105 (2008): pp. 1050–1054. Also see Wendy V. Parr, David Heatherbell, and K. Geoffrey White, "Demystifying Wine Expertise: Olfactory Threshold, Perceptual Skill and Semantic Memory in Expert and Novice Wine Judges," *Chemical Senses* 27 (2002): pp. 747–755.

6. A. Castriota-Scanderberg, G. E. Hagberg, A. Cerasa, G. Committeri, G. Galati, F. Patria, S. Pitzalis, C. Caltagirone, and R. Frackowiak, "The Appreciation of Wine by Sommeliers: A Functional Magnetic Resonance Study of Sensory Integration," *NeuroImage* 25 (2005): pp. 570–578.

7. Robert Koppel, *Bulls, Bears, and Millionaires* (Chicago: Dearborn Financial Publishing, 1997), pp. 68–75, 167–179, 129–139. Shanks's philosophy of the market as explained to me in July 2010 is this:

   We are systematic trend followers with a discretionary overlay. Roughly 80 percent of our trading is systematic. That means that that portion of our trading is determined by computer-generated signals based on extensively back-tested systems. I believe, rightly or wrongly, that trading experience can be a value-adding proposition, so we occasionally make discretionary trading decisions based on our perceptions of market conditions and our take on conditions in the world that we think may influence the markets we trade.

8. Nassim Taleb, *The Black Swan: The Impact of the Highly Improbable* (New York: Random House, 2010). See also *Fooled by Randomness: The Hidden Role of Chance in Life and in the Markets* (New York: Random House, 2001).

9. B. Knutson, C. M. Adams, G. W. Fong, and D. Hommer, "Anticipation of Increasing Monetary Reward Selectively Recruits Nucleus Accumbens," *Journal of Neuroscience* 21 (2001). Also see B. Knutson, G. W. Fong, C. M. Adams, J. L. Varner, and D. Hommer, "Dissociation of Reward Anticipation and Outcome with Event-Related fMRI," *NeuroReport* 12 (2001); B. Knutson and J. Cooper, "Functional Magnetic Resonance Imaging of Reward Prediction," *Current Opinion in Neurology* 18 (2005): pp. 411–417; and C. M. Kuhnen and B. Knutson, "The Neural Basis of Financial Risk Taking," *Neuron* 47 (2005): pp. 763–770.

10. Zhou et al., *Psychological Science,* Volume 20, Number 6, 2009.

CHAPTER 4

1. John J. Ratey, *A User's Guide to the Brain: Perception, Attention, and the Four Theaters of the Brain* (New York: Vintage, 2002), p. 17. See also the chapters on perception, pp. 48–110, and emotion, pp. 222–252.
2. Ibid., pp. 93–98.
3. Ibid., "Music and the Brain," pp. 129–146.
4. Interview with Leo Melamed: Robert Koppel and Howard Abell, *The Inner Game of Trading* (New York: McGraw-Hill, 1997), pp. 94–95.
5. Interview with Robin Mesch: Robert Koppel, *Bulls, Bears and Millionaires* (Chicago: Dearborn Financial Publishing, 1997), pp. 106–116 and over dinner in the summer of 2010 at Le Colonial in Chicago. Mesch's philosophy of the market is:

> I believe that the markets are the single portal for participants to express their opinion about value. No matter what information traders or investors rely on, whether technical or fundamental analysis, they will come up with an assessment of fair price and determine whether the market is above or below that value and will place their bets accordingly. My method reads this "collective mindset" or psychology of the market. I don't trade *my* psychology; I trade the market's psychology. I believe that the most effective way to understand the market is to understand and track investor psychology as to what they perceive as fair or unfair value and what they are actually accepting or rejecting. I use the analytical tools I developed to read market participants' opinions, which are expressed in order flows, and those opinions come from an underlying psychology or mindset about the market's value. I create charts that organize perceived value and show me where people are willing to use or not use price based on that perceived value. It's my belief that the more market participants "use" price, the more they come to accept a price as fair: Usage = Acceptance.

6. Andrew Lo, with Dmitry V. Repin and Brett N. Steenbarger, "Fear and Greed in Financial Markets: A Clinical Study of Day-Traders," *American Economic Review* 95 (2005).
7. Paul Glimcher, *Decisions, Uncertainty, and the Brain: The Science of Neuroeconomics* (Cambridge, Mass.: MIT Press, 2003). See also P. W. Glimcher, M. C. Dorris, and H. M. Bayer, "Physiological Utility Theory and the Neuroeconomics of Choice," *Games and Economic Behavior* 52 (2005): pp. 213–256.

CHAPTER 5

1. Andrew W. Lo and A. Craig MacKinlay, *A Non-Random Walk Down Wall St.* (Princeton, N.J.: Princeton University Press, 2001). See also Andrew Lo, "The Adaptive Markets Hypothesis: Market Efficiency from an Evolutionary Perspective," *Journal of Portfolio Management* 30 (2004): pp. 15–29.

2. Justin Fox, *Myth of the Rational Market: A History of Risk, Reward, and Delusion on Wall Street* (New York: HarperBusiness, 2009).
3. Alfred H. Cowles, "Some A Posteriori Probabilities in Stock Market Action," *Econometrica* 5 (1937): pp. 280–294.
4. Ming Hsu, Meghana Bhatt, Ralph Adolphs, Daniel Tranel, and Colin Camerer, "Neural Systems Responding to Degrees of Uncertainty in Human Decision Making," *Science* 310 (2005): pp. 1624–1625.
5. Daniel G. Amen, *Change Your Brain, Change Your Life* (New York: Three Rivers Press, 1998), pp. 4–24 and 82–133.
6. "Jungle Survival," *The U.S. Army Survival Manual:. Department of the Army Field Manual* 21–76, Ulysses Press, pp. 203–216.
7. John J. Ratey, *A User's Guide to the Brain: Perception, Attention, and the Four Theaters of the Brain* (New York: Vintage, 2002), pp. 19–21.
8. Reported in the ConvergEx Morning Market Briefing, April 20, 2010.
9. Eduardo B. Andrade and Dan Ariely, "The Enduring Impact of Transient Emotions on Decision Making," *Organizational Behavior and Human Decision Processes* 109 (2009).
10. J. S. Lerner and L. Z. Tiedens, "Portrait of the Angry Decision Maker: How Appraisal Tendencies Shape Anger's Influence on Cognition," *Journal of Behavioral Decision Making* 19 (2006): pp. 115–137.
11. John Tierney, "Why Brooding Shoppers Overpay," *New York Times*, February 13, 2008.
12. John Cassidy, "Mind Games: What Neuroeconomics Tells Us about Money and the Brain, Interviews with Sokol-Hessner and Colin Camerer," *New Yorker*, September 18, 2006.
13. Peter Sokol-Hessner, Ming Hsu, Nina G. Curley, Mauricio R. Delgado, Colin F. Camerer, and Elizabeth A. Phelps, "Thinking like a Trader Reduces Individuals' Loss Aversion," *Proceedings of the National Academy of Sciences, USA* 106, no. 3 (2009).
14. The anchoring experiment was conducted at the University of Chicago as shown on Nova's *Mind over Money*, April 2010.

CHAPTER 6
1. Dan Ariely, *Predictably Irrational: The Hidden Forces That Shape Our Decisions* (New York: Harper, 2008), p. 279.
2. Interview with Robert Shiller on PBS Nova's *Mind over Money*.
3. "Shiller's List: How to Diagnose the Next Bubble," *New York Times*, January 27, 2010.
4. Scott Lanman and Steve Matthews, "Greenspan Concedes to 'Flaw' in His Market Ideology," Bloomberg.com, October 23, 2008.
5. Lawrence Summers, Alan Greenspan, Arthur Levitt, and William Rainer, *Over-the-Counter Derivatives Markets and the Commodity Exchange Act: Report of the President's Working Group on Financial Markets*, November, 1999; http://www.ustreas.gov/press/releases/reports/otcact.pdf.
6. David Leonhardt, "Greenspan's Mea Culpa," October 23, 2008; http://economix.blogs.nytimes.com/2008/10/23/greenspans-mea-culpa.

7. Noel Pearson, "Comment: The Corporate Fallacy," The Monthly.com, July 2009.
8. Joseph Stiglitz, "How to Prevent the Next Wall Street Crisis," CNN, September 17, 2008.
9. Paul Krugman, "School for Scoundrels," *New York Times*, August 6, 2009.
10. "Moral Bankruptcy," *Mother Jones*, January/February 2010.
11. James Surowiecki, "Déjà Vu," *New Yorker*, May 3, 2010.
12. Interview with Leo Melamed: Robert Koppel and Howard Abell, *The Inner Game of Trading* (New York: McGraw-Hill, 1997), p. 97.
13. Interview with David Landsburgh: Robert Koppel, *Bulls, Bears, and Millionaires* (Chicago: Dearborn Financial Publishing, 1997), p. 166.
14. Interview with Jeffrey L. Silverman: Koppel and Abell, *Inner Game*, pp. 134–135.
15. Nigel Taylor, "Making Actuaries Less Human," Staple Inn Actuarial Society 15 (2000). For wishful thinking, see also D. Rosenhan and S. Messick, "Affect and Expectation," *Journal of Personality and Social Psychology* 3 (1966): pp. 38–44.

CHAPTER 7

1. Daniel Kahneman, panel discussion moderated by Jason Zweig, "Oxford Programme on Investment Decision-Making," October 24, 2004.
2. Graham comment: www.buffettsecrets.com/benjamin-graham. Also see investment principles and techniques.
3. Peter Kirsch statement as quoted in Jason Zweig, *Your Money and Your Brain* (New York: Simon & Schuster, 2007), p. 35. See also Peter Kirsch et al., "Anticipation of Reward in a Nonaversive Differential Conditioning Paradigm and the Brain Reward System," *NeuroImage* 20 (2003): pp. 1086–1095.
4. Robert Koppel and Howard Abell, *The Inner Game of Trading* (New York: McGraw-Hill, 1997), p. 142. Also see "The Importance of Trading Goals" with exercises, pp. 22–29.
5. Jack Schwager, *The New Market Wizards* (New York: HarperBusiness, 1992), p. 175.
6. Ibid., p. 441.
7. The factors that prevent investors from achieving their goals have been reported to me by colleagues, prop traders, and clients over many years. See also Koppel and Abell, *Inner Game*, pp. 21–29.
8. Schwager, *New Market Wizards*, p. 463.
9. Before becoming a fund manager, Shanks was a member of a highly successful card-counting team. As part of the interview, I asked him, as a trained card counter, what similarities he saw between card counting and professional investing. His answer follows:

   There is a wide spectrum of approaches to investing. Some are more similar to counting cards than others. Card counting is, of course, a systematic approach to blackjack; systematic approaches to trading are much more similar to card counting than, say, value investing or discretionary trading. The principal similarity is the notion of trading with an "edge," i.e., positive expectation. In blackjack, I know that if I consistently make a large bet in positive situations, I will come out ahead in the long run. If I have a trading system that has positive expectation, I have a high degree of confidence (less certain than in blackjack) that if I take every indicated trade, I will come out ahead in the long run. Any deviation from the system is suboptimal, both in systematic trading and in blackjack. While you may get lucky in the short run if you stray from the system, in the long run your performance will almost certainly be inferior to the performance you would have had had you adhered to the system. That is why discipline is so important.

CHAPTER 8

1. Daniel Kahneman et al., "Representativeness Revisited: Attribute Substitution in Intuitive Judgment," in Thomas Gilovich, Dale Griffin, and Daniel Kahneman, *Heuristics and Biases: The Psychology of Intuitive Judgment* (Cambridge, U.K.: Cambridge University Press, 2002), pp. 51–52.
2. Thomas Gilovich and Dale Griffin, "Heuristics and Biases: Then and Now," in *Heuristics and Biases: The Psychology of Intuitive Judgment*, edited by Thomas Gilovich, Dale Griffin, and Daniel Kahneman (Cambridge, U.K.: Cambridge University Press, 2002), pp. 1–4.
3. D. L. Schacter, "The Seven Sins of Memory: Insights from Psychology and Cognitive Neuroscience," *American Psychologist* 54, no. 3 (1999): pp. 182–203. Also see Daniel Kahneman et al., *Judgment under Uncertainty: Heuristics and Biases* (New York: Cambridge University Press, 1982).
4. Groupthink: Irving L. Janis, *Victims of Groupthink* (Boston: Houghton Mifflin, 1972), p. 9. See also James Surowiecki, *The Wisdom of Crowds* (New York: Doubleday, 2004), p. 183; G. Whyte, "Groupthink Reconsidered," *Academy of Management Review* 14, no. 1 (1989): pp. 40–56.
5. Amos Tversky and Daniel Kahneman, "Judgment under Uncertainty: Heuristics and Biases," *Science* 185, no. 4157 (1974): pp. 1124–1131; and Daniel Kahneman et al., "Anomalies: The Endowment Effect, Loss Aversion, and Status Quo Bias," *Journal of Economic Perspectives* 5, no. 1 (1991): pp. 193–206.
6. Maria Lewicka, "Confirmation Bias: Cognitive Error or Adaptive Strategy of Action Control?" in Mirosław Kofta, Gifford Weary, and Grzegorz Sedek, *Personal Control in Action: Cognitive and Motivational Mechanisms* (New York: Springer, 1998), pp. 233–255.
7. D. Alan Bensley, *Critical Thinking in Psychology: A Unified Skills Approach* (Pacific Grove, Calif.: Brooks/Cole, 1998), p. 137.
8. R. Thaler, "Toward a Positive Theory of Consumer Choice," *Journal of Economic Behavior and Organization* 1 (1980): pp. 39–60.

9. Framing: Amos Tversky and Daniel Kahneman, "The Framing of Decisions and the Psychology of Choice," *Science* 211 (1981): pp. 453–458.

10. B. De Martino, D. Kumaran, B. Seymour, and R. J. Dolan, "Frames, Biases, and Rational Decision-Making in the Human Brain, *Science* 313 (2006): pp. 684–687.

11. D. T. Miller and M. Ross, "Self-Serving Biases in the Attribution of Causality: Fact or Fiction?" *Psychological Bulletin* 82 (1975): pp. 213–225. See also J. Kruger, "Lake Wobegon Be Gone! The 'Below-Average Effect' and the Egocentric Nature of Comparative Ability Judgments," *Journal of Personality and Social Psychology* 77 (1999): pp. 221–232; and N. J. Roese and J. M. Olson, "Better, Stronger, Faster: Self-Serving Judgment, Affect Regulation, and the Optimal Vigilance Hypothesis," *Perspectives on Psychological Science* 2 (2007): pp. 124–141.

12. D. A. Schkade and D. Kahneman, "Does Living in California Make People Happy? A Focusing Illusion in Judgments of Life Satisfaction," *Psychological Science* 9 (1998): pp. 340–346.

13. Daniel Kahneman, Alan B. Krueger, David Schkade, Norbert Schwarz, and Arthur A. Stone, "Would You Be Happier if You Were Richer? A Focusing Illusion," *Science* 312, no. 5782 (2006): pp. 1908–1910.

14. Barry M. Staw, "Knee-Deep in the Big Muddy: A Study of Escalating Commitment to a Chosen Course of Action," *Organizational Behavior and Human Performance* 16, no. 1 (2004): pp. 27–44. See also Barry Schwartz, "The Sunk-Cost Fallacy, Bush Falls Victim to a Bad New Argument for the Iraq War," Slate.com, September 9, 2005.

15. Martin Shubik, "The Dollar Auction Game: A Paradox in Noncooperative Behavior and Escalation," *Journal of Conflict Resolution* 15, no. 1 (1971): pp. 109–111. See also C. Wald, "Crazy Money: Humans Aren't Rational, as the Recent Economic Crisis Shows. So Why Should Financial Theories Assume that They Are?" *Science* 322 (2008): pp. 1624–1626.

16. Andrew M. Colman, *Game Theory and Its Applications in the Social and Biological Sciences*, International Series in Social Psychology (London: Routledge Falmer, 1995).

17. J. S. Evans, J. L. Barston, and P. Pollard, "On the Conflict between Logic and Belief in Syllogistic Reasoning," *Memory and Cognition* 11 (1983): pp. 295–306.

18. V. Goel and R. J. Dolan, "Explaining Modulation of Reasoning by Belief," *Cognition* 87 (2003): pp. 11–22.

19. Daniel Kahneman and Amos Tversky, "The Framing of Decisions and the Psychology of Choice," *Science* 211 (1981): pp. 453–458.

20. Joel B. Cohen and Marvin E. Goldberg, "The Dissonance Model in Post-Decision Product Evaluation," *Journal of Marketing Research* 7, no. 3 (1970): pp. 315–321.

21. J. Baron, *Thinking and Deciding*, 3rd ed. (New York: Cambridge University Press, 2000), pp. 260–261.

22. S. S. Brehm and J. W. Brehm, *Psychological Reactance: A Theory of Freedom and Control* (New York: Academic Press, 1981).

23. Emily Pronin, Center for Behavioral Decision Research. See also Emily Pronin and Matthew B. Kugler, "Valuing Thoughts, Ignoring Behavior: The Introspection Illusion as a Source of the Bias Blind Spot," *Journal of Experimental Social Psychology* 43, no. 4 (2007): pp. 565–578.

CHAPTER 9

1. T. Edward Damer, Attacking Faulty Reasoning: A Practical Guide to Fallacy-Free Arguments, 6th ed. (Belmont, Calif.: Cengage Learning, 2008), p. 130. See also T. Edward Damer, *Attacking Faulty Reasoning*, 5th ed. (Belmont, Calif.: Wadsworth, 2005).
2. Roger Buehler, Dale Griffin, and Michael Ross, "Exploring the 'Planning Fallacy': Why People Underestimate Their Task Completion Times," *Journal of Personality and Social Psychology* 67 (1994): pp. 366–381.
3. Dan Lovallo and Daniel Kahneman, "Delusions of Success: How Optimism Undermines Executives' Decisions," *Harvard Business Review* (2003): pp. 56–63.
4. Aristotle, *De Sophistici Elenchi* (On Sophistical Refutations); library.adelaide.edu.au.
5. "Material Fallacies," Wikipedia, June 10, 2010. See also Douglas N. Walton, *Informal Logic: A Handbook for Critical Argumentation* (Cambridge, U.K.: Cambridge University Press, 1989).
6. Nassim Taleb, *The Black Swan* (New York: Random House, 2010).
7. *New York Times*, April 22, 2007.
8. "Ten Principles for a Black Swan Robust World," FT.com, April 7, 2009.
9. Amos Tversky and Daniel Kahneman, "Judgment under Uncertainty: Heuristics and Biases," *Science* 185, no. 4157 (1974), pp. 1124–1131.
10. Andrew Colman, "Gambler's Fallacy," in *A Dictionary of Psychology* (Oxford, U.K.: Oxford University Press); retrieved from Encyclopedia.com. See also Jonah Lehrer, *How We Decide* (Boston: Houghton Mifflin Harcourt, 2009), p. 66.
11. Ian Hacking, "The Inverse Gambler's Fallacy: The Argument from Design. The Anthropic Principle Applied to Wheeler Universes," *Mind* 96, no. 383 (July 1987): pp. 331–340. For the inverse and reverse gambler's fallacy and the law of large numbers, see "Gambler's Fallacy," Wikipedia; retrieved May 25, 2010. See also Darrell Huff and Irving Geis, *How to Take a Chance* (New York: Norton, 1964), pp. 28–29.
12. Representativeness heuristic: Tversky and Kahneman, "Judgment under Uncertainty."
13. David Hackett Fischer, *Historians' Fallacies: Toward a Logic of Historical Thought* (New York: Harper Torchbooks, 1970), pp. 209–213.
14. Amos Tversky and Daniel Kahneman, "Availability: A Heuristic for Judging Frequency and Probability," *Cognitive Psychology* 5 (1973): pp. 207–232.
15. Tversky and Kahneman, "Judgment under Uncertainty."
16. Psychological principle of the availability heuristic: A. Esgate and D. Groome, *An Introduction to Applied Cognitive Psychology* (New York: Psychology Press, 2004).

17. J. S. Carroll, "The Effect of Imagining an Event on Expectations for the Event: An Interpretation in Terms of the Availability Heuristic," *Journal of Experimental Social Psychology* 14 (1978): pp. 88–96.

18. Psychologist's fallacy: the fallacy, to which psychologists are peculiarly liable, of reading into the mind being examined what is true of the psychologist's own, especially of reading into lower minds what is true of higher. James Mark Baldwin, *Dictionary of Philosophy and Psychology*, (General Books, 2010. Originally published by MacMillan, 1901) vol. 2, p. 382. See also "A Danger to Be Avoided Known as the 'Psychologist's Fallacy,'" *British Journal of Psychology* 21 (1931): p. 243. See also William James, *Principles of Psychology* volume I. chapter vii. p. 196, 1890.

19. Atul Gawande, "The Cancer-Cluster Myth," *New Yorker*, February 8, 1999.

20. Peter Brugger, "From Haunted Brain to Haunted Science: A Cognitive Neuroscience View of Paranormal and Pseudoscientific Thought," in *Hauntings and Poltergeists: Multidisciplinary Perspectives*, edited by J. Houran and R. Lange (Jefferson, N.C.: McFarland, 2007).

CHAPTER 10

1. R. L. Solso, *Cognitive Psychology*, 6th ed. (Boston: Allyn & Bacon, 2001).

2. D. M. Eagleman, "Visual Illusions and Neurobiology," *Nature Reviews Neuroscience* 2, no. 12 (2001): pp. 920–926. See also Gregory Richard, "Knowledge in Perception and Illusion," *Philosophical Transactions of the Royal Society of London, Series B* 352 (1997): pp. 1121–1128.

3. D. Purves, R. B. Lotto, and S. Nundy, "Why We See What We Do," *American Scientist* 90, no. 3 (2002): pp. 236–242.

4. John M. Kennedy, *A Psychology of Picture Perception* (San Francisco: Jossey-Bass Publishers, 1974).

5. "Definition of Cognitive Distortions," University of Wisconsin Counseling Services; uwec.edu. See also Anand Dhillon, "Cognitive Distortions," ananddhillon.com. http://www.ananddhillon.com/blog/2008/06/cognitive-distortions/. Retrieved July 9, 2010. Also T. Ward, S. M. Hudson, and W. L. Marshall, (1995) for a definition of cognitive distortions, "Cognitive distortions and affective deficits in sex offenders: A cognitive deconstructionist interpretation," *Sexual Abuse: A Journal of Research and Treatment*, 7, pp. 67–83.

6. D. D. Burns, *Feeling Good: The New Mood Therapy*, revised and updated (New York: Harper, 1999).

7. T. Edward Damer. *Attacking Faulty Reasoning: A Practical Guide to Fallacy-Free Arguments*, 5th ed. (Belmont, Calif.: Wadsworth, 2005). See also Douglas N. Walton, *Informal Logic: A Handbook for Critical Argumentation* (Cambridge, U.K.: Cambridge University Press, 1989).

8. Hasty generalization: See Nizkor Project, www.nizkor.com/hasty-generalization.

9. Slothful induction: Stephen F. Barker, *The Elements of Logic*, 6th ed. (New York: McGraw-Hill, 2002). See also www.afterall.net/illogic for a discussion of slothful induction and ad hoc escapism.

10. John Lindow, *Norse Mythology: A Guide to Gods, Heroes, Rituals, and Beliefs* (Oxford, U.K.: Oxford University Press, 2002).

11. Misleading vividness: Nizkor Project, www.nizkorproject.org/misleading vividness.

12. Amos Tversky and Daniel Kahneman, "Availability: A Heuristic for Judging Frequency and Probability," *Cognitive Psychology* 5 (1973): pp. 207–232.

13. Mario Rizzo and Glen Whitman, "The Camel's Nose Is in the Tent: Rules, Theories and Slippery Slopes," *UCLA Law Review* 51, no. 2 (2003): pp. 539–559.

14. Whit Gibbons, "The Legend of the Boiling Frog Is Just a Legend," *Ecoviews*, November 18, 2002.

15. Nunberg, *Going Nucular: Language, Politics, and Culture in Confrontational Times* (New York: Public Affairs, 2004), p. 118.

16. Special pleading: See Nizkor Project, www.nizkor.com/specialpleading.

17. William Safire, "Make a Mountain Out of a Molehill," On Language, *New York Times*, June 14, 1987.

18. Albert Ellis, *Rational Emotive Behavior Therapy: It Works for Me—It Can Work for You* (Amherst, N.Y.: Prometheus, 2004). See also www.albertellis institute.org.

19. Albert Ellis, *Overcoming Destructive Beliefs, Feelings, and Behaviors: New Directions for Rational Emotive Behavior Therapy* (Amherst, N.Y.: Prometheus, 2001).

20. Albert Ellis, "Early Theories and Practices of Rational Emotive Behavior Theory and How They Have Been Augmented and Revised during the Last Three Decades," *Journal of Rational-Emotive & Cognitive-Behavior Therapy* 21, no. 3/4 (2003).

21. Labeling: see www.mental-health-today.com. See also Burns, *Feeling Good*. Harper, 1999.

22. E. J. Langer, "The Illusion of Control," *Journal of Personality and Social Psychology* 32, no. 2 (1975): pp. 311–328. See also E. J. Langer and J. Roth, "Heads I Win, Tails It's Chance: The Illusion of Control as a Function of the Sequence of Outcomes in a Purely Chance Task," *Journal of Personality and Social Psychology* 32, no. 6 (1975): pp. 951–955; Herbert M. Jenkins and William C. Ward, *Judgment of Contingency between Responses and Outcomes*, Psychological Monographs, no. 79 (Washington, D.C.: American Psychological Association, 1965); and L. G. Allan and Herbert M. Jenkins, "The Judgment of Contingency and the Nature of the Response Alternatives," *Canadian Journal of Psychology* 34 (1980): pp. 1–11.

23. M. Fenton-O'Creevy, N. Nicholson, E. Soane, and P. Willman, *Traders—Risks, Decisions, and Management in Financial Markets* (Oxford, U.K.: Oxford University Press, 2005). See also M. Fenton-O'Creevy, N. Nicholson, E. Soane, and P. Willman, "Trading on Illusions: Unrealistic Perceptions of Control and Trading Performance," *Journal of Occupational and Organisational Psychology* 76 (2003): pp. 53–68.

24. Illusory correlation: Brett Pelham, *Conducting Research in Psychology* (Belmont, Calif.: Wadsworth Publishing, 2006). See also L. J. Chapman and

J. P. Chapman, "Genesis of Popular but Erroneous Psychodiagnostic Observations," *Journal of Abnormal Psychology* 72 (1967): pp. 193–204. "Illusory correlation and the maintenance of stereotypic beliefs" (David Hamilton and Terrence Rose, *Journal of Personality and Social Psychology* Volume 39, Issue 5, November 1980 pp. 832–845) retrieved from Wikipedia on June 14, 2010.

25. D. A. Redelmeier and Amos Tversky, "On the Belief that Arthritis Pain Is Related to the Weather," *Proceedings of the National Academy of Science USA* 93, no. 7 (1996).

26. T. Gilovich, R. Vallone, and A. Tversky, "The Hot Hand in Basketball: On the Misperception of Random Sequences," *Cognitive Psychology* 17 (1985): pp. 295–314.

27. E. Pronin, J. Kruger, K. Savitsky, and L. Ross, "You Don't Know Me, but I Know You: The Illusion of Asymmetric Insight," *Journal of Personality & Social Psychology* 81, no. 4 (2001): pp. 639–656.

28. Introspection illusion: Timothy D. Wilson and Elizabeth W. Dunn, "Self-Knowledge: Its Limits, Value, and Potential for Improvement," *Annual Review of Psychology* 55 (2004): p. 507. See also Emily Pronin, "The Introspection Illusion," in Mark P. Zanna, *Advances in Experimental Social Psychology*, Vol. 41, (London: Academic Press, 2009), pp. 1–67.

29. Ernst Fehr and Jean-Robert Tyran, "Does Money Illusion Matter?" *American Economic Review* 91, no. 5 (2001): pp. 1239–1262.

CHAPTER 11

1. Daniel Kahneman and Amos Tversky, "Prospect Theory: An Analysis of Decision under Risk," *Econometrica* 47 (1979): pp. 263–291. See also I. Erev, E. Ert, and E. Yechiam, "Loss Aversion, Diminishing Sensitivity, and the Effect of Experience on Repeated Decisions," *Journal of Behavioral Decision Making* 21 (2008): pp. 575–597; and D. Kahneman, J. L. Knetsch, and R. H. Thaler, "Experimental Tests of the Endowment Effect and the Coase Theorem," *Journal of Political Economy* 98, no. 6 (1990): pp. 1325–1348.

2. Interviews on successful trading: Robert Koppel and Howard Abell, *The Inner Game of Trading* (New York: McGraw-Hill, 1997), pp. 77–86. See also comments by Gene Agatstein in Robert Koppel, *The Tao of Trading* (Chicago: Dearborn Financial Publishing, 1998), p. 56.

3. Jack Schwager, *The New Market Wizards* (New York: HarperBusiness, 1992), p. 468.

4. Steve Cohen interview: "What's Eating Steve Cohen?" *Vanity Fair*, July 2010.

5. Koppel, *Tao of Trading*, p. 50. I asked veteran foreign currency trader Yra Harris, who has traded on the exchange floor and has run his own shop over a 30-year career, what has been the greatest psychological challenge for him and how he deals with a series of losing trades or an extended period of drawdown. He said,

The greatest challenge for me has been not to take a trade in too early. I do a great amount of fundamental analysis and then overlay it with technicals to measure the best entry point for the lowest amount of risk. The problem becomes when to exit a trade that has been right from the start. The discipline of loss taking has never been a problem for me, but the adding to a winner has always been my weakness. When I am in a period of losing trades, I recheck my analysis to see where I have missed something. I am a big believer in global money flows, so if the market is at a turning point, I know I need to recalibrate my thinking. The markets are dynamic in nature, and the underlying themes are always in flux; therefore I need to be ever adjusting. The reason I don't like economic models is that they are too static—they may eventually be correct, but as a trader I will be broke. A serious setback has never bothered me as long as I stayed disciplined to my initial risk levels and did not pull my stops. I had a British pound/deutsche mark trade that blew up on me, but because I was true to my stops, it was the best loss I ever took. Had I hesitated, it might have been a major blow to my capital base and caused me to rethink my life in this business. But I stress that I am a very disciplined risk taker and don't put myself at career risk—small losses.

Harris added,

To be a successful trader, you have to tell yourself that you are wrong on a regular basis. Even after preparing daily and being patient to wait for my levels of entry, the trade still may not be right. As I teach new traders, you have to park your ego and let the market determine if you are correct. Most people in the world cannot admit to being wrong. I have to do it several times a day.

Another trader whom I interviewed, whom I had known as a colleague on the trading floor and who now runs an advisory service that concentrates on equities and Treasury bonds for hedge funds and professional traders, said,

I've found over the years that the best remedy for a cold streak is to take a break. For me it was sailing competitively. The concentration required to pick wind shifts, anticipate, react, and plan strategy was a total meditation that released my mind from all other thoughts. This allowed me to go back to trading with a fresh, uncluttered mind. After all, trading is just another competition. Winning is contagious, and the repetitive discipline to keep doing the right things begets more winning over time.

6. Dan Galai and Orly Sade, "The 'Ostrich Effect' and the Relationship between the Liquidity and the Yields of Financial Assets," *Journal of Business* 79, no. 5. See also Jason Zweig, "Should You Fear the Ostrich Effect?" *Wall Street Journal*, September 13, 2008.

7. G. Schraw, T. Wadkins, and L. Olafson, "Doing the Things We Do: A Grounded Theory of Academic Procrastination," *Journal of Educational Psychology* 99, no. 1 (2007): pp. 12–25.

8. Silverman interview: Koppel and Abell, *Inner Game*, pp. 127–141.

9. J. S. Lerner and L. Z. Tiedens, "Portrait of the Angry Decision Maker: How Appraisal Tendencies Shape Anger's Influence on Cognition," *Journal of Behavioral Decision Making* 19 (2006): pp. 115–137. See also "Anger Fuels Better Decisions," *Live Science*, July 2007.

10. Robert Koppel, *The Intuitive Trader* (New York: Wiley, 1996), pp. 6–8. See also Winston King, *Zen and the Way of the Sword: Arming the Samurai Psyche* (New York: Oxford, 1990).

11. Miyamoto Musashi, *The Book of Five Rings: A Classic Text on the Japanese Way of the Sword*, trans. Thomas Cleary (Boston: Shambhala Publications, 2005).

12. D. T. Suzuki, *Zen and Japanese Culture* (Princeton, N.J.: Princeton University Press, 1959).

13. The list of physical and psychological responses to loss has been compiled on the basis of what traders, investors, and clients have reported over the years as well as my own responses to loss. There have been many studies that have found similar results. See also Koppel, *The Intuitive Trader*, pp. 203–206 for ways to enhance emotional states.

14. The CME Web site offers several videos of presentations given by Shull on the psychology of trading; www.cme.com. See also her Web site, www.traderpsyches.com.

15. In e-mail and telephone interviews, I asked Shull to explain, from her perspective, how investors and traders can improve their performance based on current neuroeconomic research. She said,

> In many ways, neuroeconomics alone may not do it—at least not quite yet. Neuroeconomics tends to have a very cognitive bent to it even as it acknowledges that we need emotion to make a decision. By combining neuroeconomics with the work coming out of the disciplines of social and affective neuroscience, we start to get a much better picture of how to work with our brains as it appears they have been "designed." I have no doubt whatsoever that investors can become less "irrational," but I fully believe it is through what currently are still counterintuitive approaches of using emotion. In fact, there was a study in 2007, Seo and Barrett, where they showed that the investors who were most emotional but knew it were the most successful. Through their awareness of their emotions they implicitly gained an awareness of their biases and then were much better able to make a fully informed choice.

I also asked Shull, given the current research in neuroscience, what investors can do to make better decisions, once they are aware of the influence of irrational factors. She said,

Frankly, I think the supposition that our reflective brain is overtaken by our reactive brain is the old way to look at it. Neuroscience is proving beyond a shadow of a doubt how critical emotions, which are most associated with our so-called reactive brains, are to everything. Some of the latest research even shows that our visual cortices will not function properly if they are not correctly infused with emotional neural networks. Therefore, the emerging secret is to shift our whole idea of the value of the "reactive" brain. We need to learn to interpret the messages first as information. Everyone forgets that a feeling and an action are actually two separate psychological events. We keep attempting to revert to thinking harder, better, or smarter as a way to overpower the emotional information when the pay dirt, as least to me, is clearly in a whole new way to think about, understand, analyze, and use emotional information and energy in conjunction with intellectual and cognitive capacities.

CHAPTER 12

1. Howard Abell, *Risk Reward: The Art and Science of Successful Trading* (Chicago: Dearborn Financial Publishing, 1998). See also the foreword by Jeffrey Silverman.
2. Amos Tversky and Daniel Kahneman, "Judgment under Uncertainty: Heuristics and Biases," *Science* 185, no. 4157 (1974): pp. 1124–1131.
3. Paul Slovic, Baruch Fischhoff, and Sarah Lichtenstein, "Why Study Risk Perception?" *Risk Analysis* 2, no. 2 (1982): pp. 83–93.
4. Paul Slovic, Melissa Finucane, Ellen Peters, and Donald G. MacGregor, "The Affect Heuristic," in *Heuristics and Biases: The Psychology of Intuitive Judgment*, ed. Thomas Gilovich, Dale Griffin, and Daniel Kahneman (New York: Cambridge University Press, 2002), pp. 397–420.
5. David Brooks, "Drilling for Certainty," *New York Times*, May 27, 2010.
6. George Segal interview: I interviewed George, who was a friend and a colleague, on multiple occasions. See also Robert Koppel and Howard Abell, *The Inner Game of Trading* (New York: McGraw-Hill, 1997), pp. 79–83.
7. High-frequency trading: The *New York Times* published a series of articles on this subject, updated May 14, 2010. See also Graham Bowley's article, "Origin of Wall Street's Plunge Continues to Elude Officials," *New York Times*, May 7, 2010. Richard Ketchum's quote: "High Frequency Trading." *New York Times*, May 8, 2010. Greenspan quote: *New York Times*, April 4, 2010, in an op-ed column by Michael J. Burry, "I Saw the Crisis Coming. Why Didn't the Fed?" The Greenspan anecdote is found in the same article.
8. The TABB Group is a financial markets research and strategic advisory firm focused on capital markets. Founded in 2003 and based on the methodology of first-person knowledge, the advisory firm analyzes and quantifies the investing value chain: the fiduciary, investment manager, broker, exchange, and custodian, along with the operations that support them.
9. Quotational risk: According to the gospel of value investing, risk is generally thought to fall into distinct categories. The first is the risk of permanent

capital loss, which occurs when the fundamentals underlying a company's intrinsic value are initially assessed too optimistically or deteriorate after the investment is made. Value investors focus on this first category of risk, looking carefully at the fundamentals of the companies in which they invest. The second general category is the risk of temporary capital loss due to a quotational decline in stock price that is not materially indicative of a deterioration of company fundamentals. This kind of investment illiquidity, or quotational risk, can be very difficult for a deep value investor to guard against, as it has more to do with the financial condition of other shareholders than with the company itself.

10. Larry Carr interview: Abell, *Risk Reward*, p. 136.
11. Malcolm Gladwell, *Blink: The Power of Thinking without Thinking* (New York: Little, Brown and Co., 2005), p. 14.
12. Toby Crabel interview: Abell, *Risk Reward*, pp. 77–79.
13. Michael Lewis, *The Big Short: Inside the Doomsday Machine* (New York: Norton, 2010), p. 256. See also p. 262.

CHAPTER 13

1. Philip Goldberg, *The Intuitive Edge* (Los Angeles: Tarcher, 1983). Reprinted in 2006, it is available online at backinprint.com. Goldberg explains how to complement analytical thinking with the power of hunches and gut feelings.
2. The synoptic philosophical history of intuition comes from *Encyclopedia Britannica* and *Columbia Encyclopedia* online.
3. Mark Douglas, *The Disciplined Trader* (New York: New York Institute of Finance, 1990).
4. Jason Zweig, *Your Money and Your Brain* (New York: Simon & Schuster, 2007), pp. 9–10.
5. Saliba quotation: See Robert Koppel, *The Intuitive Trader* (New York: Wiley, 1996), preface. See also Jack D. Schwager, *Market Wizards* (New York: Collins, 1993), pp. 387–407.
6. Gary Klein et al., *Decision Making in Action: Models and Methods* (Norwood, N.J.: Ablex Publishing Co., 1993). See also Klein, *Sources of Power: How People Make Decisions* (Cambridge, Mass.: MIT Press, 1999) and *The Power of Intuition: How to Use Your Gut Feelings to Make Better Decisions at Work* (New York: Currency, 2004).
7. Gary Klein et al., "Use of a Prediction Paradigm to Evaluate Proficient Decision Making," *American Journal of Psychology* 102, no. 3 (Autumn 1989): pp. 321–331.
8. There are two additional perspectives on intuition that are of interest. The first is from Robin Mesch:

> I think intuition plays an indispensible role in trading—I see intuition as more necessary in the early part of a trade, i.e., market selection, and less important or useful in the latter part of a trade, such as timing of entry and exit or trade management. These lat-

ter elements of a trading plan are best based on quantifiable performance demands at given benchmarks that inform us regarding the structural integrity of the trade. I have built many indicators that objectify the market's order flows on short- and long-term time horizons. I always start from my initial ranking system, which can scan stocks for opportunities quite quickly. But while I rely on my objective criteria to eliminate stocks, I rely on my subjective hierarchy of criteria to ultimately select my stocks. My technical indicators weed out markets that are not offering opportunities. But when it comes down to determining the best markets that offer the greatest opportunities—i.e., market selection—my final analysis is subjective. Once in the trade, objective criteria reenter as to what type of quantifiable order flows need to show up to support and confirm my decision; subjectivity is less useful and opens the door for reactivity rather than an analytical response.

I also asked Berkeley neuroeconomist Ming Hsu based on his research, and the current state of knowledge in the field, what was the role of intuition in financial decisions. He said,

I think here much depends on one's definition of intuition. If you're restricting it to "finely honed inferential capability" of seasoned investors, I think it's clear that it plays a big part in their investment behavior. The same would go for chess grandmasters and other types of experts. They take less time to process the same information and make better decisions with that information than nonexperts. Of course, there is something special about the people who are able to become grandmasters, which is still mysterious.

9. Daniel Kahneman interview: Conversations with History, Institute of International Studies, University of California Berkeley, February 7, 2007.
10. Daniel Gilbert, "The Weight at the Plate," *New York Times*, August 4, 2010.
11. Antonio Damasio, "The Somatic Marker Hypothesis and the Possible Functions of the Prefrontal Cortex," *Philosophical Transactions of the Royal Society of London, Series B* 351 (1996): p. 1413. See also Sandra Blakeslee, "In Work on Intuition Gut Feelings Are Traced to Source: The Brain," March 4, 1997 and "Tracing the Brain's Pathways for Linking Emotion and Reason," December 6, 1994 in the *New York Times*.
12. Antonio Damasio, *Descartes' Error: Emotion, Reason, and the Human Brain* (New York: Penguin, 2005).
13. Antonio Damasio, *The Feeling of What Happens: Body and Emotion in the Making of Consciousness* (New York: Mariner, 2000).
14. Antonio Damasio, *Looking for Spinoza: Joy, Sorrow, and the Feeling Brain* (New York: Mariner, 2003).
15. Somatic markers hypothesis: A. R. Damasio, D. Tranel, and H. Damasio, "Somatic Markers and the Guidance of Behaviour: Theory and Preliminary

Testing," in *Frontal Lobe Function and Dysfunction*, ed. H. S. Levin, H. M. Eisenberg, and A. L. Benton (New York: Oxford University Press, 1991), pp. 217–229. See also E. T. Rolls, "Consciousness in Neural Networks," *Neural Networks* 10 (1997): pp. 1227–1240.

16. Klein, *Power of Intuition*, pp. 11–35. See also the preface.
17. Ibid., p. 6.
18. Interview with Antoine Bruguier via e-mail and telephone in 2010. Bruguier, a researcher at Caltech, published a paper with Caltech professors Peter Bossaerts and Steve Quartz, "Exploring the Nature of Trader Intuition," No. 10-02 in the Swiss Finance Institute's research paper series. After several conversations by phone with Bruguier, I asked him to elaborate on certain points raised in the paper. My questions and his answers follow:

In light of "Exploring the Nature of Trader Intuition," what do you feel are the practical implications for traders and financial firms that manage trader risk?

If the results of this paper are confirmed, they would have very important implications for traders. They are a reminder that trading is essentially a social activity and that, while it may be possible one day to model the behavior of the markets, the current simple models are not sufficient to capture all the effects. Please note that we are not saying that all mathematical models are junk, just that they have to be taken as approximate. Of course, these tests might be used for recruitment methods, as a part of a battery of other tests. As to the question whether one can improve his or her ToM abilities, this remains to be seen. I think it is likely that it is possible, but that may be overspecialization toward these tests as opposed to broad ToM. My inclination is to believe that ToM can be improved, because so many other human faculties can improve with training. I don't have any data on this, though, so please note that so many hypotheses and models break down when tested with real-life data. But that is essentially my point: one should not get carried away by elegant mathematical descriptions; they have to be tested when humans are in the mix.

What are the practical implications of your work in theory of mind for individual investors and financial firms?

For individual investors, I would be cautious about the results. They certainly do not mean that following hunches is a winning strategy. There are some mathematical impossibilities and human biases that can be very misleading. For financial firms, I want to be careful (because there are things I don't understand about what they do). It seems to me that many approaches are based on assumptions (Gaussian error distributions, etc.) that may or may not hold. I think modeling in that case would be much more experimentally driven even if it means giving up on the mathematical elegance. The results of the papers are certainly not as elegant as they could be, but they have been tested with experiments. There is also one aspect that you didn't ask me about: regulations. Humans are not always rational and do not always make the best decisions for themselves. This is likely to be the case in financial markets too.

In your opinion, how can sophisticated investors benefit from the current research in neuroeconomics?

I think one possible benefit is for the creation of new models. It seems to me that markets are often approached as a physical system whose laws have to be discovered, a bit like one would try to discover the laws of planetary motion. I would probably try to approach as a chess game, where one understands that the opponent's behavior depends on your own behavior (also, markets are not necessarily zero-sum games). I know some of my answers are vague, but I don't want to stretch the results toward something that is not supported by the data.

19. Interview with Denise Shull via e-mail over several months and in Chicago at the Ritz-Carlton.
20. Klein, "Where Do Our Hunches Come From?" *Power of Intuition*, pp. 20–35.
21. Ibid., p. 35.

CHAPTER 14

1. Robert Koppel, *Bulls, Bears, and Millionaires: War Stories of the Trading Life* (Chicago: Dearborn Financial Publishing, 1997). I've also had my own ups and downs in the market, which I wrote about in Chapter 1 of that book, "A Personal Tale," pp. 1–8. Also see pp. 8–16. Pat Arbor: pp. 4–5.
2. Sandner interview: Ibid., Chapter 2. See also Robert Koppel and Howard Abell, *The Inner Game of Trading* (New York: McGraw-Hill, 1997), pp. 87–106.
3. Ibid., p. 71.
4. Lillian Comas-Diaz et al., *The Road to Resilience*, American Psychological Association Practice Directorate publication; www.apa.org, retrieved July 6, 2010.
5. Martin Seligman and Mihaly Csikszentmihalyi, "Positive Psychology: An Introduction," *American Psychologist 55*, no. 1 (2000): pp. 5–14.
6. Sydney Smith, ed., *The Human Mind Revisited: Essays in Honor of Karl A. Menninger* (New York: International Universities Press, 1978).
7. American Psychological Association. *Psychological Resilience Questionnaire*; www.apa.org, retrieved July 18, 2010.
8. Seligman and Csikszentmihalyi, "Positive Psychology: An Introduction," pp. 6–8.
9. Positive Psychology: Current researchers in positive psychology include Martin Seligman, Ed Diener, Mihaly Csikszentmihalyi, Christopher Peter-

son, Carol Dweck, Barbara Fredrickson, Sonja Lyubomirsky, Kennon Shel-
don, Jonathan Haidt, Shelley Taylor, C. R. Snyder, Robert Biswas-Diener,
Donald Clifton, Albert Bandura, Charles S. Carver, Michael F. Scheier, and
Ilona Boniwel.

10. Positive psychology research studies published as Research Summaries by
the University of Pennsylvania's Positive Psychology Center, 2010.

11. Profile of and interview with Martin Seligman: Stacy Burling, "The Power of
a Positive Thinker, *Philadelphia Inquirer*, May 30, 2010.

12. Seligman and trading: Robert Koppel, *The Intuitive Trader* (New York: Wiley, 1996), pp. 212–213.

13. Mihaly Csikszentmihalyi, *Flow: The Psychology of Optimal Experience*
(New York: Harper & Row, 1990). Seligman has described Csikszentmihalyi as the world's leading researcher in the field of positive psychology.
He says that Csikszentmihalyi's work on improving lives has been important in his own effort to encourage psychologists to focus on building human strengths. "He is the brains behind positive psychology, and I am the
voice," said Seligman. Csikszentmihalyi is working with Seligman to engage
young psychologists to focus on prevention and building human strength.
Csikszentmihalyi is also a leading researcher on creativity. He explored the
lives of more than 90 of the world's most creative people, such as scientist
Jonas Salk, to find out how creativity has been a force in their lives. He's
discovered that some highly creative people find satisfaction by inventing
careers for themselves, like a scientist who creates a new field of study. These
findings are described in his book *Creativity: Flow and the Psychology of
Discovery and Invention* (New York: HarperCollins, 1996).

CHAPTER 15

1. Technical analysts identify price patterns and trends and attempt to exploit
them. While they employ various tools, the study of price charts is the primary one. Technicians search for patterns, such as head and shoulders, double tops and bottoms, reversal patterns, flags, channels, spikes, and gaps.

2. Jon Elster, *Sour Grapes: Studies in the Subversion of Rationality* (Cambridge, U.K.: Cambridge University Press, 1983), p. 123.

3. Leon Festinger, *A Theory of Cognitive Dissonance* (Stanford, Calif.: Stanford University Press, 1957).

4. Lee Lowenfish, *Branch Rickey: Baseball's Ferocious Gentleman* (Lincoln:
University of Nebraska Press, 2009).

5. P. Salovey and D. Grewal, "The Science of Emotional Intelligence," *Current
Directions in Psychological Science* 14, no. 6 (2005). For emotional intelligence, see also the Wikipedia article on this topic.

6. Adriaan de Groot and Fernand Gobet, *Perception and Memory in Chess:
Heuristics of the Professional Eye* (Assen, Netherlands: Van Gorcum,
1996).

7. Fernand Gobet, Alex de Voogt, and Jean Retschitzki, *Moves in Mind: The
Psychology of Board Games* (Hove, U.K.: Psychology Press, 2004).

8. Dennis Holding, *The Psychology of Chess Skill* (Hillsdale, N.J.: Erlbaum, 1985).

9 Pertti Saariluoma, *Chess Players' Thinking: A Cognitive Psychological Approach* (London: Routledge, 1995).

10. G. Campitelli, F. Gobet, and A. Parker, "Structure and Stimulus Familiarity: A Study of Memory in Chess-Players with Functional Magnetic Resonance Imaging," *Spanish Journal of Psychology* 8, no. 2 (2005): pp. 238–245. A grandmaster and an international chess master were compared with a group of novices in a memory task involving both chess and nonchess stimuli, varying the structure and familiarity of the stimuli, while functional magnetic resonance images were acquired. The pattern of brain activity in the masters was different from that in the novices. The two masters showed no differences in brain activity when different degrees of structure and familiarity were compared; however, novices did show differences in brain activity in such contrasts. The most important differences were found in the contrast of stimulus familiarity with chess positions. In this contrast, there was extended brain activity in bilateral frontal areas, such as the anterior cingulate and the superior, middle, and inferior frontal gyri; furthermore, posterior areas, such as the posterior cingulate and cerebellum, showed great bilateral activation. These results strengthen the hypothesis that when performing a domain-specific task, experts activate different brain systems from those activated by novices. The use of the experts-versus-novices paradigm in brain imaging contributes to the search for brain systems involved in cognitive processes.

11. In the same interview, Mesch also said,

> I don't think you can avoid getting caught in a Black Swan Event. The best you can do under those circumstances is recognize these moments for what they are as soon as possible and act without hesitation or hope. Overall, I like to know on the front side, while building my entry and exit scenario for the trade, where the structural out point would be that would actually tell me that the trade idea is wrong. Then I create the trade entry in accordance with proper risk/reward parameters in line with the company's risk tolerance. Many traders use price and not structure as the starting point for setting risk, and I think that brings a lot of emotion into the trade when it goes against them because it creates doubt and second-guessing about whether they really need to exit their trade for any other reason beyond risk/reward.

12. Robert Koppel, *Bulls, Bears and Millionaires: War Stories of the Trading Life* (Chicago: Dearborn Financial Publishing, 1997), pp. 68–74. See also pp. 129–138.

13. In the same interview, I asked Mesch what has been her greatest psychological hurdle. She said,

One of my biggest psychological hurdles to overcome was my mis-understanding that the market could be forced to fit my personal clock speed rather than shift to connect more directly to market time. My mistake was coming into the market as a long-term trader and exiting like a short-term trader or vice versa; or shortening my time frame in order to gain more trader control through external controls such as ever-tighter stops or, on the flip side, lengthening my time frame and stops to avoid being wrong. We already try to impose false time constraints on order flow by organizing the market into artificial constructs such as day, week, month, etc., versus or-ganizing the market according to its natural flow of market time—a market time that has an organizing principle of order flow and time cycles that are bracketed by the beginning and end of the auction process that moves toward consensus. Overcoming this hurdle has definitely been a blend of both discovering and clarifying my per-sonal internal clock speed, which is more of an investment rhythm, and it compels me to organize auctions that are moving at that tempo. I got into the industry because I've always been attracted to understanding and unlocking systems and patterns. Perhaps that's why the bulk of my career has been in the field of building systems, creating methods for understanding the markets, and supporting and coaching traders. In my current capacity, I develop portfolios for money managers and trading firms. I'm using my proprietary tools, systems, and methodology for investing rather than trading, which is more congruent with my personal trading clock and is far more gratifying.

14. David Brooks, "History for Dollars," *New York Times*, June 7, 2010. In the column, Brooks wrote,

Technical knowledge stops at the outer edge. If you spend your life riding the links of the Internet, you probably won't get too far into The Big Shaggy either, because the fast, effortless prose of blogging (and journalism) lacks the heft to get you deep below. But over the centuries, there have been rare and strange people who possessed the skill of taking the upheavals of thought that emanate from The Big Shaggy and representing them in the form of story, mu-sic, myth, painting, liturgy, architecture, sculpture, landscape and speech. These men and women developed languages that help us understand these yearnings and also educate and mold them. They left rich veins of emotional knowledge that are the subjects of the humanities. It's probably dangerous to enter exclusively into this realm and risk being caught in a cloister, removed from the market and its accountability. But doesn't it make sense to spend some time in the company of these languages—learning to feel different emotions, rehearsing different passions, experiencing different sacred rituals and learning to see in different ways? Few of us are hewers of wood. We navigate social environments. If you're dumb about The Big Shaggy, you'll probably get eaten by it."

For Further Reading

Akerlof, George A., and Robert J. Shiller. *Animal Spirits: How Human Psychology Drives the Economy, and Why It Matters for Global Capitalism*. Princeton, N.J.: Princeton University Press, 2009.

Amen, Daniel G. *Change Your Brain, Change Your Life*. New York: Three Rivers Press, 1998.

Ariely, Dan. *Predictably Irrational: The Hidden Forces That Shape Our Decisions*. New York: Harper, 2008.

Ariely, Dan. *The Upside of Irrationality: The Unexpected Benefits of Defying Logic at Work and at Home*. New York: Harper, 2010.

Bear, Mark F., Barry W. Connors, and Michael A. Paradiso. *Neuroscience: Exploring the Brain*. Baltimore, Md.: Lippincott Williams and Wilkins, 2006.

Benartzi, Shlomo, and Richard H. Thaler. "Heuristics and Biases in Retirement Savings Behavior." *Journal of Economic Perspectives* 21, no. 3 (2007): pp. 81–104.

Berns, Gregory. *Iconoclast: A Neuroscientist Reveals How to Think Differently*. Boston: Harvard Business Press, 2010.

Bernstein, Peter L. *Against the Gods: The Remarkable Story of Risk*. New York: Wiley, 1996.

Bossaerts, Peter, Kerstin Preuschoff, and Ming Hsu. "The Neurobiological Foundations of Valuation in Human Decision Making under Uncertainty." In *Neuroeconomics: Decision Making and the Brain*, edited by Paul Glimcher, Colin Camerer, Ernst Fehr, and Russell Poldrack. Amsterdam: Elsevier, 2008.

Camerer, Colin, and Richard H. Thaler. "Anomalies: Ultimatums, Dictators and Manners." *Journal of Economic Perspectives* 9, no. 2 (1995): pp. 209–219.

Camerer, Colin, George Loewenstein, and Matthew Rabin. *Advances in Behavioral Economics*. Princeton, N.J.: Princeton University Press, 2003.

Carter, Rita. *Mapping the Mind*. Berkeley: University of California Press, 1999.

Cootner, Paul H. *The Random Character of Stock Market Prices*. Cambridge, Mass.: MIT Press, 1964.

Damasio, Antonio. *The Feeling of What Happens: Body and Emotion in the Making of Consciousness*. New York: Mariner, 2000.

Damasio, Antonio. *Looking for Spinoza: Joy, Sorrow, and the Feeling Brain.* New York: Mariner, 2003.

Damasio, Antonio. *Descartes' Error: Emotion, Reason, and the Human Brain.* New York: Penguin, 1994.

Douglas, Mark. *The Disciplined Trader.* New York: New York Institute of Finance, 1990.

Fredrickson, B. L., and D. Kahneman. "Duration Neglect in Retrospective Evaluations of Affective Episodes." *Journal of Personality and Social Psychology* 65 (1993): pp. 45–55.

Gazzaniga, Michael S., Richard B. Ivry, and George R. Mangun. *Cognitive Neuroscience: The Biology of the Mind.* New York: Norton, 2008.

Gilovich, Thomas. *How We Know What Isn't So: The Fallibility of Human Reason in Everyday Life.* New York: The Free Press, 1993.

Gladwell, Malcolm. *The Tipping Point: How Little Things Can Make a Big Difference.* Boston: Back Bay Books, 2000.

Gladwell, Malcolm. *Blink: The Power of Thinking without Thinking.* New York: Little, Brown and Co., 2005.

Gladwell, Malcolm. *Outliers: The Story of Success.* New York: Little Brown, 2008.

Glimcher, Paul W. *Decisions, Uncertainty, and the Brain: The Science of Neuroeconomics.* Cambridge, Mass.: MIT Press, 2003.

Glimcher, P. W., and N. Kanwisher. "Cognitive Neuroscience Editorial Overview." *Current Opinion in Neurobiology* 16 (2006): pp. 127–129.

Glimcher, P. W., M. C. Dorris, and H. M. Bayer. "Physiological Utility Theory and the Neuroeconomics of Choice." *Games and Economic Behavior* 52 (2005): pp. 213–256.

Glimcher, Paul W., Colin Camerer, Russell Alan Poldrack, and Ernst Fehr. *Neuroeconomics: Decision Making and the Brain.* New York: Academic Press, 2008.

Graham, Benjamin. *The Intelligent Investor: A Book of Practical Counsel,* 4th rev. ed. New York: Harper & Row, 1985.

Graham, Benjamin, and David L. Dodd. *Security Analysis,* 6th ed. Foreword by Warren Buffett. New York: McGraw-Hill, 2008.

Hsu, Ming, Meghana Bhatt, Ralph Adolphs, Daniel Tranel, and Colin Camerer. "Neural Systems Responding to Degrees of Uncertainty in Human Decision Making." *Science* 310 (2005): pp. 1624–1625.

Kahneman, D. *Attention and Effort.* Englewood Cliffs, N.J.: Prentice-Hall, 1973.

Kahneman, D. "A Perspective on Judgment and Choice: Mapping Bounded Rationality." *American Psychologist* 58 (2003): pp. 697–720.

Kahneman, D., and D. Lovallo. "Timid Choices and Bold Forecasts: A Cognitive Perspective on Risk-Taking." *Management Science* 39 (1993): pp. 17–31.

Kahneman, D., and A. Tversky. "Subjective Probability: A Judgment of Representativeness." *Cognitive Psychology* 3 (1972): pp. 430–454.

Kahneman, D., and A. Tversky. "On the Psychology of Prediction." *Psychological Review* 80 (1973): pp. 237–251.

Kahneman, D., and A. Tversky. "Prospect Theory: An Analysis of Decision under Risk." *Econometrica* 47 (1979): pp. 313–327.

Kahneman, D., and A. Tversky. "Choices, Values and Frames." *American Psychologist* 39 (1984): 341–350.

Kahneman, D., and A. Tversky. "On the Reality of Cognitive Illusions." *Psychological Review* 103 (1996): pp. 582–591.

Kahneman, D., and A. Tversky (eds.). *Choices, Values and Frames*. New York: Cambridge University Press, 2000.

Kahneman, D., E. Diener, and N. Schwarz (eds.). *Well-Being: The Foundations of Hedonic Psychology*. New York: Russell Sage Foundation, 1999.

Kahneman, D., J. L. Knetsch, and R. H. Thaler. "Experimental Tests of the Endowment Effect and the Coase Theorem." *Journal of Political Economy* 98, no. 6 (1990): pp. 1325–1348.

Kahneman, D., P. Slovic, and A. Tversky. *Judgment under Uncertainty: Heuristics and Biases*. New York: Cambridge University Press, 1982.

Kahneman, D., A. Krueger, D. Schkade, N. Schwarz, and A. Stone. "Would You Be Happier if You Were Richer? A Focusing Illusion." *Science* 312, no. 5782 (2006): pp. 1908–1910.

Klein, Gary. *The Power of Intuition: How to Use Your Gut Feelings to Make Better Decisions at Work*. New York: Currency, 2004.

Koppel, Robert. *The Intuitive Trader: Developing Your Inner Trading Wisdom*. New York: Wiley, 1996.

Koppel, Robert. *Bulls, Bears, and Millionaires: War Stories of the Trading Life*. Chicago: Dearborn Financial Publishing, 1997.

Koppel, Robert. *The Tao of Trading: Discovering a Simpler Path to Success*. Chicago: Dearborn Financial Publishing, 1998.

Koppel, Robert, and Howard Abell. *The Inner Game of Trading: Creating the Winner's State of Mind*. New York: McGraw-Hill, 1997.

Lefèvre, Edwin, and Jon D. Markman. *Reminiscences of a Stock Operator Annotated Edition*. Newark, N.J.: Wiley, 2009.

Lerner, J. S., and R. M. Gonzalez. "Forecasting One's Future Based on Fleeting Subjective Experiences." *Personality and Social Psychology Bulletin* 31 (2005): pp. 454–466.

Lerner, J. S., and D. Keltner. "Beyond Valence: Toward a Model of Emotion-Specific Influences on Judgment and Choice." *Cognition and Emotion* 14 (2000): pp. 473–493.

Lerner, J. S., and D. Keltner. "Fear, Anger, and Risk." *Journal of Personality and Social Psychology* 81, no. 1 (2001): pp. 146–159.

Lerner, J. S., and P. E. Tetlock. "Accounting for the Effects of Accountability." *Psychological Bulletin* 125, no. 2 (1999): pp. 255–275.

Lerner, J. S., J. H. Goldberg, and P. E. Tetlock. "Sober Second Thought: The Effects of Accountability, Anger, and Authoritarianism on Attributions of Responsibility." *Personality and Social Psychology Bulletin* 24 (1998): pp. 563–574.

Lerner, J. S., D. A. Small, and G. Loewenstein. "Heart Strings and Purse Strings: Carryover Effects of Emotions on Economic Decisions." *Psychological Science* 15, no. 5 (2004), pp. 337–341.

Lerner, J. S., R. M. Gonzalez, D. A. Small, and B. Fischhoff. "Effects of Fear and Anger on Perceived Risks of Terrorism: A National Field Experiment." *Psychological Science* 14 (2003): pp. 144–150.

Lewis, Michael. *The Big Short: Inside the Doomsday Machine.* New York: Norton, 2010.

Lo, Andrew W., and Jasmina Hasanhodzic. *The Heretics of Finance: Conversations with Leading Practitioners of Technical Analysis.* New York: Bloomberg, 2009.

Lo, Andrew W., and A. Craig MacKinlay. *A Non-Random Walk Down Wall Street.* Princeton, N.J.: Princeton University Press, 2001.

Loewenstein, George. *Exotic Preferences: Behavioral Economics and Human Motivation.* New York: Oxford University Press, 2008.

Lowenstein, Roger. *When Genius Failed: The Rise and Fall of Long-Term Capital Management.* New York: Random House, 2000.

Mackay, Charles. *Extraordinary Popular Delusions and the Madness of Crowds.* 1841. Reprint, New York: Harmony Books, 1980.

Markowitz, Harry. *Portfolio Selection: Efficient Diversification of Investments*, 2nd ed. New York: Wiley, 1959.

Patterson, Scott. *The Quants: How a New Breed of Math Whizzes Conquered Wall Street and Nearly Destroyed It.* New York: Crown, 2010.

Paulson, Henry M. Jr. *On the Brink: Inside the Race to Stop the Collapse of the Global Financial System.* New York: Business Plus, 2010.

Pinker, Steven. *How the Mind Works.* New York: Norton, 1997.

Politser, Paul. *Neuroeconomics: A Guide to the New Science of Making Choices.* Oxford, U.K.: Oxford University Press, 2008.

Ratey, John J. *A User's Guide to the Brain: Perception, Attention, and the Four Theaters of the Brain.* New York: Vintage, 2002.

Rotella, Robert F. *Elements of Successful Trading: Developing Your Comprehensive Strategy through Psychology, Money Management, and Trading Methods.* New York: New York Institute of Finance, 1992.

Schkade, D. A., and D. Kahneman. "Does Living in California Make People Happy? A Focusing Illusion in Judgments of Life Satisfaction. *Psychological Science* 9 (1998): pp. 340–346.

Schwager, Jack D. *Market Wizards: Interviews with Top Traders.* New York: Collins, 1993.

Schwager, Jack D. *The New Market Wizards: Conversations with America's Top Traders.* New York: Harper Business, 1992.

Shefrin, H. M., and Richard H. Thaler, "Interpreting Rationality in Hierarchical Games." *Economic Letters* 5 (1980).

Shefrin, H. M., and Richard H. Thaler. "An Economic Theory of Self-Control." *Journal of Political Economy* 89, no. 2 (1981): pp. 392–406.

Shermer, Michael. *The Mind of the Market: How Biology and Psychology Shape Our Economic Lives.* New York: Holt Paperbacks, 2009.

Shiller, Robert J. *Irrational Exuberance.* 2nd ed. New York: Broadway Business, 2006.

Shiller, Robert J. *The Subprime Solution: How Today's Global Crisis Happened, and What to Do about It.* Princeton, N.J.: Princeton University Press, 2008.

Simon, Herbert. *Models of Man.* New York: Wiley, 1957.

Simon, Herbert. *Administrative Behavior*, 3rd ed. New York: The Free Press, 1976.

Simon, Herbert. *Models of Thought*. Vols. 1 and 2. New Haven, Conn.: Yale University Press, 1979.

Simon, Herbert. *Models of Bounded Rationality*. Vols. 1 and 2. Cambridge, Mass.: MIT Press, 1982.

Simon, Herbert. *Models of My Life*. New York: Basic Books, 1991.

Slovic, P. Review of *Risk in Perspective: Insight and Humor in the Age of Risk Management*, by Kimberly M. Thompson. *Risk Analysis* 25 (2005): p. 493.

Slovic, P. "Affect, Reason, and Mere Hunches." *Journal of Law, Economics and Policy* 4, no. 1 (2007): pp. 191–211.

Slovic, P., and E. Peters. "Risk Perception and Affect." *Current Directions in Psychological Science* 15, no. 6 (2006): pp. 322–325.

Slovic, P., M. Finucane, E. Peters, and D. G. MacGregor. "The Affect Heuristic." In *Heuristics and Biases: The Psychology of Intuitive Judgment*, edited by T. Gilovich, D. Griffin, and D. Kahneman, pp. 397–420. Cambridge, U.K.: Cambridge University Press, 2002.

Slovic, P., M. Finucane, E. Peters, and D. G. MacGregor. "Rational Actors or Rational Fools? Implications of the Affect Heuristic for Behavioral Economics. *Journal of Socio-Economics* 31 (2002): pp. 329–342.

Slovic, P., M. Finucane, E. Peters, and D. G. MacGregor. "Risk as Analysis and Risk as Feelings: Some Thoughts about Affect, Reason, Risk, and Rationality." *Risk Analysis* 24, no. 2 (2004): pp. 1–12.

Slovic, P., E. Peters, M. L. Finucane, and D. G. MacGregor. "Affect, Risk, and Decision Making. *Health Psychology* 24 (2005): pp. S35–S40.

Slovic, P., E. Peters, J. Grana, S. Berger, and G. S. Dieck. "Risk Perception of Prescription Drugs: Results of a National Survey." *Drug Information Journal* 41, no. 1 (2007): pp. 81–100.

Slovic, S., and P. Slovic. "Numbers and Nerves: Toward an Affective Apprehension of Environmental Risk." *Whole Terrain* 13 (2004/2005): pp. 14–18.

Small, D. A., J. S. Lerner, R. M. Gonzalez, and B. Fischhoff. "Emotion Priming and Attributions for Terrorism: Americans' Reactions in a National Field Experiment." *Political Psychology* 27, no. 2 (2006): pp. 289–298.

Smitten, Richard. *Jesse Livermore: The World's Greatest Stock Trader*. New York: Wiley, 2001.

Sokol-Hessner, Peter, Ming Hsu, Nina Curley, Mauricio Delgado, Colin Camerer, and Elizabeth Phelps. "Reappraising Loss Aversion: Manipulating Choices with Emotion Regulation Strategies." *Proceedings of the National Academy of Sciences* 106 (2009): pp. 5035–5040.

Soros, George. *The New Paradigm for Financial Markets: The Credit Crisis of 2008 and What It Means*. New York: Public Affairs, 2008.

Soros, George. *The Soros Lectures at the Central European University*. New York: Public Affairs, 2010.

Steenbarger, Brett N. *The Psychology of Trading: Tools and Techniques for Minding the Markets*. New York: Wiley, 2002.

Stiglitz, Joseph E. *Freefall: America, Free Markets, and the Sinking of the World Economy*. New York: Norton, 2010.

Stiglitz, Joseph E. *The Stiglitz Report: Reforming the International Monetary and Financial Systems in the Wake of the Global Crisis*. New York: New Press, 2010.

Sunstein, Cass, and Richard H. Thaler, "Market Efficiency and Rationality: The Peculiar Case of Baseball." *Michigan Law Review* 102, no. 6 (2003): pp. 1390–1403.

Taleb, Nassim Nicholas. *Fooled by Randomness: The Hidden Role of Chance in Life and in the Markets.* New York: Random House, 2001.

Taleb, Nassim Nicholas. *The Black Swan: The Impact of the Highly Improbable.* New York: Random House, 2010.

Taylor, S. E., J. S. Lerner, R. M. Sage, B. Lehman, and T. Seeman. "Early Environment, Emotions, Responses to Stress, and Health." *Journal of Personality* 72 (2004): pp. 1365–1393.

Taylor, S. E., J. S. Lerner, R. M. Sage, D. K. Sherman, and N. K. McDowell. "Portrait of the Self-Enhancer: Well Adjusted and Well Liked or Maladjusted and Friendless?" *Journal of Personality and Social Psychology* 84 (2003): pp. 165–176.

Taylor, S. E., J. S. Lerner, D. K. Sherman, R. M. Sage, and N. K. McDowell. "Are Self-Enhancing Cognitions Associated with Healthy or Unhealthy Biological Profiles?" *Journal of Personality and Social Psychology* 85 (2003): pp. 605–615.

Thaler, Richard H. "Judgment and Decision Making under Uncertainty: What Economists Can Learn from Psychology." In *Risk Analysis in Agriculture: Research and Educational Developments.* Presented at a seminar sponsored by the Western Regional Research Project W-149, Tucson, Arizona, June 1980.

Thaler, Richard H. "Maximization and Self-Control," a commentary on "Maximization Theory in Behavioral Psychology," by Howard Rachlin, Ray Battalio, John Kagel, and Leonard Green, in *Behavioral and Brain Sciences* 4 (1981), pp. 403–404.

Thaler, Richard H. "Illusions, Mirages, and Public Policy." In *Environmental Impact Technology Assessment and Risk Analysis,* edited by V. T. Covello et al. NATO ASI Series, 1983.

Thaler, Richard H. "Illusions, Mirages, and Public Policy." *Public Interest* (Fall 1983).

Thaler, Richard H. "Illusions, Mirages, and Public Policy." In *Judgment and Decision Making: An Interdisciplinary Reader,* edited by Hal Arkes and Kenneth Hammond. Cambridge, U.K.: Cambridge University Press, 1986.

Thaler, Richard H., and Cass R. Sunstein. *Nudge: Improving Decisions on Health, Wealth, and Happiness.* New York: Penguin, 2009.

Tversky, A., and D. Kahneman. "Availability: A Heuristic for Judging Frequency and Probability." *Cognitive Psychology* 5 (1973): pp. 207–232.

Tversky, A., and D. Kahneman. "Judgment under Uncertainty: Heuristics and Biases." *Science* 185, no. 4157 (1974): pp. 1124–1131.

Tversky, A., and D. Kahneman. "The Framing of Decisions and the Psychology of Choice." *Science* 211 (1981): pp. 453–458.

Zweig, Jason, *Your Money and Your Brain: How the New Science of Neuroeconomics Can Help Make You Rich.* New York: Simon & Schuster, 2007.

Index

ABOUT THE AUTHOR

Robert Koppel is the author of critically acclaimed books on the psychology of trading and money issues, including *The Inner Game of Trading* and *Money Talks: Candid Conversations about Wealth in America*. His books have been widely featured in the media and translated into many languages.  He is a former member of the Chicago Mercantile Exchange (CME), a hedge fund partner, and president of his own division of Rand Financial. Koppel was the senior business writer for Onmoney.com. His work has been covered in *The New York Times*, *The Wall Street Journal*, and other leading financial publications. Koppel has appeared on CNN, CNBC, and National Public Radio. He lives with his wife in Chicago.